THE WORLD OF
SAN BERNARDINO

by

IRIS ORIGO

A HELEN AND KURT WOLFF BOOK

HARCOURT, BRACE & WORLD, INC.

NEW YORK

FIRST PUBLISHED IN THE UNITED STATES IN 1962
LIBRARY OF CONGRESS CATALOG CARD NUMBER: 62-16733

PRINTED IN ITALY
FOR HARCOURT, BRACE & WORLD, INC., NEW YORK, N. Y.

CONTENTS

ACKNOWLEDGEMENTS

My grateful acknowledgements are due to the Librarian of the Biblioteca Laurenziana, Florence, for permission to reproduce Plates XIVa and XIVb, and to the Librarian of the Biblioteca Queriniana, Brescia, for permission to reproduce Plate XX; to the Directors of the Museum of Fine Arts, Boston, Mass., and of the Yale University Art Gallery for permission to reproduce Plates VIIIa and VIIIb; to the Soprintendenza alle Gallerie, Milan, for permission to reproduce Plates Vb, VII and XXXb, and to the Soprintendenza ai Monumenti e Gallerie degli Abruzzi e Molise for permission to photograph and reproduce the death-mask of San Bernardino.

I also wish to express my indebtedness to Padre Martino Bertagna, O. F. M., Superior of the Convento dell'Osservanza, Siena, for the loan of books and for his valuable advice, to Professor Enzo Carli for permission to reproduce Plates IX and XI from his book, *I Primitivi Senesi*, to Madame René van der Hoeden for allowing me to reproduce the picture by Francesco di Giorgio in the Wauters Collection, Brussels, to Marchesa Nannina Fossi for a similar permission with regard to the picture by Sano di Pietro from the Rucellai Collection, and to Contessa Vittoria Forquet and Principessa Sobilia Carafa della Roccella for allowing me to photograph and reproduce Plate XXXI from the scroll in the Palmieri Collection, Siena.

LIST OF ILLUSTRATIONS

SOURCES OF THE PHOTOGRAPHS

Alinari, Florence: Pl. VIIa, XIII, XVIII, XXII, XXIII, XXIV, XXV, XXVI, XXVII, XXIX. Altimani, Milan: Frontispiece. Anderson, Rome: Pl. XIX. Biblioteca Queriniana, Brescia: Pl. XX. Braun, Mulhouse: Pl. IX, XI. British Museum, London: Pl. XXVIII. Gabinetto Fotografico Nazionale, Rome: Pl. XVIa, XXI. Grassi, Siena: Pl. I, II, III, IV, Va, VI, VIIb, XII, XVa, XVb, XVIb, XXXa, XXXI. Soprintendenza, L'Aquila: Pl. XXXII. Museum of Fine Arts, Boston: Pl. VIIIa. Pineider, Florence: Pl. XIVa, XIVb. Private Collection, Frankfurt: Pl. Xa. Soprintendenza alle Gallerie, Milan: Pl. Vb, XVII, XXXb. Wauters Collection, Brussels: Pl. Xb. Yale University Art Gallery, New Haven, Conn.: Pl. VIIIb.

PRINCIPAL EVENTS
IN THE LIFE OF SAN BERNARDINO

1380   September 8. Bernardino is born in Massa Marittima, the son of Tollo degli Albizzeschi of Siena, and Nera degli Avveduti of Massa.

1386   After the death of his father and mother, Bernardino is handed over to the care of his mother's sister, Diana.

1391   Bernardino is sent to Siena, to the house of his father's brother, Cristoforo degli Albizzeschi.

1392-99 Attends school in Siena, first with Maestro Onofrio di Loro and then with Maestro Giovanni da Spoleto, and afterwards studies canon law at the University.

1400   During an outbreak of the plague, nurses the sick in the Ospedale della Scala, and is afterwards dangerously ill.

1402   September 8. Enters the Franciscan Order and goes as a novice to the hermitage of Il Colombaio on Monte Amiata.

1403   September 8. Takes his final vows.

1404   September 8. Celebrates his first Mass.

1405   Is nominated a preacher and delivers his first sermon, at Seggiano.

1408-16 Preaches around Siena and in Ferrara (?), Siena, Pavia, Padua, and Mantua. Visits La Verna.

1417   A novice in Fiesole has a vision, telling Bernardino to go and preach in Lombardy. Preaches on his way in Ferrara (?) and Genoa (?).

1418   Preaches in Genoa and Mantua and in many places in Liguria and Piedmont. Arrives in Milan and preaches daily there.

1419-20 Delivers a course of Lenten sermons in Milan, and preaches in many cities of Lombardy and in the Canton Ticino.

1421   Gives further course of sermons in Milan. Brings peace to Crema. Is appointed Vicar of the Observants in Umbria and Tuscany.

1422-3 Preaches in Venice, Bergamo, Verona and other cities of the Veneto.

1424   Preaches in Bologna, where his orthodoxy is attacked, in Florence and in other parts of Tuscany.

1425   Preaches again in Santa Croce in Florence, and in Tuscany and Umbria.

1426   Preaches in Todi and Viterbo. Is summoned to Rome by Pope Martin V on a charge of heresy. Declared innocent, preaches eighty sermons in St. Peter's, and evangelizes the Marches.

1427   Is nominated Bishop of Siena, but refuses the honour. Gives course of sermons in Siena.

1428-9 Preaches again in the Marches, in Arezzo, in Lombardy and Venice.

1430   Takes part in the Franciscan Chapter in Assisi. Returns to the Marches.

1431   Returns to Siena, preaches in the Romagna and the Marches, refuses the Bishopric of Ferrara. Pope Eugenius IV issues a Bull of Exculpation in his favour.

1432-3   Makes friends with the Emperor Sigismund, in Siena, and accompanies him to Rome for his Coronation. Sets down his sermons at La Capriola.

1435   Preaches in Gubbio. Refuses the Bishopric of Urbino.

1438-9   Is again charged with heresy at the Council of Basle and is defended by the Duke of Milan. Is appointed Vicar General of the Observant Order in Italy. Preaches in Aquila and Perugia. Attends the Council for the Reunion of the Greek and Latin churches, in Ferrara and Florence.

1440   Appoints Fra Giovanni da Capistrano as his assistant. Frequent visits of inspection to convents of the Observants.

1441   Visits Florence and Assisi again. Preaches in Perugia from the new pulpit in the piazza. Attempts to make peace in Florence between Pope Eugenius IV and Siena.

1442-3   Offers his resignation as Vicar General and retires to La Capriola. Death of his close friend and companion, Fra Vincenzo. Goes to Milan to preach at the Duke's invitation and delivers farewell sermons in Pavia, Ferrara, Padua, Venice (?) and Verona.

1444   Preaches in Massa Marittima. Returns to La Capriola, and from there, after a farewell sermon in Siena, sets forth on his last journey to Aquila, where he dies, in the Convent of San Francesco, on the eve of the Ascension. His possessions are brought back to Siena. His body remains in Aquila.

1450   Is solemnly canonized on Whit Sunday by Pope Nicholas V.

2

PREFACE

IT is not possible to live in Tuscany without becoming familiar with San Bernardino's emblem: its golden rays, encircling the monogram YHS, are still set on the front wall of the Palazzo Pubblico in Siena[1] but they may also be seen in much less stately places: above the doorway of small country churches, over wayside shrines, on the wall of some crumbling farm or castle, or on the vault of what was perhaps once a chapel and is now a stable or a cellar. This is where San Bernardino came, the emblem tells; this is where he spoke.

His face, too, is almost equally familiar. He lived in an age of great painters and – since he was canonized only six years after his death and the cities and convents in which he had preached all wanted a picture or a statue of him as soon as possible – his portraits were painted by men who had known him by sight or, soon after, by artists who scrupulously followed these models. Sassetta, perhaps the most Franciscan in spirit of the Sienese painters, was working during San Bernardino's lifetime in the Convento dell'Osservanza near Siena which he had founded, and only seven months after the saint's death, painted a portrait of him in the oratory of the Ospedale della Scala, where he had nursed the plague-stricken in his youth. This, however, has unfortunately been destroyed and the only extant portrait certainly painted from the living model is the one by Sassetta's pupil, Pietro di Giovanni d'Ambrogio, when the saint, although only forty-six years old, had already the looks of an old man. (Plate 1). This, with a wooden bust by an anonymous contemporary[2] and the pictures by Sano di Pietro and Vecchietta, are the models on which subsequent portraits of him were based. In all of them we see the same small spare figure, the straight thin neck above the wide cowl, the hollow cheeks –

for, owing to his privations, he had lost all his teeth by the time he was forty – the determined, pointed chin and deep-set, rather small brown eyes, the fine-drawn bones, the look of gentleness and suffering. It is a face on which the privations of the ascetic and the humility of the saint have not wholly effaced the look of the aristocrat and scholar – and in some pictures there is also a hint of ironic humour in the corners of the thin mouth.

After these portraits, and those of many other Sienese painters and sculptors, comes a long series of works by great artists from other parts of Italy. Most of the portraits of the Sienese school are now in the Pinacoteca of Siena, but some may still be seen in the little country towns for which they were originally ordered. There they have an especial significance. The narrow streets and faded brick houses, the churches and convents which knew San Bernardino's own footsteps, the unchanged landscape, the very faces of the population – still cast in so much the same mould as the shrewd, garrulous, factious *Senesi* whom he rebuked and mocked and loved – form a fitter setting for these portraits than any public gallery. Here, one feels, the saint is still at home.

His memory, too, is still green in the countryside of Siena, and especially on the wild, lonely slopes beneath Monte Amiata where he spent his novitiate. The peasant who showed us the track to the ruins of his remote hermitage, Il Colombaio – leading a donkey very like the saint's own, for he was going to fetch a load of wood – spoke of him with affectionate familiarity, as of a relation who had died only a short time ago. Of the convent – standing in a little hollow in the hills, with the winding river-bed of the Orcia at its feet – nothing remains but the belfry and a few crumbling walls; ilex trees and juniper bushes grow in the cloister, thyme and wormwood pave the floors. But our guide took us to a spot from which it was still possible to make out the outline of the nave and of the cells, and showed us a sheltered clearing where the friars' vineyard

1. San Bernardino: *Pietro di Giovanni d'Ambrogio.*

II. San Bernardino: *Anonymous Contemporary*.

stood, as well as their olive grove and orchard. Sometimes, he said, the parish priest of Seggiano used to walk up there to say Mass on an improvised altar set up on the grass, against what was left of the church wall, and the peasants would walk there in procession from the nearest farm, bearing the church's Cross. The last Mass had been said only a few years before, when, after a series of severe hail-storms, they had decided to call upon San Bernardino for help. "And there has been no more hail." The peasant told us, too, how one evening recently, at dusk, a naughty boy had climbed up into the belfry wearing a cowl over his head, and the peasants who saw him from a distance had cried out, "San Bernardino has come back!" For several months afterwards, he added, his wife had been afraid to bring out his meals to him in the fields. Finally he told us to notice, on our way back to Seggiano, a great grey boulder beside the track. "They say that the boys of Seggiano used to throw stones at San Bernardino's ankles, but one day, when he reached that turn of the path, he suddenly vanished, and the stones fell only against a bare rock. And ever since it has been called *il masso di San Bernardino*" (San Bernardino's rock).

This book is partly based on the biographies of San Bernardino's contemporaries[3] and has also made use of the information gathered by later biographers and, in particular, of the important new material recently published in the *Archivum Franciscanum Historicum*, in the *Studi Francescani*, and especially in the *Bollettino di Studi Bernardiniani*, and also in the critical and biographical essays collected by Franciscan scholars and historians and published on the fifth anniversary of the saint's death.[4] On the same occasion an exhibition in Siena – the *Mostra Bernardiniana* – brought together, not only many of the less familiar works of art representing the saint, but also some of his manuscripts and personal possessions.[5] The more modern biographers I have consulted – including the only Life in English, written in 1913 by A. G. Ferrers Howell – are listed in the bibliography, while specific works on the period and monographs consulted for single chapters are mentioned at the beginning of the notes for each chapter.

The main source, however, for any Life of San Bernardino must be his own words: his Latin sermons, as he himself set them down for his own use and for that of his friars, but above all, his sermons in the vulgar, which have only recently become available in their entirety, as they were written by scribes in shorthand on wax tablets, while the saint was speaking. The use of shorthand was of course not uncommon in San Bernardino's time, but it was practised in a highly idiosyncratic manner, since each scribe more or less invented his own abbreviations as well as making use of the customary ones, and spelling was also very much a question of personal taste. Moreover, as becomes very obvious in reading these particular sermons, there was often a considerable difference in skill between one scribe and another. The man who set down – as we shall describe later on – the sermons which the saint delivered in Siena in 1427, did so with great accuracy and gusto, while the one who wrote down the Florentine sermons in 1424 was obviously unable to keep up. "[San Bernardino] gave many fine parables and good and useful doctrines," he wrote, "about the workings of the conscience, which I, the scribe, did not take down, owing to their length and my lack of time. I only wrote what he said about the Holy Gospels." And he brought one sermon to an end with the words: "I, the scribe, could not set down more, for lack of tablets on which to write."

Padre Cannarozzi, in the preface to his scholarly and definitive edition of the saint's hitherto unpublished sermons, suggests that the passages most fully reported were those which especially moved or interested his congregation, but this is only a supposition. It would certainly appear that many of the parables and stories in the Florentine course of 1425, and also in the one delivered in Siena later in the

6

same year, were omitted, to our great loss. But though the transcriptions of the sermons are in some cases uneven and incomplete, more than enough has come down to us to give an extremely vivid picture both of the man and of his times. At any period in history, the formulated ideas which are set down in words are only the outer crust of a vast body of unformulated assumptions, beliefs and fears – of "doctrines felt as facts" – so deeply embedded, so universally taken for granted that men seldom bother to express them, nor are aware that they are constantly changing, but which colour their imaginations and shape their behaviour. It is these ideas – the imaginative background which forms the "climate" of a period – that San Bernardino brings to light for us, with a vividness equalled by hardly any other writer of his time. The picture which he paints may be framed and annotated by the works of such chroniclers as Villani and such novelists as Sacchetti and Sermini, by the domestic letters of Ser Lapo Mazzei, the treatises on domestic life or trade of Fra Giovanni Dominici or of the merchant Paolo da Certaldo, and perhaps most of all, by the direct, unvarnished records left by the domestic chroniclers of the Tuscan Trecento and Quattrocento. But none of them, as a social historian, equals San Bernardino. He would have smiled to hear himself described in this manner, for the title would have seemed to him a very trivial one compared with that of preacher, but though he was certainly one of the greatest popular preachers of his time, it is also as a historian that he should be read. His interest was in men's hearts, and it was these that he sought to move. And since he considered every facet of human life to have some interest or importance, he ended by painting some pictures as detailed and as brilliant as those which illustrated the missals of his brother-monks. It is as if a series of miniatures had been turned into a newsreel of the early fifteenth century, a minute, faithful documentary. Here are the young gallants of Siena, "all full of cock-a-doodle-doo," and the pretty girls who spend the days on the terraces at the top of their houses, washing their fair hair again and again and bleaching it in the sun. Here are the purse-proud merchants who – after one of the preacher's most impassioned appeals for clothes for poor debtors in prison – respond only with a gift of two sheets, two pairs of breeches and a pair of broken shoes. Here is the whole world of dishonest tradesmen, of usurers and gamblers, of ignorant priests and fanatical friars, of unjust rulers and wretched prisoners, of the factious, the plague-stricken and the hungry. And the world of women is there, too: *Monna Pigra* and *Monna Sollecita* (Madam Lie-abed and Madam Earlybird), jostling each other for a good place at the sermon, the old widow with "a little plot of scented herbs – marjoram, thyme and basilisk"; the wife who, when she goes to confession, tells only her husband's sins; the young girl "who runs to the window as soon as she hears a horse's hooves, and wants to see everything and know everything"; the over-indulgent mother and the corrupt procuress. All these are described not only with the passionate fervour of a great reformer, but also with the compassion and irony of a man who, for all his saintliness, had a great deal in common with the people to whom he spoke.

San Bernardino has been compared to the genial Florentine merchant and novelist who wrote some fifty years before him, Franco Sacchetti, and the resemblance goes beyond their common delight in a good story or their racy use of the Tuscan tongue. It lies rather in their common taste for life itself – hard, earthy, real, but illumined by a touch of poetry and by their love for the people about whom they spoke. Their characters are the coarse, money-loving, quarrelsome, humorous, loquacious men and women of any little Tuscan town, always glad to play a trick upon a neighbour or to give him the rough side of their tongue, always ready for a good joke, a good fight or a good meal – washed down with pungent Tuscan wine over a game of dice, under a pergola of vines – always swift to repentance, and equally swift to sin again. It was, perhaps, because San Bernardino understood them all so well, that they, too, were so much at ease with him. Every great man – whether poet, ruler or saint – transcends the outlook of his own period; but there is also a part of him that still belongs to it. San Bernardino's vision of God belongs to eternity, but in his view of the world around him he was very much a man of his own time, a period of unrest and transition. Though his dry common-sense led him to dismiss the grosser forms of superstition and he was unusually sceptical with regard to the popular prophecies about the Second Coming, he differed not at all from the simplest members of his congregation in his attitude to signs and portents and to the physical presence of angels and devils: good and evil took on for him, as they do for each successive generation of men, the forms in which he expected them to appear. Though he steadily and fervently rejected the attitude of his fellow-citizens towards vengeance as a moral obligation and towards the need for party strife, though he combated monastic ignorance and aristocratic idleness and expressed enlightened views on marriage and the dignity of women, he fully shared, and did not hesitate to express, the harsh prejudices of his contemporaries with regard to witches, usurers and Jews. He was intensely a man of his time, too, in his lively interest, not only in all sorts of men, but in every kind of profession, trade and manner of life, and in the adaptability which made him welcome everywhere. For over forty years he travelled across Italy on foot, and there was nowhere where he was not at home: in the universities of Padua and Florence and in the dark shops of the cobblers, apothecaries and corn-merchants round the market-place; in the bookshops in Piazza della Signoria, looking for rare codices; in the *palazzi* of the knights to whom, by birth, he himself belonged, and for whom he once composed a sermon on "the things that constitute true nobility"; in the prisons and hospitals, or talking to small boys in the street about how they slung their slings; warming his tired bones in the chimney-corner of a poor farmhouse; and even chatting on the highroads with the "locusts" of the day, the dreaded soldiers of fortune, and confessing that, for all his reprobation of their calling, he would dearly love to see a battle, just for once.

It is into some of these worlds that this study will try to follow him.

I. THE FALSE AND THE TRUE VOCATION

La vraie éloquence se moque de l'éloquence.

PASCAL

I

ON Friday, August 15, 1427, the Cathedral bell of Siena called
Sovana[1] tolled, as usual, at dawn, – but the city was already
awake. Long before sunrise, in the dark Piazza del Campo, Fra Bernardino degli Albizzeschi had set up his altar before the Palazzo
Pubblico and had said his Mass by the light of two guttering tapers,
and from their barred shops and shuttered houses the citizens had
hurried down the steep, narrow streets to get themselves a good
place – for this was the Feast of the Assumption, and at dawn
Fra Bernardino was to preach to the *Signori* of the Council and the
assembled citizens. The pulpit, adorned with a piece of red brocade,
had already been set up, and beside it, on a dais hung with a fine
tapestry, sat the city officials, while in the square a low canvas
partition separated the men from the women – the women wearing
long, seemly cloaks with white or black shawls covering their heads,
the men in the garments of their station: the long merchant's gown,
the short gay cloak of the young nobleman, or the drab tunic of
the craftsman. As the sun rose over the piazza – its first rays catching
the summit of the slender rose-coloured tower beside the Palazzo
Pubblico, then slowly bringing light to the whole honey-coloured
square – the Cathedral bell began to toll. As it ceased, the preacher
rose, held up the tablet bearing the monogram of the name of
Jesus, and slowly made the sign of the Cross, while the congregation
fell upon their knees. Then he began to describe "how our glorious Mother went to Heaven, and the delight that she aroused in
Paradise."[2]

All this is not surmised, but recorded. Two artists of the time,

11

Sano di Pietro and Neroccio di Bartolomeo, painted the scene,[3] and in addition we have the account of a singularly accurate eye-witness, who fully realized the value of what he had chosen to do. This was a poor craftsman of the wool-guild[4] named Benedetto di Maestro Bartolomeo – a man, according to his own account, "with a wife and several children and few possessions" – but so enraptured by Bernardino's preaching that he gladly gave up some hours of his day's work, so that no word should be lost. Day after day, he settled himself in a quiet corner of the Campo with a set of waxed tablets, drew out a stylus and wrote down, in a self-taught shorthand, everything that the preacher was saying. "No slightest word," he said, "came out of that holy mouth, that I did not set down." When the sermon was over, he gathered up his tablets and went home, carefully transcribed what he had written on parchment in long-hand, waxed a fresh set of tablets for the next morning – and only then turned to his own day's work.[5]

From the first, Fra Bernardino's sharp, bright little eyes fell upon him – and now and again he slowed down for his benefit or even, when there was some point to emphasize, leaned forward and addressed him directly. On the first day he seems to have taken him for a public accountant, an *abbachista*. "You there, you *abbachista*, have you drawn up your account?" But then he realized what the man was doing, and spoke to him again. "Set it down even as you did last time, and then practise it; for to write it down will fix it well in your memory." Gradually the preacher came to depend upon this faithful listener and would draw his attention to an important passage. "Scribe, set this down" – "mark this well, scribe" – "St. Peter replied – lo, scribe, hear this good word." When there was a Latin quotation or a Biblical reference, he emphasized it: "So says our *Paolozzo*.... Take heed, scribe, and write with care. I will say it in such a way that you will understand it, and then I will repeat it again, so that you can seize it well." And, word for word, Bene-

III. The Sermon in the Piazza del Campo: *Sano di Pietro*.

IV. Il Colombaio.

detto set it all down – even the interruptions and the preacher's exclamations, which suddenly bring the whole scene before our eyes. "Lo, wait a moment, for a saying from Gregory to this purpose comes to my mind." A dog ran across the piazza and distracted the whole congregation. "Hit that dog, send him away, hit him with your slipper."[6] The great bell-tower called the *Mangia* rang the hour, and Bernardino interrupted himself, "Let the bell toll, first."[7] Other interruptions, too, were faithfully noted. The public fountain called the Fonte Gaia, not far from the pulpit, was the habitual meeting-place of peasants and middlemen, where they argued and bartered interminably, as they marketed their wheat, wine and cattle. But this, the preacher protested, was not fitting, while he was speaking. "You men by the fountain, bartering your wares, do it elsewhere. Do you not hear me, you men by the fountain?"[8] He had innumerable devices to catch his hearers' attention. "Now I will tell you a very fine parable. Listen well, for it will surely please you." Any sign of inattention was at once marked, and pounced upon. "I see a woman who, if she were watching me, would not be looking where she is. Listen to me, I say!" If what he was saying was not welcome to his congregation, he was at once conscious of their restlessness: "I am well aware that you do not like listening to me, and I look for signs of it: you twist your head, you turn away, you put your hand to your head."[9] Yet he insisted that they should at least hear him out. "Go not, take not your leave, wait – and perhaps you will hear things that you will never hear again." And when finally the congregation's attention was visibly flagging – and we must remember that some of his sermons lasted for four hours, and that his hearers had been listening on their feet or on their knees – he leaned forward and drew out of his habit a piece of parchment. "Hark to the letter I received this morning!" All leaned forward, agape. "Lo, you prefer an unread letter to the word of God!"[10] Then, when the interpolation was over, he would slap his own

13

cheek sharply, crying "*A casa!*" (home again) – and would take up the thread of his remarks.

The friar who was thus speaking in the Piazza del Campo had not always meant to be a preacher. Some twenty-six years before, in the spring of 1401, he was wandering, a devout but most uncertain young man, about the wooded hills between Siena and Massa Marittima, which were then mostly covered with forests or with a thick undergrowth of scrub-oak, myrtle, juniper and laurel. His intention, according to his own account, was "to live not like a man but an angel" – that is, to lead a hermit's life – and for this purpose he had bought himself a pilgrim's robe and a Bible (wrapping it in a goatskin to shield it from the rain) and was roaming from one hill to the next, in search of a site for his hermitage. "And I looked," he said, "first at one hill and then at another and entered first one wood and then another, seeking where I might roost and saying to myself, 'Lo, this would be a fine place!' and then, 'Lo, this would be better still!'" At last, since he could not make up his mind, he decided to go home again, to discover there whether he was indeed capable of leading so austere a life. He thought he would start his experiment with a meal of unseasoned, bitter wild herbs, and, going out of the Porta Follonica to the west of Siena, bent down and picked a thistle. For the first time, he thought, he might permit himself to scrape the earth off it and wash it, and then, he relates, "in the name of the blessed Jesus . . . I placed it in my mouth and began to chew. I chewed and chewed – it would not go down. 'Let us try,' said I, 'a sip of water.' In vain! The water went down, the thistle stayed in my mouth." He tried again and again failed: the prickly plant stuck in his throat. "And thus," Fra Bernardino concluded, "with a mouthful of thistle the temptation was cast out – for a temptation it was, and not a vocation." "But the saints of the past, in the time of the Holy Fathers," objected one of his hearers, "how did they fare? For they lived on herbs. . . . And San Francesco, what did he do, who

14

fasted forty days without touching a crumb?" "He could do it," Bernardino replied, "and I could not!"[11]

It was nearly twenty-six years before he told this story against himself, having by then discovered his true calling. He had become one of the greatest popular preachers of Italy.

Of his early life, no more need be told than the steps which led him to his vocation. The son of Nera degli Avveduti and Tollo degli Albizzeschi – a Sienese nobleman who had been sent as Governor of the fortified city of Massa Marittima in the Maremma – he was born in Massa on September 8, 1380, the birthday of the Madonna and the year of the death of St. Catherine. Before he was six he had lost both his parents, and the rest of his boyhood was mostly spent under petticoat government. His first foster-mother was his mother's sister, Diana, who brought him up until he was eleven, at which time he was sent to Siena, to the care of his father's brother and sister-in-law, Cristofano and Pia Albizzeschi. But it was two other women who then became his chief mentors – his cousin Tobia and his aunt Bartolommea – both of them gentle, pious widows, who strictly conformed to the high standard of self-discipline and decorum required of women who had lost their husbands, and who always wore the conventional widow's garb, a long dark cloak which fell from the head to the feet and almost concealed the face. "You are not as you used to be," Bernardino said many years later, in a sermon addressed to the women of Siena. "I see a widow today . . . with her forehead bare and her cloak drawn back to show her cheek. And how she shapes it over her brow! That is a prostitute's gesture."[12]

Monna Bartolommea's piety was that of Mary; Monna Tobia preferred Martha's. Bartolommea was an Augustinian Tertiary and her life was given up to contemplation and prayer. Summer and winter, she slept on straw and rose from her pallet to pray at midnight, and again when the great Cathedral bell rang at dawn. Tobia was much younger, but she must have had an unhappy marriage behind her, for she spoke of a return to matrimony as "stepping back three paces," and declared that she would never wish to "sell her poor flesh" again. She, too, was a member of the Third Order, but a Franciscan, and her time was spent in the seven works of mercy: she nursed the sick, took gifts to hospitals and prisons, and kept her heart and door open to all who asked for alms. "When a beggar comes to your door," she said to Bernardino, "put a loaf under his cloak, but so secretly that you are hardly seen, even by yourself." Bernardino was very fond of her, and when she died, a vision of her came to him in the midst of a sermon which he was preaching far away, in a church in Milan: he saw her ascending straight to heaven, like a saint.

The boy, however, was not brought up entirely by these virtuous ladies. Like other boys of his age, he relates, he made "bows and arrows, slings and other such oddities . . . and thought it a fine thing." He attended first the grammar school of Maestro Onofrio di Loro and then the school of rhetoric of the celebrated Maestro Giovanni da Spoleto. A good-looking boy – not tall, but active and slender, with a determined chin, fair hair, a finely chiselled nose and mouth, and a great sweetness of expression – he did not escape the attentions of one of the young men who had given Siena the reputation of being more addicted to sodomy than any other town in Italy, but he appears to have been well capable of taking care of himself, since he retorted by soundly punching his assailant on the chin. Several years later, when he was preaching in the Piazza del Campo, one of his friars observed this man listening to him, in tears.[13]

As he grew older, he also took a course at the university in canon law, which was then considered a preparation not only for an ecclesiastical career, but also for any important office. He delighted in poetry, but, according to his own account, "could not enjoy the Bible or any other holy books – indeed when I read them, I fell asleep." And he also relates that when someone suggested that he should become a friar, "I merely laughed at him and at the friars. I said that if God called me, I would go, but otherwise not."[14]

Nevertheless at the age of eighteen, while still leading on the surface a life very similar to that of any of his friends, he joined the Confraternity of *I Disciplinati di Santa Maria della Scala*, a company of flagellants who held their meetings at midnight, in the underground vaults beneath the great hospital in the Cathedral Square. Here Bernardino, after a careful scrutiny of his petition (for the confraternity was aristocratic and chose its members with care), was received on the night of Holy Thursday, 1398. The low, vaulted chapel into which he descended held nothing but a bare stone altar and, around the walls, a row of stalls, from which the other members of the Confraternity, wrapped in black cloaks, watched him in silence behind the narrow slits of their masks. He presented the customary gift – a wax candle weighing one pound – to the prior, watched the ritual washing of feet, and then, as the lights, one by one, were extinguished, he heard the leather thongs falling, in silence and darkness, on the bare shoulders of the flagellants. Then, when the discipline was over, the voices rose and fell in a penitential *laude*:[15]

> *Peccator, ch'ora qui siete, – con Madre Maria piangete,*
>   *ch'è con tanta avversità:*
> *ch'ella vede il suo figliuolo – pendere in croce con duolo,*
>   *e verun conforto non ha . . .*
> *– Figliuol mio angelicato, mai non facesti peccato,*
>   *e se' in tanta estremità! –*
> *Per la gran doglia infinita, cade in terra tramortita,*
>   *che sentimento non ha.*

17

Evening after evening Bernardino went back there – until, two years later, his first call came. The epidemic of the Black Death which swept over Italy in 1400 (almost as severe as the first outbreak half a century before) invaded Siena too – having been brought there, it was believed, by pilgrims on their way to the Roman Jubilee. The hospital was so crowded with the dead and dying that, to counteract the terrible stench, the prior made an attempt at fumigation by lighting fires in every room. But in vain. The stench was blown out with the smoke through every door and every window-crack, and soon the disease, too, spread from house to house, from street to street. In the hospital, in the course of the first few weeks, nine priests died, seven doctors, five clerks and ninety-six attendants, and no one was willing to take their place: the dying lay untended, the dead unburied. The prior issued an appeal for help, and Bernardino – with twelve of his friends, all under twenty – volunteered for hospital service and for four months, until the disease died down with the coming of winter, never set foot again outside the wards. It was then – in the long bare rooms in which there was not enough food, nor drugs, nor linen, nor nurses, nor even pallets, among the stench of the dead and the cries of the dying – that Bernardino learnt the value of the only gift he could still bestow: a look of pity. Later on he would say to his congregation: "Can you not give a loaf? Well, give a crumb. Can you not give wine? Give wine and water. . . . Can you not succour a sick man? Grieve with him at least; show him your compassion."

After leaving the hospital, Bernardino spent four months in bed, between life and death, in the house of one of his friends, and when he recovered, the turning point of his life was already near. He spent another year, until her death, looking after his aunt Bartolommea, who had become both blind and deaf, but during all this time his mind was in a turmoil. "Do you know what one's mind is like, when one cannot choose between the things that are entering

18

it? It is like the sea in a storm, or water with lotus-dye in it, turbid."[16]

That his vocation was to enter a religious Order, he now felt certain, but he could not decide which it should be. Should he join, as his aunt advised, the Mendicant Order of the Augustinians, whose convent, Lecceto, was only a few miles away? Or should he enter one of the recently founded Preaching Orders, the Dominican or the Franciscan?

It was probably at about this time that he made a journey to Northern Italy which may well have influenced his choice. In 1401 St. Vincent Ferrer, a Spanish Dominican who was then at the height of his renown, was preaching in Piedmont, and Bernardino went to Alessandria to hear him. Of all the preachers of his time, he was perhaps the one whose character and methods were most likely to appeal to the young man. Though he could speak only Spanish and Latin, his enthusiasm and personal magnetism held his audience spellbound wherever he went. His sermons were not delivered in churches, but from a pulpit set up in an open square or field, from which a small flag waved to indicate the direction of the wind and to tell his hearers where they might place themselves best. His themes were not abstract points of doctrine, but were directly related to the daily lives of his congregation: he spoke about the scandals and dissensions of the day, and called men back to penitence and prayer. Wherever he went, his main purpose was to bring back peace, and he brought with him – in addition to a long procession of penitents who followed him from city to city – not only choirboys to sing the Offices and priests to hear confessions, but a notary to set down formally in writing the numerous pacts of reconciliation which were brought about by his words. This mixture of fervour and practical common sense was equally characteristic later on of Bernardino himself. After the sermon, in spite of the crowd of penitents surrounding the Dominican, the younger man succeeded in speaking to him alone. What they said to each other we do not know, but on the next morning, as St. Vincent was bidding his congregation farewell, he told them to give thanks to God, for they had among them "a young man who in a few years' time will be celebrated throughout Italy and whose apostolate will bear great fruit . . . and though I am older than he, yet he will be honoured before me by the Church."[17]

During this time of uncertainty, Bernardino moved to a little house which he owned near one of the city gates – the *casa degli orti*, so called because it stood among some of the garden-plots of leeks and onions, of rosemary and sage, which brought the Tuscan countryside within the city walls. Here he spent his days in solitude and prayer, and it was here – looking beyond the walls over the lunar landscape formed by the bare clay hills of the Sienese countryside, windswept and pale – that "the temptation" of a hermit's life came to him and was rejected. A few months later, his true call came.

One night, when he had fallen asleep in his oratory, he dreamed that he was outside the city walls at Fonte Nuova and saw a great house on fire, with flames and smoke coming out of the windows. Only one window was still untouched, and in its opening stood a friar with outstretched arms, calling upon St. Francis to save him. And indeed the room in which he stood was spared, while all the rest of the house was destroyed by the flames.[18]

Bernardino believed the meaning of this dream to be that the Franciscan Order alone would save him from the flames kindled by the flesh and the devil. He at once gave away everything he had,[19] and, in the church of San Francesco, on September 8, 1402, he was received as a novice and was clothed in the Franciscan habit – dear to him because, he said, it was made by St. Francis in the shape of a Cross. "Even as he [St. Francis] bore Christ Jesus crucified within his heart, so he wished to wear the Cross as his habit, for love of Him." The date, the feast-day of the Madonna, was Bernardino's birthday, and this was the date he also chose, in the following year,

20

for his final profession and, a year later still, for his first Mass and first sermon.

Preaching on the anniversary of this day in Siena, twenty-five years later, he told his hearers how great a significance this date held for him: "I would have you know that this is my birthday, and also the day on which I was born again; for now it is twenty-five years since I put on a friar's habit, and twenty-four since I made my vows of poverty, chastity and obedience. And I pray God that I may also die upon this day."[20]

The little community to which he was sent for his novitiate was one which followed the strict Rule of the Observance: a lonely mountain hermitage on the slopes of Monte Amiata above Seggiano called Il Colombaio – the pigeon-cote, from the large number of wood-pigeons which nested in the surrounding woods. The region, to this day, is a wild one, though the lower slopes of the hills are now planted with flourishing olive trees and an occasional stony vineyard. But as you climb the hill leading to the convent by the track up which Fra Bernardino must often have trudged, the trees become fewer; soon there is no vegetation left but an occasional tuft of juniper or broom, and the wind blows freely over fold upon fold of hills to the sea. In Bernardino's time it must indeed have been, as an early biographer described it, "a most devout and harsh place" (*devotissimum et asperrimum*). Most of the hillside was given up to forest and of the valley-bed to swamp, while the road was nothing more than a stony track formed by the infrequent passage of men and beasts. The convent itself (like other Franciscan foundations in their first years) had at first consisted only of a few rough huts clustering round a little church of grey stone, and the story was told that when once one of the friars had attempted to make himself a little more comfortable, St. Francis himself had appeared to him in a vision, to upbraid him for this insult to Lady Poverty. But by the time of Bernardino's novitiate, there was already a small dwelling-place of rough stone, set on a slightly sheltered southern slope, and here the friars had cleared some undergrowth to plant a vineyard, an olive grove, a wheat-field and a little kitchen-garden. In summer their fields suffered from drought, and in winter they were often snow-bound for weeks.

Some of the most austere of the Friars Minor or members of the Third Order had, at various times, spent a period of retreat there – among them the Blessed Giovanni of La Verna, who had fled from Siena to avoid the honours awarded to him by its citizens, the Sienese Tertiary Pietro Pettinaio, and the Blessed Giovanni Colombini, the founder of the Gesuati, who had wandered, *"pazzo per Cristo"* (mad for the love of Christ), all over these bare hills and valleys. Another brother, Fra Guido da Salvena, had possessed a holy simplicity very similar to that of St. Francis' Brother Juniper. One story about him tells how, in his old age, a young friar came to his cell one day and found him weeping bitterly, and on inquiring the reason was told to come nearer, whereupon Fra Guido took up his staff and beat him soundly. "I have done this," he then said, "so that you may remember better what I will now tell you" – and he proceeded to foretell the troubles which would be brought upon the Franciscan Order by the fanaticism of the friars who had broken away to form the sect called the *Fraticelli*.[21]

At Il Colombaio the friars endured cold and heat, hunger and thirst, and Bernardino also learned to bear what he himself admitted to be the hardest trial of monastic life, the constant company of his fellows. "Some are naturally melancholy, others ill-tempered, others merry; some are young, some old: and you must fit yourself to the temper of each." At least one of his brother-friars, indeed, appears to have been offended by his dry and caustic Sienese jokes, and was seen in tears after Bernardino's death, muttering, "Father, father, forgive me for murmuring against you."[22]

Like his fellow friars, Bernardino helped to nurse the sick in the neighbouring villages and at the time of the *questua* – the periodical begging from door to door for food or alms, on which many poor convents subsisted – he walked barefoot from farm to farm with a sack on his shoulder. Sometimes the village boys threw sharp stones at his thin, bare ankles, or laughed at the raggedness of his short habit. Once a woman asked him into her house and tried to persuade him to make love to her, not desisting until, taking up his discipline, he thrashed her soundly. Sometimes a housewife would keep him waiting at her door for an hour and once one threw a hard loaf at him out of the window.[23]

After a year – once again, on the feast-day of the Madonna – Fra Bernardino took his final vows, and after two years he was ordained, said his first Mass, and at once preached his first sermon in the little parish church of Seggiano. He was so nervous that, before entering the pulpit, he almost fainted, and his voice was so weak and hoarse that he could scarcely be heard. But he persevered. A few weeks later, on a hot summer's day, he cast off his habit, took up a heavy wooden Cross upon his naked shoulders, and thus, half-naked, led two other friars down the steep mountain track, calling upon God's mercy, until they reached Seggiano and there set up the Cross. "The villagers ran indoors, crying that the friars of Il Colombaio had gone mad," but after a while curiosity called them back, and when Fra Bernardino began to preach about the Passion, he did so "with such fervour of love" that they were all moved to tears. "And when the friars went home again, all the men who had heard him followed, weeping."[24]

For some time after this we hear nothing more about his preaching. "He lay hidden," says his biographer Maffeo Vegio, "and his name was obscure and unknown." Young as he was, however, he was appointed as the *Guardiano* (Superior) of Il Colombaio and in 1405 he was officially appointed a preacher by the new Vicar General of the Franciscan Order. It must have been in those years that he

23

served his apprenticeship as a preacher, addressing the friars and villagers in the Tuscan convents and villages he visited. Sometimes, too, he would pause upon his way to speak to little groups of country-folk at wayside shrines, on the threshing-floors of farms, in castle courts, or even in stables or barns, where his emblem still bears witness to his passage. The peasants working in the fields – themselves as stunted and half-starved as their cattle and dressed in rough unbleached wool of the same colour – would lift up their heads to see the little group pass: first a small grey donkey, led by a barefoot friar and laden with a rough folding altar, a sheaf of sermons and a couple of holy books, and then, walking in the dust behind them, another little friar, so thin that the folds of his short habit hung loose upon him as on a scarecrow and flapped against his slender ankles, yet walking with his head erect, with the sun sometimes making a halo of the soft, fair hair around his tonsure, and glancing round him with a look of great gentleness and humour. "*Povertade va leggera, Vive allegra e non altera.*" Always, until the last months of his life, his feet were bare – as a symbol of the casting off of all earthly ties. "If you would reach eternal life, bare your feet – that is, cast off your affections. . . . Shoes are of leather, belonging to a dead beast. Cast them off, cast them off!"[25]

It must have been at this time that Fra Bernardino acquired the fluency and ease which give his Italian sermons their especial flavour. He learned to hold the attention of the peasants with a lively image or an arresting story, and did not hesitate to mimic familiar sounds to tickle their ears – the buzzing of a bumble-bee in a barrel, *rush*, *rush*, "so loud that some men, thinking it was a small trumpet, called out, 'To arms, to arms!'" or the croaking of a frog, "You know what the frog says: she says *quà, quà, quà!*" Describing how a child could be weaned by putting some bitter ointment on its mother's breast, he said: "He draws his mouth away from the nipple, *tpu, tpu,* and spits."[26] He invented nicknames, too, to raise a laugh:

a careless housewife was "*Madama Aruffola*" (Madam Shaggy-head), a girl who was always at the window, "*Monna Finestraiuola*" (Miss Window-gazer), and to make eyes at her was to *balestrare* (literally, shoot), while the young men who did so were "full of cock-a-doodle-doo."

The images that he chose, too, were ones that a countryman could understand. If a man puts a heavy load on his donkey's neck, he said, or on its tail, the beast cannot carry it: it must be set in the right place. So God places each man's burden where he is fit to bear it. For the Angel of Death, who would bring vengeance upon sinners, he used the familiar image of a reaper: "Have you not seen such a man? He rests his sickle upon the ground, with the handle in his hand – and as he stands there he thinks, 'Where shall I strike?' And so he stands in suspense. But when he has made up his mind, he raises his sickle and sweeps it round!" When he told his hearers to think over what he had said, he said that they should ruminate, like their oxen. "When you go home or to your shops or vineyards, ruminate as you go – *ruguma, ruguma.*" When he bade them go to Mass, he told them to be "like the sheep cropping grass, in the midst of flowers – and so should you feed on God's word." He explained to them, step by step, how they should behave during the service and emphasized that they must not stay outside in the porch, talking about their oxen. "'How is it going with your ox? How much have you ploughed? How many men are hoeing your vineyard?' And they don't come into church, until just before the Elevation!" There was once a saint, he said, San Giovanni Elemosinario, who, on seeing that his church was empty, went out into the porch himself in all his vestments, and the people said he must be going mad. "'You don't come into the church,' he replied, 'to do what you should. So, since I am your shepherd, I will stay with my sheep and herd them!'"[27] Moreover, Fra Bernardino also understood the needs of seed-time and harvest, by which the lives of countrymen are ruled, and adapted himself to them. If he arrived during the vintage, when every hour of daylight is valuable, he held his sermons at night, or rather so early in the morning that by dawn the sermon had nearly reached its end.

One day he preached outside the city walls of Siena, at a place still know as L'Alberino (the little tree), because it was here that, according to tradition, St. Francis placed in the ground a staff which budded into a tree, and on another occasion, the feast-day of Sant'Onofrio, when a crowd of pilgrims and merrymakers had gathered on a hill near the saint's chapel, he climbed up into an olive tree, and addressed the astonished crowd from among its branches.[28] Soon afterwards, too, he preached for the first time in Siena itself, but at first he did not find it easy to hold his congregation's attention. For several years he suffered from some trouble in his throat (possibly an abscess on the vocal chords) which prevented him from speaking audibly, and this became so serious that he was on the point of asking to be released from the duty of preaching at all. One day, however, in answer to his prayers, he was suddenly healed – so completely and permanently that one of his early biographers could only attribute it to a miracle: a ball of fire, he said, had descended one night to touch the saint's throat as he knelt in prayer, healing him for ever.[29] From this time his voice became, as his hearers all agree, unusually musical, clear and penetrating, and also remarkably rich in its modulations – "now sweet and gentle," wrote a contemporary, "and now sad and grave, and so flexible that he could do with it whatever he would."[30]

But he also had another obstacle to overcome. This was that the kind of sermon he chose to preach seemed so plain and easy, so concerned with everyday matters, that his hearers could hardly believe it to be worth hearing. "They marvelled greatly at the curious manner of his preaching," and, for all his exertions, they sometimes did not even wait to hear him out. Three times, "prostrated by bitterness of spirit," he declared that he would never preach again – then, once again, "he humbly submitted to the burden." Yet even in later years, when great crowds gathered to hear him, he would sometimes walk away after preaching, "in as great dejection as if he were being led to execution," conscious only of all that he had failed to say.

Soon after his appointment as a preacher, he was sent from Il Colombaio to a little hermitage outside Siena, on a wooded hill-top not far from Sant'Onofrio.[31] Since the hermitage belonged to the Ospedale della Scala, it was not difficult for him to obtain it as a gift (in return for a nominal yearly gift of a wax candle to the Hospital, since the Friars Minor might accept no possessions) and here he and his friars began to build another convent – *pauperculum nidulum* (a little nest of little paupers) – chiefly with their own hands. This small convent – named La Capriola, but known in Siena simply as the Convento dell'Osservanza – was the place to which, whenever he could, he "came home to roost," and which still bears the mark of his work and of his spirit. It is a very Tuscan site, looking down towards Siena over gently sloping hills (now planted with olives and vines, but then mostly wooded) – remote enough, at least in his time, to be entirely peaceful, yet near enough for him to see the walls of his city, with the arch of Porta Ovile and the great tower of the *Mangia*, and to hear the chiming of the bells. It was here, rather than in the harsh wilderness of Monte Amiata, that he really belonged. From here he occasionally continued to preach – in the Cathedral of Siena in 1410 and possibly also in Ferrara and Padua – until in 1417 he was transferred to another convent at the top of the Fiesole hill above Florence, set in the midst of a cypress-wood and looking down over the whole valley of the Arno. This, like Il Colombaio, followed the strict Observant Rule. The friars were cloistered, only allowing two of their number to go out once a week to beg for their daily bread, "so that" – according

27

to a contemporary – "when their clogs were heard, men and children would hurry to their windows and doors, to look upon these holy friars with devotion, and the mothers would say to their daughters, 'Learn from the friars of the Observance to walk modestly, with your eyes upon the ground.'"[32]

It was here that Fra Bernardino found two men who were to become his closest disciples and collaborators, Fra Giovanni da Capistrano and Fra Giacomo della Marca, and also that at last, by means of one of the convent's novices, his wider call came. One night when Fra Bernardino was away in Florence, this novice sprang up from his pallet and ran up and down the narrow passages of the convent, rousing all his brothers from their sleep by crying, "Fra Bernardino, Fra Bernardino, do not hide the talent that God has given you! Go to preach in Lombardy!" For three successive nights this scene was repeated and when the friars complained of the disturbance of their night's rest, the novice replied that an irresistible impulse had compelled him to speak.[33]

Perhaps, had the incident occurred sooner, Fra Bernardino would not have obeyed, but now he himself must have felt that he was ready. In the company, as usual, of one other friar and of his little donkey, he set forth for the North upon his mission.

II

The precise route which he followed upon this journey to the North is somewhat uncertain,[34] but he seems to have paused first in Ferrara, where the plague was raging, and then to have made his way to Genoa, where he gave a course of Advent sermons, and unmasked a drunken impostor, Giovanni Vodadeo, who – dressed only in lambskins – was playing upon the credulity of the people. In the following year (1418), after preaching again in Genoa and also

V. A. The Sermon to the Confraternity: *Vecchietta*.

quak in edificatione monasterii fratres hortatus fuerit   quak malus fu

V. B. Building the Convento dell'Osservanza: *Giacomo da Lodi*.

VI. Vision of Fra Bernardino: *S. Figuera & R. Thomas.*

in Mantua, he visited many cities of Liguria and Piedmont (encountering the members of various heretical sects), and before the end of the year had arrived in Milan, a city then ruled by the last of the cruel and ambitious Visconti, Duke Filippo Maria – a treacherous, superstitious and bigoted tyrant.[35] At this time Milan was a flourishing city of some two hundred thousand inhabitants, but its great Cathedral was not yet completed and its three principal churches were Sant'Ambrogio, Sant'Eustachio and San Vittore al Corpo. Fra Bernardino, however, did not dare to enter the pulpit of any of these, and spoke instead in a little suburban church. His future biographer, Maffeo Vegio – then a boy of twelve – was taken by his preceptor to hear "that good little friar" (*bonum illum fraterculum*) and was struck by his natural dignity, his coarse and shabby habit, his gift for communicating his ideas and the great beauty of his voice.[36] Others, too, must have observed these qualities, for Fra Bernardino was asked to return in the following spring, to preach a series of Lenten sermons, and it was during the first of these that his congregation suddenly saw their preacher caught up, in the midst of his discourse, in a vision – that of the ascension to heaven of his cousin Tobia. When, on sending a courier to Tuscany, the answer came back that this vision must indeed have taken place at the very moment of Tobia's death, the news swiftly spread that a new seer had come to Lombardy. Fra Bernardino's success was assured: the Milanese – naturally devout, and also fond of anything new – hurried to his little church "like so many ants."[37] When Easter came, it was difficult to find enough priests to hear confession and to administer Holy Communion, and his converts included a knight from Monza called Cristoforo, who left Visconti's service to join the Observants, and was later on beatified.

It was during these sermons that Fra Bernardino, for the first time, displayed for the crowd's adoration a gilded tablet bearing his celebrated monogram of the letters of Jesus' Name. During the whole course, he refrained from referring to any worldly matters or to the sins of the city in which he was preaching, but spoke only of divine love – "as high as hope, as long as faith and as wide as charity."[38] One day, however, he received a complaint: one of his congregation came to ask him to descend to more earthly matters and to dwell especially upon the sin of usury – to which, he said, the Milanese were much addicted. After he had left, Fra Bernardino inquired who he might be – only to learn that he was himself the most merciless usurer in the city, who had hoped that the friar's eloquence might induce all his rivals to go out of business![39]

Even the suspicious Duke Filippo Maria developed an unwilling respect for this unworldly preacher and invited him to come back, but on one of Fra Bernardino's subsequent visits to Lombardy, in 1439, he may have regretted his invitation. By then, twenty years after his first visit, many of Fra Bernardino's converts were scattered or had been corrupted by the despotism of their tyrant, who demanded from his subjects an almost idolatrous reverence. This Fra Bernardino could not allow, and in one of his first sermons – which took place in the Duke's own presence – he plainly told the Milanese to refrain from giving to Caesar what was due only to God. On the following day, threats of torture reached him from the Duke and, when these failed to alarm him, an attempt was made to corrupt him instead: some courtiers came to his cell, bearing a bowl containing five hundred gold ducats. Fra Bernardino sent them back laughing and saying, "I value them no more than so many flies!"[40] The Duke sent the money a second time, with a message that if Fra Bernardino did not want it himself, he could make use of it for his friars. Again the preacher refused, but when, at a third attempt, the Duke's courtiers suggested he should use the coins to free the wretched debtors in the prisons, he took them at their word, and, taking the Duke's envoys with him as witnesses, presented some of the prisoners with their freedom. From that time, according to

Surio, the Duke "dismissed his suspicion and hatred and held him [Bernardino] in great reverence."[41]

This story, however, belongs to the later period of Fra Bernardino's apostolate. During the fifteen years which followed his first sermons in Milan his voice was heard in every important town of Northern and Central Italy, as well as in many villages and hamlets, and wherever he went, some witnesses of his passage may still be found in some convent or church founded in his honour, in some shrine or relic, or in the echo of a legend. The mere distance that he covered – when we consider that, until the last months of his life, he always went on foot, refusing even to ride upon his donkey – is remarkable. Wherever there was a Franciscan community, he would spend the night there, but sometimes, too, he would take shelter in a farm or a shepherd's hut or in one of the great walled abbeys or hospices, on the roads to Rome, whose privilege it was to give hospitality to pilgrims, preachers and wayfarers. ("Each time that you shelter a pilgrim, you shelter Christ.") Often, indeed, these lonely abbeys – standing in the fertile oases they had made for themselves in the midst of waste lands – were the places where the latest tidings from all over Europe could best be heard: news of wars and treaties, of a Pope's election or a Prince's marriage, of an outbreak of pestilence or a prosperous harvest. "Know you not," said Fra Bernardino in one of his sermons, "when a letter comes from a King, how sweet it is to go and hear that letter?"

When at last, after a long day's tramp, he reached a city at nightfall and found a lodging, he would retire early, to spend most of the night in looking over his sermons and preparing himself for the next day. Long before dawn he was already setting up his altar in the square; he would celebrate Mass at sunrise, and afterwards preach for two or three hours, before the day's work began. Then, as the sun rose higher and the shops opened and the housewives hurried indoors to their daily tasks, the little grey, spare figure set off again upon the road.

Between 1419 and 1421 he walked, preaching almost daily, over the greater part of Lombardy and through the gentle green plains and spacious towns of the Veneto, perhaps even visiting Lugano and Bellinzona, in what is now Switzerland, and then crossing the Alps by the pass which still bears his name – and after his return, preaching on the shores of the Lake of Garda. In Bergamo, where his congregation was small and inattentive, he made use of an innocent stratagem: "My friends," he said, "I invite you all next Sunday to the sermon and beseech you to bring as many others with you as you can – men and women, old and young, peasants and craftsmen . . . because I must read you a letter which has come straight to me from Heaven, assuredly inspired by the Holy Ghost and addressed by God Himself to the city of Bergamo." On the Sunday morning, when the church was packed with curious listeners, he drew out a great sheet of parchment on to which he had copied, "with a fine initial letter," the Epistle to Pergamum in the Apocalypse. This he made the text of his discourse, and it appears to have been eloquent, for from that day his church was always crowded.[42]

In 1422 he preached, for the first time, in Venice, a city which he praised for the strength and stability of its government and for its freedom from party strife. Here he preferred to live, not in the prosperous convent of the Conventuals, I Frari, but in the poor little one of the Observants, but he preached – since no church was large enough to hold his congregation – in Piazza San Polo, and sometimes rowed out across the lagoon to the lonely little island, green with cypresses, of San Francesco del Deserto, to visit the convent which St. Francis himself had founded on his way back from the Holy Land.

His main subject when he spoke to the Venetians was the one closest to their hearts – trade – and so great was his success that the Doge, Tommaso Mocenigo, said he would grant him any wish: whereupon he asked for the gift to the Carthusians of the island of Sant'Andrea al Lido, and the foundation of a hospital for the plague-stricken on another island, Santa Maria di Nazaret. Both desires were fulfilled, and he also left behind him two prophecies, both of which came true: that the ships of Venice would sail towards the hills, and the Venetian horses cross the sea. The first was accomplished when, in 1438, some Venetian ships were taken to the Lake of Garda to guard the borders of the Veneto against the Duke of Milan; the other when, in 1464, Venetian troops went to fight the Turk in Morea.[43]

During this period Fra Bernardino also spoke in almost every other city of the Veneto, in Verona and Vicenza, Bassano and Treviso, Conegliano, Belluno and Feltre, and perhaps even went, according to one tradition, as far East as Istria, to Pola and Pirano. In Padua he gave a course of sixty sermons, addressing not only the crowds that flocked wherever he went, but also the magistrates of the city and the teachers and scholars of the great university – and he candidly admitted that this was a deep satisfaction to him. "Nowhere else have I dared," he said later on, "to preach such profound truths as in your Padua, because here I knew that I was being heard by most virtuous doctors and men skilled in every discipline, whereas elsewhere I might not have been understood and would have been in danger of being considered a heretic or a conceited ignoramus."[44]

And indeed, when he addressed the crowd in Bologna, precisely this occurred, for an unlettered friar began to preach against him, accusing him of heresy. Nevertheless, here too the great church of San Petronio was not large enough to hold his congregation and he was obliged to preach instead in the open square, and an equal success attended the two courses of Lenten sermons which he delivered in 1424 and 1425 in Santa Croce in Florence.

It is not necessary and indeed would be extremely difficult – since many places claim, on rather insufficient evidence, the honour of his presence – to follow Fra Bernardino's progress in every city in which he preached. It was not until 1432 that he at last allowed himself a period of rest and retirement at La Capriola, to set down and revise his sermons. He had been preaching, almost daily, for twenty-eight years.

Wherever he spoke, the whole population flocked to hear him. The Cathedral bell warned the faithful that the sermon was about to begin, and no shop opened its shutters until he had ended. However exhausted he might have been on arriving, when once he had begun to speak, he was tireless. "I think," he would say to his congregation, "your prayers must be renewing my strength." Sometimes, too, he surmised that it was his own pleasure in preaching that strengthened him. "I wax fat thereon," he said. "I weigh a pound more after speaking, than I did before."[45] At the sermon's end a long procession would make its way through the streets, headed by the city's magistrates and officials, with Fra Bernardino in their midst, bearing the standard with his emblem, and followed by the whole population. Then, when he had gone indoors, he would often receive visits from men who had suffered a change of heart. One of them came to vow that he would never again belong to a faction or take part in civil war; another, to announce that he had left his mistress and made peace with his wife; a usurer came to give back his ill-gotten gains, and the owner of a gambling house, to close his tables. A rich man brought a purse full of gold for Fra Bernardino's poor; a beautiful young woman, in tears, offered her cosmetics, her jewels, or her yellow hair. And the effect of his words continued even after he had gone away. Empty churches were suddenly filled; misers untied their purse-strings and gave donations to hospitals or prisons; prostitutes and criminals determined to spend the rest of their lives doing penance in a monastery or convent, rich men who had cast their debtors into prison, forgave them and set them free; men who had been waging an implacable vendetta, suddenly made peace with their enemies. "We were so full of piety after hearing him," said a chronicler of Viterbo, "that we felt as if we had all become saints."

What was the secret of Fra Bernardino's success? Part of it was undoubtedly due to something very simple, if achieved with great pains: his congregation understood every word that he said. An aristocrat and a scholar, preaching in a period in which the formal scholastic tradition still encouraged preachers to make abstruse and elaborate addresses, he held that no sentence should be spoken that was not intelligible to the simplest of his hearers. "Be clear! be clear!" he cried, "let your hearer go away satisfied and enlightened, not confused." And he told the story of a friar who spun his arguments so fine, so fine, "as fine as the linen your daughters spin," that one of his brethren, "a friar so coarse that he was quite confounded," could only say at the end, "My brother spoke of the highest and noblest things you ever heard! He spoke so high, that I couldn't understand a word!"

None of Fra Bernardino's hearers could have said the same. To be clear, he always maintained, was a preacher's first duty: "Wrap not up your speech, speak plain and open. Call a loaf, a loaf; say with your tongue, what you hold in your heart."[46]

He once declared that to his mind the three things most to be coveted in this world were great eloquence, deep scholarship and a virtuous life – and that what is known as eloquence consists simply in three things: "to speak clearly, briefly, and well." By clearness, he explained, he meant "the art of speaking so as to bring the high matters of the heavens and of holy theology and astrology as close, as if you could touch and feel them with your hand." Of brevity, he said that it was the speech of angels. "Read, when the Angel Gabriel came down to the Virgin Mary, how briefly he spoke. Only the essential and what was needful."[47] And as to speaking well, with

35

beauty of form, he said that it was like placing a good wine in a fine glass or cup, instead of in a coarse, dark bowl. "You will delight in it more, though it be the same wine."[48]

Again and again, in varying words, he repeated his principle: "A preacher must bring light." "For example I will take the sun, the most splendid thing one can mention. The sun holds in itself three things – light, heat and strength – and so is the word of God." And elsewhere he added, "The men who lack God's word, even though they attend Mass, are like the world without the sun." He even went so far as to say that if a man had only time either to hear a sermon or go to Mass, "you should let the Mass go, rather than the sermon." This is a curious statement to our ears, but it should be related to a time when unlettered men had no idea of what was going on during the Mass, and the only means of teaching them was through the spoken word. "How could you believe in the Holy Sacrament on the Altar, but for the preaching you have heard . . . and how, but for sermons, would you know what sin is? All that you know comes from the words that enter your ears."[49]

He never had recourse to any of the theatrical devices of some preachers of his time, such as reminding his congregation of the approach of death by suddenly holding up a skull or a skeleton, or concealing a man beneath his pulpit to simulate the cries of the damned, or to blow a trumpet announcing the Day of Judgment. Nor did he deliberately play upon the feelings of the crowd, since he had little faith in either the efficacy or the durability of such emotions. "Tears," he said, "belong to women and children, whose hearts are easily moved by poets' fables and epitaphs of the dead. I remember to have seen many and even evil men burst into tears on hearing about Our Lord's Passion . . . and then I have seen them return to their vices. . . . It would be more salutary if they wept, not for the Passion, but for its cause, their own sins."[50]

He did not, however, hesitate to illustrate his meaning with stories

36

and parables. "Preachers," he himself said, "are not to be criticized when, in order to render plain those high matters which are beyond us, they do so with simple and tangible examples, for in this lies the art of making oneself clear." Sometimes, too, he used the device of imaginary dialogues, which broke into the course of the sermon with vivid, crisp little scenes – dialogues between buyers and sellers, between countrymen and townsmen, between husband and wife, between two ignorant priests or two chattering women, and often, between the preacher himself and some imaginary member of his congregation. "'Wait a while.' – 'What is it?' – 'They're soldiers.' – 'But what will they do?' – 'Nothing but harm.' – 'Where are they going?' – 'They mean to go to Siena.' – 'What for?' – 'To seize the goods and possessions [of the Sienese] which are so fine, to dwell in their houses, which are so comfortable, and to live a little at their expense, to make up for the hard time they have had.'"[51]

He once compared a preacher to "a fencer, who sometimes uses his rapier's point and sometimes the flat of the blade, and sometimes attacks from the front, and then from the side or rear".[52] He, too, thrust and struck – but above all, he never failed to make his hearers laugh. He made fun of their superstitions and their follies, of their long trains and hats "like bats and owls," of their intolerable quarrelsomeness, of the foolish friar who let a gambler borrow his money and the lovesick girl who looked for a charm to get a husband; and his hearers, recognizing their own portraits and those of their neighbours, laughed – laughed and remembered.

An instinct which he himself could not account for, told him a great deal about every place he visited, the moment he arrived there. "When I enter a city," he said, "all the good and evil that is done in it comes into my head . . . everything that smells sweet or that stinks . . . and this is not through confessions. How can I explain it? When I was a secular, I thought I knew everything about the world, both good and evil, but according to what I have learned since, I knew and understood nothing. Then, after I had become a confessor, I learned a great deal more. But since I have ceased hearing confessions, I know more still."[53]

In addition, however, to this instinct, he took great pains to find out, before coming to a place, its customs and its troubles; he knew which town was divided into factions or oppressed by a tyrant, which had recently been invaded by enemy troops or attacked by the plague – and just as, when he wandered over the fields and hills of the Sienese countryside, he had shown his hearers that he knew about the hazards of the vintage and the harvest, so, in Venice, he made himself familiar with the habits of the little tradesmen whose shops lie close to the Rialto, and in Milan, with the art of making cuirasses and coats of mail. In Lombardy, he preached especially against civil war; in Venice, on trade and usury; in Tuscany, against sodomy and avarice. He would try, too, to master beforehand the dialect of each region, and sometimes would enliven a familiar tale by quoting a bit of dialogue in dialect, as when he made a pilgrim reply to a question in broad Milanese. "*Donde se', compagnone? – So' de Milano mi. – Che mestiere fai? – Mi so far de fustani.*"[54] His stories are often taken from familiar sources – St. Gregory's *Dialogues*, the *Legenda Aurea*, or the collection of popular tales in *Il Novellino*; at least one of them comes from the *Arabian Nights* and several, including the famous story of Ghino di Tacco, from the *Decameron*. But each of them is told again with the dry humour, the sharp eye for the revealing trait, the moral drawn without unctuousness or pedantry, which are Fra Bernardino's own hallmark. He treated the saints and Holy Fathers to whom he referred with affectionate, semi-humorous familiarity. St. Joseph is "the most cheerful old man there ever was . . . and yet the foolish painters will portray him as a melancholy old man, resting his cheek upon his hand."[55] St. Paul is "*Pavolozzo nostro*" (our Pauly), St. Jerome "*barba canuta*" (the greybeard), Alexander of

Hales "*Alisandro gentile*" (the courteous Alexander). He quoted them often, but most of all he liked to use the words of the Gospels. "There was a time," he said in middle age, "when I did not use [the Gospels] much . . . a time when I squeezed out all my knowledge, and never saw much fruit. But for fifteen years past, I have seen that this is better." To quote from the Gospels, he said, "is like being in a meadow full of flowers. You pluck this flower and that and then another – and then you make yourself a little garland."[56]

But at this point one must be careful. It is easy to overemphasize the colloquial, popular elements in Fra Bernardino's preaching, the anecdotes and parables that enliven it, the crisp phrases which evoke the very accents of his voice, and to remain with the impression that his sermons in the vulgar were nothing but brilliant improvisations, the emotional appeals of a mediaeval revivalist. Nothing could be further from the truth. Brought up in the strict scholastic tradition of the *ars concionandi*, Fra Bernardino never wholly broke away from it. All his sermons, whether intended for delivery in Italian or to be set down in Latin for his brother-friars, were constructed within the approved mediaeval scaffolding: first the *pro-thema* (an invocation to God and the Saints) and then the *thema* (the text), taken from the Scriptures, followed by the intricate divisions and subdivisions of its development, and leading up to the peroration and summing-up. To a modern ear, this structure sometimes seems both artificial and wearisome: the twelve damsels of the Virgin Mary, each representing her virtues, the seven sins of the Magdalen, the "twelve laws of the merchandise of Divine Love," and so forth – these seem cumbersome and sometimes faintly distasteful devices. But they were entirely in harmony with the taste of the times and in mediaeval oratory they formed the essential framework of a discourse, breaking up its monotony and serving as a valuable prop to memory, when the moment came for the preacher to sum up. "Today you have heard . . ." "Gathering up what I have said . . ."

Sometimes, too, the preacher would add that if there was anything that one of his hearers had not understood, he was to come to him as soon as the sermon was over. "I will explain and he will be satisfied."

He considered a preacher's vocation so exacting as to be incompatible with any other duty. "I have renounced," he said in middle age, "every other task. . . ." He even refused to hear confessions or to administer baptism. "The Lord has not sent me," he quoted from St. Paul, "to baptize, but to spread his word." After he had become famous, many people came to ask for his practical advice on worldly matters, but he refused to give it. "One man comes to me who has a quarrel with his wife, saying, 'For the love of God, make peace between her and me.' Another says, 'I am owed money by such a man, he is tormenting me, mocking me, I am in sore straits.' Well, what would you have me do? I am neither *podestà* (Mayor) nor Captain of the City. . . . If a boy is turned out of his home by his father, he comes to me. . . . If a woman is sent away by her husband, she comes to me – if she runs away from home, *he* turns to me. . . . And some of them begin their tales a thousand miles away." One man even came to him to complain of the corruption of his parish priest. "You would have me be Pope, Bishop, Rector, and Officer of the Merchants' Guild; I am to do all that is fit for those who hold these offices. Well, I cannot do everything! Let each man perform his own office. . . . When you need to go to the *Signori*, do not come to me, for I can do nothing for you . . . and I should instead be preparing a sermon to God's glory."[57]

Not all preachers, in Fra Bernardino's opinion, were fit for their high vocation. They were, he said, of three kinds. "Some have the life and not the doctrine . . . others have the doctrine, but not the life," and finally, there were a few who had both. "And of such is it said, 'He who shall both do and preach, the same shall be called great in the Kingdom of Heaven.'" A good preacher, he said, must always adapt himself to an audience made up of all kinds of hearers – he must convince the intellectual, move the feelings of the emotional and arouse the fears of the hardened sinner. But above all, he must always be brave enough to speak the truth, "for few men are so ignorant and blind as not to distinguish between a flatterer and a man who sets forth the truth."[58]

It is on these grounds – not as a subtle theologian nor an original thinker, but as a man never afraid to speak the truth and capable of moving the hearts of both the simple and the learned – that one can claim that Fra Bernardino was one of the greatest popular preachers of Italy, and in this, too, he was following the traditions of his Order, since the task given by Pope Innocent III to St. Francis had been "to preach penitence to all men" – not, as was ordered to St. Dominic, to combat heresy or expound theology. "I have learned," said Fra Bernardino, "from our father St. Francis, who says in his Rule, 'Go, speak to the people of virtue and vice, of the glory and the pain.'"[59] Many preachers of his time, following St. Augustine's definition of the preacher as *divinarum Scripturarum tractator et doctor*, still used the text of the day's Epistle or Gospel merely as a starting-point from which to launch themselves upon long, learned (and often, to their hearers, totally incomprehensible) theological or philosophical disquisitions. Bernardino broke away from this tradition. He used the text as a starting-point for the illustration and elucidation of some simple problem of human conduct, or for the description of some virtue or vice, and the men who heard him came away fully informed as to what, in his opinion, God's will for them was. In these respects Bernardino was an innovator, developing, in the direct tradition of St. Francis, a new school of preaching – and his method was followed by his disciples.

There is, moreover, one other trait that is peculiarly his own: the intensity of his delight in his own calling. In the midst of his harshest denunciations of sin, his most eloquent exhortations to repentance, this note of sheer pleasure rings out. "Oh, one cannot live without delight! A student cannot learn anything well, unless he delights in his book, a priest cannot say Mass well, if he feels not delight; nor can a preacher ever preach well, unless he delights in preaching."[60]

This "delight" – the most irresistible of gifts – is very Franciscan, and so is Bernardino's spontaneous, contagious pleasure in the beauties of the visible world. This earth, he admits, is only "the stable of the Lord's horses," in comparison with the splendours of Paradise, but its beauty entranced him, as it had St. Francis himself. There is a legend that once, as a little boy, Bernardino was found up a cherry tree, telling the cherries that they should be grateful to their Creator "for making you, with no trouble of your own, so beautiful, so sweet to the taste and so much loved by men," and on another occasion, among the branches of a fig tree, preaching – in lack of any other audience – to the vines.[61]

Later on, it was with infinite, detailed delight that he described the loveliness of flowers, trees and plants, each marked by the touch of God's own hand, the wooded hills round Siena, the ebb and flow of the tide at Venice and the "little wind" which, rising at nightfall, "strikes the waves and brings forth a sound, and this is the voice of the waters." "Do you know in what the understanding of nature consists? It is when, through natural things, you know God . . . and through the things you can see, build up a ladder to reach eternal life."[62]

After more than five hundred years his sermons still have the freshness of the early dawns on which his congregation first heard them. In all their devotion, they are never solemn and never arid; his voice is always warm, and he often has time to laugh. "If Lorenzo de' Medici reflected the intellect of the Quattrocento," wrote Bontempelli, "and Fra Savonarola its wrath, San Bernardino was its heart."[63]

II. THE WORLD OF WOMEN

Che dirai tu delle donne di Siena?
Che ne dirò? che le fur fatte in cielo.
Acconce, sconce, in cuffia, in treccia, in velo,
Formose sono, e la città n'è piena.

ANTONIO CAMMELLI*

I

A MONG the portraits drawn by Fra Bernardino, none are more vivid than those of the women of Siena and Florence. They pass before us, a frieze of brightly-coloured, swiftly-moving figures, as convincing and alive as if we had met them in the Piazza del Campo or Piazza Santa Croce this morning. Here are all the women of his congregation, the fine ladies in their grotesque high headdresses and trailing gowns, the pious old crones in long black cloaks, the stout peasant-women with country baskets, and the pretty girls ogling their young men across the curtain which divided the square. For each one of them he had a penetrating glance, a smile or a frown, and also, to hold their flagging attention, a good story, in which they might see themselves in a mirror. He described the delicate old lady who, when she pleased, could cover more ground in a day than a strong man on horseback, and told the tale of the penitent harlot who, as she stood idly listening to his sermon, was suddenly struck, as by lightning, by the realization of the blackness of her sins, so that, crying out the single word, "Mercy!" she fell to the ground and died. "And I believe," said Fra Bernardino, "that she passed away to glory."[1] And for the fine ladies there was the story of Madonna Saragia, an extremely greedy woman, who wished to seem very refined. She told one of her peasants to bring her a basket of ripe cherries ("fine big ones, from the Marches"), and began to gobble them up in handfuls, while he stood by and watched her. A little later her husband came home and she, picking up some cherries,

43

began to toy with them delicately – "seven bites to a cherry" – and then, turning to the peasant, asked him condescendingly, "How do people eat cherries, out there in the country?" "Madonna," said he, "they eat them just as you did yours, in your room this morning, in great handfuls!"

Perhaps it was partly because Fra Bernardino had lived in a wholly feminine household as a boy that he understood all these women so well, but it was also because so large a part of his congregation was always made up of them – some brought to the Campo by genuine piety, some (as he well knew) merely because his sermons had become the fashion, and many others, because there were so very few gatherings to which an honest woman could go. Early in the morning as he spoke, there were always a few of them who would hurry to the Campo to get themselves a good place, even before the bell summoning the congregation had begun to toll, and these he regarded with some exasperation. "The square is so large and fine that if you come when the bell tolls, it will be soon enough, and each of you will get a good place. And do not come before dawn, as you like to do; for so you will have a bad night, and when the sermon begins you will fall asleep!" Besides, if these good women arrived so early, the late-comers would then try to elbow and jostle their way in front of them. "*Monna Pigra* (Madam Lie-abed) arrives and wishes to sit in front of *Monna Sollecita*" (Madam Earlybird), and the whole square echoed with their cries. "*O donne,* how shameful is it that, when I am saying Mass, you make a clamour like a bag of rattling bones. One calls, 'Giovanna,' another, 'Caterina,' yet another, 'Francesca!' Oh, it is a fine devotion with which you follow the Mass!"[2]

But then the sermon would begin, and gradually, in the warm morning sunlight, the women who had got up too early would indeed begin to doze off, even though they rubbed their eyes and pinched themselves to keep awake. "I see two women sleeping beside each other, and each is the other's pillow. . . . Women, if you were spinning and went to sleep, you would break your thread. I have spun, and now I shall begin to weave." However large the square, however thick the crowd, Fra Bernardino's sharp little eyes seemed to be everywhere. While he was speaking of the pit into which Lucifer fell, he caught sight of another sleeper. "Beware," he cried to her, "lest you fall into the same pit!" And again, raising his voice, "You sleeper, waken, hark to what I have to say! Have you heard, you sleeping woman?" He noticed, too, which of them had brought her husband and daughters with her, and which had left them at home. "The wise woman has brought her daughter with her to the sermon; the less good one, has left her in bed." And to another, "Woman, get up at once, go and call your husband!" "But I have called him." – "I say, go and call him." – "But if I lose my place?" – "No, you will not lose it, there is room enough." – "Oh, I shall never be able to get out!" – "I tell you, go and call him."[3]

To regard the churches as places of entertainment, was very common in Fra Bernardino's time. Often they were used for gambling or dancing[4] – as in the fairly recent days when, in many villages, the church was the only building large enough for the population to gather in – and sometimes also for parodies of the Mystery Plays or for such survivals of the old Roman *Saturnalia* as the *festa dei pazzi* (the fools' feast), celebrated during the twelve days between Christmas and the Epiphany, in which an "Archbishop of Fools" was solemnly consecrated in church and distributed false indulgences to "penitents" masked as pulcinellas or harlequins, who burned excrement as incense and played dice upon the altars.[5] Even Fra Bernardino's congregation did not hesitate to bring to church with them, as well as their weeping babies, their dice, their hawks and their hunting dogs with bells. "The child cries, the hawk flies about and the bells tinkle." But above all, both men and women

45

came to enjoy each other's company. "There are some women so bold and shameless that they trifle with young men even inside the church," he said, "and the girl's mother, too, becomes her own daughter's procuress, making her sit on the church benches, while her suitor gapes at her, following every movement she makes. . . . Shame upon you, shame! And they say, 'Oh, she goes to church so devoutly!' Does she indeed seem devout to you, behaving like that and gesturing to her admirer? And he goes about saying, 'I fell in love with her in church!'"[6]

And the preacher went on to describe these young gallants, "in a tunic, with a page's haircut and long slit hose, polishing the benches with their sparrow-hawks, and with their dogs on a leash. . . ." "One stands here and the other there, one keeps his arm on his friend's shoulder and his eyes keep darting round; and then the women rise and go to the Hospital [the chapel of Santa Maria della Scala] for the Pardon, and the young men go out arm in arm and form an aisle and the women pass between them and one man stares at them and another makes some gesture. . . . You have turned the church into a brothel with your behaviour, and with all your darts and grimaces. You would do better to stay at home!"[7]

He had harsh words, too, for the woman who only made herself fine for such public occasions, and neglected herself at home. "When she goes to church, she is all adorned, painted, garlanded, so that she seems *Madonna Smeraldina* (literally "my lady Emerald", i.e. a fine lady), and at home she is a slut. . . . Shame upon you, for you should look finer and more seemly in your own room with your husband than among so many folk in the Bishop's palace!" On the whole, too, he seems to have preferred Martha to Mary. "Have you a sick man at home? – 'Yes!' – Do not leave him to come to the sermon! Have you children? – 'Yes!' – Do not leave them. . . . First take heed to the things that are needful at home, and then come to the sermon." He added, however, that those who *had* come, should take pains not to lose a single word, especially when he was speaking of the Virgin Mary. "Take great heed, for if the stones could do so, even they would come to hear." And after the sermon, he told each one to spread the good word to the old and the sick and the children who had been left at home. "O women, I will make preachers of you all!"[8]

The Sienese ladies of Fra Bernardino's time were renowned all over Europe for their beauty, grace and elegance. *"Dolce 'l guardo, il parlar e dolce 'l viso,"* the poet Antonio Cammelli wrote about them, ["sweet in their looks and speech, sweet in their face"] – only adding, for he was no friend to Siena, that it was a pity that such charms should be wasted on such swine as the Sienese.[9] The *Story of Two Lovers* by Aeneas Silvius Piccolomini (who became Pope Pius II) described the Emperor Sigismund as exclaiming to one of his barons, on his arrival in Siena in 1432, "Did you ever see any women like these? I wonder whether they are human beings or angels." And the future Pope also wrote elsewhere that these charmers were "full of wit and grace, knowing how to play in- struments and dance, and even how to write in Latin and in verse."[10]

Fra Bernardino himself, indeed, approved of such gifts – in moderation. "A woman's beauty and a fine grace are given to her by God, if only she uses them well. . . . I would have you be adorned and delicate, but with discretion in all things, and modestly."[11] At that time elaborate high headdresses were being worn – and very charming some of them must have been on a pretty woman, al- though perhaps absurd on an old or ugly one. When the Emperor Frederick III passed through Tuscany in 1460 and saw the Florentine and Sienese ladies, he wrote that "they all seemed to have come from the hands of Andrea Mantegna," and added that "the variety of their headdresses made them seem to belong to every nation, some looking like angels, others like French or Flemish women, and yet others like Indians, Arabs or Chaldees."[12]

But Fra Bernardino saw these creations with a very different eye. "You wear so many vanities upon your head," he cried, "that it is shameful. Some wear battlements, some fortifications and some towers as large as that one [pointing at the tower of the Piazza del Campo, in which he stood]. I see upon these battlements the devil's banner.... I see one woman with a headdress shaped like tripe, and others like a pancake or a plate. Some fold the rim up and some down.... Could you but see yourselves, you look like so many owls and hawks.... O women, you have made a god of your head!"[13]

There was, indeed, very little in the fashions of the day that did meet with Fra Bernardino's approval. Very wide sleeves, which he called *ale* (wings), were often worn, slashed in silver or embossed in velvet, and these distressed him on account of their wastefulness. "One may say that a woman's gown has two cloaks, one on either side" – but, he added, if war came and the dreaded soldiers of fortune entered the city, "your wings, women, will be cut off." Sometimes these great sleeves were held up over a woman's head during a shower, sometimes she flung them "first over one shoulder and then over the other, because they get in your way. What a waste of stuff and of energy!"[14]

Equally wasteful and wrong, to his mind, were the long, sweeping trains, "like a snake," which every lady of fashion wore. They were, he said, the devil's own invention. "God made both men and women without a tail.... And tell me, what happens to a woman's train, when she walks down the road in summer? It stirs up the dust and in winter it is covered with mud.... And if she asks her maid to clean it, she will upbraid that sow, her lady."[15]

Then there were the high-heeled shoes, *pianelle*, made with many layers of leather beneath the sole, and a painted heel. "If a woman has a short daughter, she wishes her to seem tall, and makes her wear a pair of *pianelle* as high as a span, and dresses up her head, too, so that she seems a different person ... so that, between her head

VII. A. Fra Bernardino's Congregation: *Neroccio di Bartolomeo*.

VII. B. A Sienese Wedding: *Sano di Pietro*.

VIII. A. Ladies in Hats and Trains: *Attributed to Aollonio di Giovanni.*

VIII. B. Ladies of Siena: *Master of the Jarves Cassone.*

and her feet, she has added half an ell to her stature."[16] "One third of the Sienese ladies," said a wit of the day, "is made of wood!"[17]

Like all other women, too, they liked to change their fashions as often as possible. "You say to your husband," Fra Bernardino remarked, "'I want a gown in such a fashion, I want it made like that woman's, trailing as much as hers upon the ground.' Well, you get it – and in a few days' time you find yourself so weighed down by so much stuff that your shoulders ache, and you say, 'I cannot wear it . . .' and you have it shortened to a new fashion." And he went on to tell the tale of a woman who, seeing a prostitute wearing a dress with a new cut, borrowed it and put it on her daughter, to show the model to her own dressmaker. "Were I your husband," cried the preacher, "I would give you such a mark with hands and feet that you would remember it for a long time! Are you not ashamed to dress up your daughter, and yourself too, in the garments of a whore?"[18]

It was easy, he said, to measure a woman's worth at a glance by her appearance. "So one knows the wool-merchant's shop by his emblem . . . and the monk by his habit, black or white. . . . By what is without, you may tell what is within. I mean that when a woman wears a harlot's gown, I know not whether she is so within, but what I do see, seems to me a bad sign. . . ."[19]

The most reprehensible habit of all, in his eyes, was the fine art which the Sienese ladies called *delicatura* – the use of hair-dyes and ointments, of beautifying waters and cosmetics. Their beautiful fair hair was made fairer still by spending whole days on the roof-tops, "bleaching their hair in the sun, washing and drying, washing and drying again" – and apparently the Florentine ladies also did the same, for he complained of their washing their hair "three times a week" and then drying it in the sun, "and not even in a private place, but in the squares and streets." "And meanwhile," he added, "time flies . . . and if they spent as much of it on their soul as they do

49

on beautifying their bodies, they would turn into St. Catherine!"[20] He tells us, too, that they used, to whiten their skins, not only asses' milk, but washes of sulphur and sublimate, which often produced a most unpleasant smell. "Some there are among you whose mouth stinks from your cosmetics, some who reek of sulphur, some who anoint themselves with this and that, and stink so much in the presence of your husbands that you turn them into sodomites. How many of you have teeth which have rotted from so much painting? Bear in mind that this is the Devil's work, to weaken both your husband and yourself, and thus get both your souls. Do not wonder if your husbands cannot bear the sight of you: it is your own fault."[21]

What most deeply offended Fra Bernardino in all this was that it was a form of deceit, a repudiation of God's intention. "Do not hate yourself, for you are hating your Maker. . . . He has made [a woman] small, and you put stilts under her to make her seem tall; He has made her dark, and you paint and smear her to make her seem pale; He has made her yellow, and you paint her red. You are improving on God, a good painter. . . ."[22]

During the years in which Fra Bernardino was preaching, a long series of "sumptuary laws" were passed both in Siena and Florence, attempting to restrict all these extravagances of fashion and especially the value of the stuffs that the women wore, and of their jewels and ornaments. These laws were as inconsistent as they were ineffective. At one moment, trains were forbidden by law in Siena from June to mid-September, and were only allowed in winter, if their wearer draped them over her arm; then in 1427 – perhaps owing to Fra Bernardino's influence – they were entirely forbidden; a little later on, they were back again, but might only be of a specified length. In 1412 a statute was passed forbidding the Sienese ladies to wear any gown of silk, velvet or cloth of gold, but their protests must indeed have been violent, since it was revoked after a single month.[23]

When Fra Bernardino told them that the height of their *pianelle* should be no more than a couple of fingerbreadths, they pretended that they had thought he meant two fingers *long*,[24] and when the statutes forbade them to wear golden or silver garlands, they replaced them by wreaths of pearls. As to furs, ermine, in theory, was forbidden in Florence to anyone but knights and their ladies, and miniver (the fur of the small grey and white squirrel called *menu vair*) might be worn only by knights, magistrates and doctors, while in Siena ermine was only allowed to trim a collar or a sleeve. But in practice these furs were worn by anyone who could afford to buy them. Above all, it was found quite impossible to limit the value of the stuff used for the ladies' gowns. Restrictions were laid upon silks embossed in velvet, and also upon the rich oriental damasks and brocades, woven with silver and gold, embroidered with precious stones and reflecting all the colours of the rainbow, which often formed part of a bride's trousseau. But we have only to look at the pictures of the time to see how often, in spite of every statute, these beautiful gowns were worn, and indeed in the very year in which Fra Bernardino's voice was protesting in the Piazza del Campo, the city's legislators admitted their own powerlessness, stating that "the immoderation of women in dress is a great defeat for the men, since as soon as the statutes forbid one fashion, they find another which is worse and even more costly!"[25] Moreover these same legislators were also, at the same time, encouraging such extravagance, for they were granting a yearly subsidy to an enterprising young Sienese artisan, Nello di Francesco, who had introduced the art of silk-making into his own city – thus greatly diminishing the yearly importation of fine stuffs from Florence, Lucca and Venice, and enabling the Sienese ladies to buy their silks at home.[26]

All this, of course, laid a great burden upon the economy of the State and made it extremely difficult for a man to get his daughters married, since their dowry included not only these costly garments but also jewels and exquisite linen. "How can one describe," Fra Bernardino asked, "the luxuries which one may often find not only in the palaces of the great, but in the houses of common citizens? Consider the size and softness of the beds: there you will find silken and linen sheets, with borders of fine gold embroidery, precious coverlets . . . painted and provocative of lust, and gilded and painted curtains." Most of these objects, he declared, came from ill-gotten gains, but this their owners preferred to forget. "You give your daughter to a man in marriage, but neither he nor his father and mother consider where her chattels have come from, nor what her dowry is made of. . . . Sometimes, indeed most often, it is the fruit of robbery and usury, of a peasant's sweat or a widow's blood, of the very marrow of widows and orphans. Were you to take one of these gowns and press it and wring it out, you would see, gushing out of it, a human being's blood."[27]

Fathers came to dread the birth of a girl-child, in view of the large dowry they would have to provide for her, and every year the prices in the marriage-market rose. In 1384 a prosperous Florentine merchant, Lapo Niccolini, was content to receive a dowry of 700 florins with his first bride, but when, twenty years later, he married again, he required 1000 florins from his second, and at the middle of the fifteenth century, Alessandra Macinghi Strozzi, who was looking for a wife for her son, contemptuously wrote that 1000 florins was a mere craftsman's dowry. "He who takes a wife wants money," she firmly wrote, referring to the bride as "suitable merchandise."[28]

Moreover, there were not a few young men who, rather than provide the luxuries which their bride would require, preferred to remain unmarried. "There are many," said Fra Bernardino, "who do not take a wife and do not want to do so, on account of the additional expense," and by the middle of the fifteenth century the situation in Florence had become so serious that Leon Battista Alberti, in his famous treatise *Della Famiglia*, was obliged to suggest that fathers should leave a share of the family estate only to those sons who had married "at a reasonable age."[29] The truth was, too, that there were a good many young men who were not sorry to have any excuse, since their own inclinations lay in other directions. The list which Fra Bernardino drew up of the qualities which a wise mother should look for in her son-in-law is informative, since it included not only the obvious positive virtues of honesty and industry, and the possession of a peace-loving and God-fearing nature, but several important negative qualities: the chosen bridegroom should not be a gambler, taverner or drunkard – "as fiery as a dragon at home" – nor a magician nor astrologer, nor, above all, a sodomist. "There are some men," he said, "who have a beautiful wife, wise and honest and of good repute, and the devil enters the husband's eyes. Owing to the evil vice of sodomy, he cannot bear to look at her, and she seems to him a worthless country wench."[30]

II

In his denunciations of women's frivolity and vanity – a theme dear to preachers since the days of Tertullian and St. Jerome – Fra Bernardino's thunder has somewhat conventional accents. But when he is preaching about marriage itself and about the relationship between man and wife, it is his own voice that we hear, with all the humour and compassion, the dry commonsense and warm humanity, with which he regarded the complicated predicament of life. He devoted five of his sermons in the vulgar to the problems of marriage,[31] calling them *prediche scuopri-magagne* (sermons to lay bare the hidden sores), and in all of them he expressed himself extremely plainly. Most of the troubles of married life, he said, were

53

due to "a gross and foolish popular ignorance," and this was often encouraged by the reluctance of most preachers to touch upon this delicate subject – sometimes from a dread of being laughed at or criticized, and sometimes because of their own inner lack of purity. "What then should you do, Fra Bernardino?" he asked himself. "If for fear of being bitten by the malicious or from false shame, or for any other reason, you remain silent, you will be damned, for it is your duty to preach and to bring people back to salvation . . . . Speak out, then, and let other men say what they please!"[32]

In dealing with such matters, he said, he would try to be "like a cock on a dunghill . . . with his wings drawn up high, so as not to sully them. So is the preacher, who must come into the mud to speak of your sins, but in such a way as not to be sullied. . . . And you, woman, do not fall asleep, but hearken to the sins that you have never confessed, for I have decided to show them to you, so that you may guard against them." With great frankness of speech and fullness of detail, he told his listeners what the duties of marriage were, as well as which practices were permitted, and at what times. But after laying down these rules, he added that the best guide for any woman – in marriage as in the rest of life – was *Madonna Discrezione*, my lady Discretion. "She will teach you how much and when and how, and if you follow her advice, you will never sin. And if you do not understand her, I would have you go to her sister. . . . She is called *Madonna Coscienzia*."[33]

He had harsh words for young women who used their ignorance as an excuse for not performing their marriage duties as they should. "And I say the same of any profession or trade." He mimicked a young bride excusing herself, "'Oh, oh, I knew nothing and know nothing!'", replying, "That does not excuse the sin. . . . The girl who is to be married has chosen her trade and must know how to perform it honestly and purely. If she does not, she is sinning; but her mother has sinned still more, for not having taught her what she should know. It is like sending her off to sea with no biscuit." Some women, he said, did not even bring their daughters with them to his sermons, "saying they do not want them to learn many things that are said therein, 'for they do not even know what sin is.' Alas, you do not know what you are saying! Let your daughter know what it is against which she must guard herself. . . . Do you think that they cease to be sins, because she does not know about them?"[34]

It was still the general custom in Tuscany for a girl's husband to be chosen by the head of the family, with no reference to her own wishes. The strength and compactness of the family, not the happiness of the individual, were what mattered. But that in this, as in many other matters, there was already some discrepancy between theory and practice, is shown not only in Fra Bernardino's sermons, but in many other documents of the time. The difficulty is, which of them are we to believe? Are we to follow what is implied in the exhortations of preachers and moralists and in the ribald tales of Sacchetti and Sermini, or to trust to what we can glean from private letters and domestic chronicles? The latter are probably nearer to the truth, but they are too few and often too incomplete to present a picture in the round. Undoubtedly, however, Fra Bernardino was one of the first monastics to proclaim that a girl should have a voice in choosing her husband, and he also told with some gusto the story of at least one occasion on which one of them asserted her rights. A very short young man, he said, had been taken by his brothers to meet his future bride, a fine tall young woman. "Finally he was asked, 'Well, does she please you?' – 'Indeed she does.' But she, looking at his little stature, cried, 'But you do not please me!' – and it served him right."[35]

Undoubtedly, too, Fra Bernardino was among the first to defend a woman's right to be treated with both kindness and courtesy, and to lift up his voice against the corporal punishment which was still explicitly permitted by the statutes of most cities. Both in Siena and Florence a man might still beat his wife for even a small offence, and that this was by no means a dead letter is shown by Fra Bernardino's description of husbands, "like madmen on a chain, who are more able to bear with a hen who lays them a fresh egg every day, than with their own wife.... As soon as she says one word more than you think fit, you take up your stick and begin to beat her; yet you have patience with the hen who cackles all day long, for the sake of the egg she will lay!"[36] His own view was that "a wise man should never beat his wife, whatever fault she may commit," but should instead use "threats and good examples" – and above all, treat her with respect. "She needs help in her fragility ... and if she thinks herself despised, she will do worse instead of better."[37]

Moreover he affirmed – and this was then a new and odd idea – that a husband had no right to ask of his bride virtues which he himself did not possess. "What do you want your wife to be like?" he asked a young man. "I want her to be honest." "But you are dishonest: that will not do." And again, "'I want her to be temperate' – and you are always at the tavern. You shall not have her. 'I want her not to be greedy.' But you are always eating liver patties. You want her to be active, and you spend the whole day in idleness; you want her to be sweet-tempered, and you storm if a straw lies across your path; you want her to be good, beautiful, wise and well-mannered, with every virtue. I tell you, if you want such a woman, be like that yourself!"

He gently reminded young bridegrooms, too, that it was hard for a young girl who had been brought up all her life with her own family, "to go off, as soon as she is married, with her husband to another neighbourhood, to converse with people she does not know, leaving her father and mother, her brethren and kinsfolk, all for the love of the husband she has taken.... You must therefore show her great compassion and consideration," he concluded, "and love her as much in yourself alone, as she used to be loved by her whole family."[38]

He did not tell the wives he was addressing to become either Beatrices or Griseldas, but practical, tolerant and loving partners. "Between husband and wife there should be the most singular friendship in the world. . . . If one of them is virtuous and the other sinful, they will never agree, but if they are both good and love each other with true love, such friendship will spring up between them that it will be a paradise on earth." In such a true and equal relationship the total submission once required of women was no longer needful. "In the flesh," he said, "the husband is greater than the wife and should be obeyed in all things that are honest and permitted, but in the spirit a wife is her husband's equal." And he went on to point out that "God did not make a woman out of a bone of Adam's foot, so that he should tread her underground, nor out of a bone of his head, so that she should dominate him; but he made her out of his rib, which is close to his heart, to teach him to love her truly, as his companion."[39]

In such remarks as these, we may indeed feel in Fra Bernardino a foretaste of the spirit of the Renaissance, which only a few years later would lead Baldassarre da Castiglione to write in *Il Cortegiano*: "A woman must no longer be sold in marriage, for she has the same right to life and happiness as a man. She must be free to learn what she will, to choose a man as she pleases."

It must, however, be admitted that when it came to housekeeping, the preacher's list of a good wife's tasks was somewhat formidable. "She takes care of the granary and keeps it clean, she takes care of the oil-jars. . . . She sees to the salted meat. . . . she sees to the spinning and the weaving. She sells the bran, and with the proceeds gets the sheets out of pawn. She looks after the wine barrels, and notes whether they have broken hoops or if one of them is leaking. She sees to the whole house." And he went on to describe the life of a man who had no wife to care for him, but only a maidservant or a concubine. "If he is rich and has some oil, it gets spilled. . . . And in bed, do you know how he sleeps? He sleeps in a trough, and once he has put the sheet on it, he does not take it off again, until it is torn. The room where he eats has melon rinds, bones and bits of salad on the floor, without their ever being swept away. And the table? The cloth upon it is not changed until it is soaked. He rubs the plates a little; the dog licks them and washes them. . . . Do you know how he lives? Like a brute beast. . . . It is the woman who rules a house!"[40]

Again and again, Fra Bernardino repeated that the value of a good wife is "above rubies." "What is the most beautiful and useful thing in a house? Is it to have many obedient and well-dressed servants? Is it to own fine ornaments – silver and stuffs and curtains and velvets? Is it to have healthy, obedient, pleasant children? No, it is to have a beautiful, tall wife, who is good, modest, honest, temperate. . . . If she is full of charity, faith, humility, rectitude and patience and, besides all this, is capable of bearing you children – how great should be your mutual friendship! . . . This is the first thing that you should seek in her, goodness, and then the other things – but first of all, goodness." "When such a one truly loves her husband," he said elsewhere, "she feels such anguish when you are ill, that it equals your own. . . . She does not sleep or take off her clothes, she scarcely eats. And I tell you that a husband cannot come home to a good wife without her seeing in his eyes, whether he is happy or sad. If he is happy, she will be content; if not, she will grieve and will comfort him as best she can. With her he can lay down the burden of every trouble."[41]

That marriage was not always like this, however, Fra Bernardino would have been the first to admit. In one of his most vivid passages, he described the contrast between the triumph of a happy young bride riding to her husband's house, and what awaited her later on.

"She rides all adorned, with loud music and sounds of great rejoicing; she gathers a crowd as she goes down the street, and it is paved with flowers. She has so fine a dress, embossed in silver, and jewels and rings upon her fingers, she is painted, her hair is combed and dressed and garlanded, she has a headdress and shines all over with gold. She is riding in such great triumph as has never been seen before!" And then, pretending to interrupt himself, he called to her, "Oh, oh, oh, how high do you think you have risen? oh! oh!" And the narrative went on. "Then she reaches her husband's house and is received with great feasting . . . and for three days her husband seems bewitched and enchanted by her, and then in eight days' time she goes back to her father's house. And during all this time, as is the custom, it is a feast-day. . . . But however it may be, it soon comes to an end. If she is beautiful, her husband becomes jealous; if he is a fine young man, *she* becomes jealous; and so grief and anxiety enter in. . . . She may find stepsons and love them so little that she grudges them even their food. . . . or if she finds a daughter-in-law, or one comes soon after, peace lasts a very short time. And oh, oh, oh, if there is a mother-in-law – I will say nothing: you know it for yourselves. Little peace; the happy time is soon over."[42]

And finally he dwelled upon the fate – which appears to have been far from unusual – of the wife whose husband, after those first few days, became totally indifferent to her. "She is fit to have children, she is a good housewife, attentive, attractive, tall, young, of good family, with a good dowry – and she has a husband who cares for her no more than if she were made of straw. Oh, how much compassion she deserves! If she bears this patiently, that alone will suffice for her to deserve eternal life." "Women, women," he cried, "I am on your side – because you love your husbands better than they love you."[43]

After the wives, the mothers. To them, too, Fra Bernardino had a great deal to say, for, like his contemporary Ser Lapo Mazzei, he considered the mother's role in a household to be that of "the ship's mast." Whatever storms blew in the sails, she must stand fast. He realized, too – at a time when no one considered it unusual for even a delicate woman to have twelve or fourteen children and to be old by thirty-five – how hard her life could sometimes be. "When she is pregnant, she has the labour of her pregnancy; she has that of giving birth to her children and of caring for them and bringing them up, and she has also that of caring for her husband, when he is ill; she has the burden of the whole house to bear.... All this labour is the woman's alone, while the man goes off singing.... See to it, husband, that you help her to bear her burdens." Once, he said, a woman had said wistfully to him, "Messer Domeneddio does what he thinks best, and all that he does is right. But the woman alone has the burden of the children in many things: she alone carries them, she bears them and brings them up, and often with great trouble. If only God had given one part of all this to the man, at least in giving birth!" And Fra Bernardino commented, "I think she was right!"[44]

But however sympathetic he might be about a mother's burdens, he was also quite uncompromising about her duties. To hand over one's baby to a wet-nurse (often in a remote farmhouse, from which it did not return for a couple of years) was then the custom of both the prosperous burgher and the noble, but he resolutely opposed it. "You give your child," he said, "to be suckled by a sow, where he picks up the habits of his nurse.... And when he comes home you cry, 'I know not whom you are like: this is no son of ours!'" Children, he said, were like plants: when a man set in the soil of Siena a peachstone from one of the fine peach trees of San Gimignano, it only bore tiny, shrivelled fruit. "You have brought the seed here, but not the soil!"

Fra Bernardino's tenderness for small children and his understanding of their ways are quite unmistakeable, and it is plain that he must often have watched a mother with her baby. "She swaddles him round and round, she cleans and washes him when it is needful, she rocks him to sleep when he cries, she amuses him with little toys; she calls him to her, and sometimes shows him a cherry." He describes a very little boy falling down in the muddy road, "and he is little and cannot get up again without help. And he cries, 'Mamma, help me!' and his mother pulls him up."[45] When he walks through the streets of Siena, he always has an eye for the children's games, "as they cry, 'bread and candles, candles and bread!' and sometimes lie down on the ground as if they were dead, with crosses made of reeds," and when he meets the older boys, he stops to ask them how they use their slings. "You hold one of the strings back with your finger, don't you, and wind it round and round like this?"[46]

But for all this, Fra Bernardino was no more a sentimentalist about children than about their elders. He told the parents who cared only for their offspring "in the body," without also shaping their characters, that they fully deserved all the trouble that would certainly be theirs. "Look at the madness of the fathers and mothers who, when their children are five or six years old, teach them to say this and that, *messer sí* and *messer no*, make your bow and say: 'I thank you, sir,' and tell them not to take money if it is offered them – and all that is good. But when they are ten or twelve years old and need wiser teaching, you neglect them, and so you have the most shameless young men in the world – and all because of the coldness of their parents' love."

A wise man, he said, had once remarked to him that a child committed more sins between the ages of eight and fifteen, than at any other time in his life. Children of that age were natural liars, pilferers and tale-bearers, "and no higher than a fist, before they are chambers of vanity, especially the girls," and moreover – since they naturally repeated whatever words they heard – they also frequently fell into the sin of blasphemy. "Their eyes are hardly dry before they have nothing but blasphemies in their mouths.... And this is the fault of their parents and of those who should rule over them and correct them, who attach no importance to their sins and make excuses for their ignorance, saying, 'It is only their youth!'"[47]

The seven duties which, to his mind, good parents should teach their children were love, fear, reverence, obedience, long-suffering, imitation and support – "and the first of these duties is love." But in this, too, he was no sentimentalist and had no illusions about the spontaneity of these emotions, quoting St. John Chrysostom's image of a tree, in which the sap flows from the roots to the branches, but not back again,[48] though he did not, apparently, draw the conclusion that an upbringing as strict as that which he commended would hardly be likely to promote great affection and tenderness. The absolute authority of a father over his children – based both on the Roman *patria potestas* and on the traditions of the Germanic code giving a man power of life and death over his children, so long as they "shared the same bread" – was taken for granted by everyone in the society that he knew. Sons and daughters addressed their parents as *messer padre* or *madonna madre*, and were forbidden to sit without permission in their presence. "At least twice a day" (these maxims belong to Fra Giovanni Dominici, a famous preacher in Florence) "let them kneel down reverently at their father's and mother's knee and ask their blessing . . . and on rising, bend their head and kiss their father's hand.... They should not presume to speak in their father's and mother's presence, even when they are bearded men, but only to listen and answer."[49] Corporal punishment was, of course, not only permissible but right. "A son," wrote Fra

Giovanni elsewhere, "is his father's and mother's *thing (cosa del padre e della madre)* and may therefore be beaten as much as they wish."[50] And he added that the benefits of such beatings – which should not be confined to childhood, but were equally necessary for a son of twenty-five – were double: if the children deserved the punishment, they would discover what justice was; and if they did not, they could practise patience. These theories were shared by Fra Bernardino. "You, father, never laugh in his presence. Foster his reverence for you, and let his mother be the one to comfort him." The father should not spare the rod, but should also remember that the grave demeanour of a wise parent obtains greater respect than the beatings of a foolish one. Both parents should insist on constant good manners and on little services. "Let them say, '*messer sí*' and '*messer no*', and bow their heads . . . Treat them like slaves: make them serve you in little things and great: let them take off your shoes and wash your feet, rub your back, fetch your nightcap and slippers . . . not for your sake, but for their own." It was the father's duty, too, to take his sons to Mass, to warn them against gambling and dishonest contracts, and to shield them from bad habits and bad company. "If you see your son going out with young men of evil customs or running after women, and you see him come home like a wounded swine and he answers you angrily and eats little and sleeps less, you may know that he is in love. If then, out of negligence, you do not chastise him, you are committing a mortal sin." And when the father had grown old, it was still his son's duty to bear with his slightest whim. "Men are not like oxen, which grow tougher as they grow older. . . . If [your father] is ill, irascible in speech and stormy in temper, bear with him. If he seems forgetful and childish, strew his path with roses."[51]

As for daughters, an even more complete submission was required of them. Not only could they be beaten or bullied into a marriage they disliked, but they could also be disposed of – especially if ugly or deformed – in a convent. "I have heard," said Fra Bernardino, "that if you have [a daughter] who is blind or lame or crippled, you at once place her in God's service: you put her in a convent. . . . And when they are grown-up, they curse their fathers and mothers, saying: 'They put me there so that I should have no children, but I will have some, to spite them!'"[52]

This custom was one which Fra Bernardino whole-heartedly condemned; but, except for a passing reference, he did not concern himself with conventual education. His teachings were confined to the way in which a mother should bring up her daughter at home – with a discipline hardly less severe than that of a monastic rule. If he did not go quite as far as his fellow-preacher, Fra Giovanni Dominici, who required a little girl to be separated from her brothers at the age of three, and who adjured her father never to smile at her, "lest she fall in love with his virile countenance," he did demand that she should lead, from the age of twelve, a life in which she was never for a moment idle, and never out of her mother's sight. She should be the first in the house to rise; she should be set to work so hard that she had neither time nor inclination to look out of the window, and when she went to early Mass with her mother, she should muffle herself so closely in her cloak that no part of her face could be seen. It was her mother's part to teach her her prayers, (the Lord's Prayer and Hail Mary five times at rising and at bedtime, and grace at meals) and to see that she never told lies or mentioned the Devil, and made the sign of the Cross whenever she went out of the house. As to book-learning, he did not entirely disapprove of it – indeed he admitted that some women of his time were "more learned than a man" – but he firmly insisted that they were, and should remain, a minority, and that for most girls the chief purpose of learning to read was "to purge them of vanity." "Do you wish them to be honest? Make them learn to read. For I warn you that they cannot remain without any pleasure, and if they take

IX. Fine Linen and Curtains: *Paolo di Giovanni*.

x. A. Studious Young Ladies: *Domenico Veneziano.*

x. B. "La Finestraiuola": *Francesco di Giorgio.*

pleasure in the Scriptures it will be good, while if they do not, they will find their delight instead in vanities."[53]

The main object, however, of a girl's education was always the same: to prepare her for marriage by habits of obedience and industry, and by skill in every household task. "Teach them to sew, to cut out, to spin, to sweep, to cook, to wash their own heads and their brothers', to do the household washing and to serve at table. Let them not be like the girl, who when she went to her husband, could not cook an egg!" Again and again, he repeated these injunctions: "Does the house need sweeping? Let her [your daughter], sweep it. Are there dishes to be washed? Let her do it. . . . 'But there is the maid!' – Let her be; make the girl do it, not because it is needful, but for practice. Let her look after the babies, and wash their napkins; if you do not accustom her to do everything, she will turn into nothing but a lump of flesh. . . . If she has no love for household matters, you will see her become crazy and forgetful and wholly given up to vanities, to painting and anointing and combing herself... and always at the door or window" (usciaiuola e finestraiuola).[54]

Never should a girl be left, even for a moment, to her own devices. "Keep your eye upon her! If she does not stay quietly at home spinning and weaving, but runs to the window at every sound – then, if you don't chastise her, you will see her bring you to shame. If you want to punish her fitly, take her pulse and say, 'Oh, what a face you have today! You must have a fever,' and then send for the barber and let him draw three pints of blood, and it will decrease her heat."

Any outside influence whatever was to be feared. "Be always watching, and if they go into any room, always go with them. Beware how you let them go to feasts or weddings. . . . Let them have nothing to do with the servants. Let them not have too much converse even with their relations; for if you then find them pregnant, you need not ask how such a thing came about. Do not trust them

65

in your kinsmen's houses. Let them never, never, never, be alone, even when they are talking to each other. And never, never, never let them sleep with their own brothers, as they begin to grow bigger: for the Devil is subtle.... Hardly trust her even to her father, when she has reached the age of marriage."[55]

Above all, a mother must beware of ever leaving her daughter at home alone, even for a single hour. As soon as she was out of the door, he said, one of the old women who were the professional match-makers of Siena would knock at it, perhaps on the pretext of washing the girl's hair, or "with a basket of little bottles to make her fine." "First she will start by flattering the silly child, saying, 'Oh, what a pity it is that you are not painted and adorned! You are the prettiest girl in the city and you sit there like a sheep. Let me tell you what to do.'" And then, when the girl is "jumping up and down with delight," she will go on to say: "'I bring good tidings: there is someone who feels for you the greatest love in the world, true love!'"[56]

Such was the theory. In actual practice, however, it is plain that this constant watchfulness was not possible, especially in the working-classes, and that the natural Italian tenderness and gentleness towards children often broke down the strictness of these rules. Fra Bernardino admits that though it was the father's role to be feared, it was equally the mother's to comfort the child afterwards. "There must be a father's virility and a mother's compassion." And he went on to describe the fond, foolish mother, who, "when her little son wants anything, gives it to him at once, and when he cries, puts a fig into his hand, even though she knows that it is bad for him." Elsewhere, too, he spoke (though with disapproval) of the custom of allowing little girls to go *alle madonne*, that is, to pester the rich ladies of Siena in the street on feast-days, "pulling at their sleeves and asking for small coins" – and, from the very frequency and vigour with which he attacked their foolishness, we may be

66

pretty sure that there were more than a few mothers who did allow their daughters to go in the evenings to parties in their neighbours' houses, and who not only spent all that they could and more to make them fine, but were convinced that if they could dance well and sing sweetly, this would increase their chances of getting a good husband.[57]

But it would appear that it was Fra Bernardino who, even in worldly terms, was right. The old-fashioned virtues which the Church demanded were also still those that a man looked for in his bride, and we even find his contemporary, Giovanni Morelli, telling his son to inquire into the characters of the grandmother and mother of the girl he had chosen. "Make sure that they too were honest and bashful women." He added that the bride herself should be, above all, "peace-loving and not arrogant, as reasonable and intelligent as it is in a woman's nature to be, and also, if possible, not too vain, and not always wanting to go to parties and weddings."[58] Even as late as 1469, when customs had become freer, Marietta Strozzi, the daughter of a most virtuous mother, Alessandra de' Bardi, nearly lost her chance of marriage, because she had been allowed too much freedom – and in particular, had taken part in a snowball fight one evening with some young men. "She has beauty and a good dowry," wrote the elder brother of her suitor, "but there are drawbacks which outweigh even these advantages. She was left very early without father and mother . . . and it would be no matter for surprise that there should be some stain."[59]

IV

There was moreover one category of women for whom Fra Bernardino's precepts still followed the strictest mediaeval tradition: it was extremely undesirable, in the fourteenth century, to let yourself become a widow. Possibly the pattern which Fra Bernardino set before them had partly been shaped by the two pious women who had brought him up, Bartolommea and Tobia, but it also reflected the public opinion of his time. "The widow," he declared, "who knows how to demean herself is half a saint." It is plain, however, that he did not consider that many women of his congregation had attained this standard. His advice to them is rather based on the assumption that they would constantly be assailed by temptations, and particularly by those of vanity, idleness and lust. Idleness, he said, should be combated by filling every hour with some small task, and chiefly by working for the poor. "It is more pleasing to God, that you should sew a shift yourself and give it to a poor man, than that you should give him money for two shifts." Vanity and desire must be quenched by an unceasing self-discipline. Widows should eat and drink frugally and never sleep on a feather-bed, but, fully dressed, on straw. "If you eat well, drink well and sleep well, you'll come to a bad end!" And as to their possessions and ornaments, "You should behave like the Jewish women, who, when their husband dies, bury all their goods with him. If you used to wear headdresses with ornaments, pretend that you have buried them, and so with your clothes and all your other vanities. And bury your eyes, too, with him [your husband]; keep them modestly cast down." A widow's choice of company, too, was extremely restricted. "You should always seek the company of ripe and wise women of good repute. And have no familiarity with any man, not even with priests and monks, save with a ripe old confessor. And do not go out, save when no one can see you [i. e. for the first Mass at dawn]. . . . In all things you must be mature, chaste and solitary."[60]

A handsome young widow, he said, would probably very soon be approached by some old procuress (even more insistent than the match-makers who lay in wait for young girls), anxious to "feed upon her flesh" by arranging a second marriage for her. She would come indoors "to sell rosaries and coral beads," and then, as soon

68

as they were alone, would begin her lament: "'Oh, how my heart grieves for you, wasting your time away! You are young, you should have a husband.' And then she adds, 'I well know who it is that loves you!'... 'You must realize that you are thought the most beautiful woman in this place.' And with such airs and graces, she praises you so much that the devil enters into your body.... Tell her never to come to your house again! And if she does, when she reaches the top of the stairs, give her a push and throw her down them.... And for the love of God, try to remain a widow – if you can."[61]

The general agreement that a widow should not marry again was not only a religious principle: an economic consideration was also involved. To keep family fortunes intact, it was the custom, if a widow was childless, for her dowry to be returned to her own family, and, in that case, she herself went home again with it. Her position, then, was seldom enviable. Even though a wise father would sometimes set aside in his will a portion of the family fortune for this eventuality, Fra Bernardino thought it necessary to adjure her relatives not to behave to her, "as a dog does, when he sees another dog arriving,"[62] and any partial independence she had acquired as a wife was lost again, forever. She was again as subject to her father's rule as she had been as a child, dependent upon him for every crumb she ate and every stitch she wore – or if he had died, she was equally dependent upon her brothers. Perhaps, however, the widow had children. In this case she was very little better off: she remained with her former husband's family; but there, too, she was subject to the new head of her husband's family and often had very little say in her children's upbringing, although she was expected to be more strict than other mothers, to make up for the loss of their father's beatings. "If you have been left a widow," said Fra Bernardino, "supply in yourself a father's nature, too. Show them both sweetness and severity, [awaken] both love and fear."

69

"You must become half a man; keep your children under the heel of your clogs. . . . Teach them, when they are of the right age, with slaps and floggings."[63]

It is perhaps hardly surprising that, in view of the demeanour required of them, many young widows should have set their hearts on marrying again at any cost, and should meanwhile have made themselves very disagreeable at home. "She complains," said Fra Bernardino about one of them, "of her mother-in-law and sister-in-law, saying 'My maid is rude to me, she is too much for me, I can't say a word to her without her answering me back as if I were her donkey.' And so, too, [she complains] about her peasant, 'It is very plain that there is no man in the house!' And sometimes, too, she looks at her children, sighing, 'Oh, my poor neglected children, who will look after you? How will you manage? Everything goes wrong with you.' In all this, what she wants is a husband. Well, let her go and get one!"

He advised her, however, to meditate first on the perils of a second marriage, and the picture he drew was not encouraging. "If you are old and marry a young man . . . he will not be able to bear the sight of you, but will keep another woman and spend all your money, and desert you and mock at you. If you are young and take an old man . . . he will be so jealous that you will never be able to go out without receiving a good warming (*riscaldatoia*). . . . If you have children and he has children, they will never like each other. If you love yours more than his, or caress them more, you will be in trouble. . . . Whatever you do, if you marry again, you will never know a happy day."

Yet if, in spite of all this, she was still determined to carry out her plan, Fra Bernardino was the first to tell her not to be impeded by the dread of public opinion. "Learn that if you live in the world, even though you do all the good that you can, you cannot avoid evil being said of you." And he told the story of "a wise and virtuous

70

Roman matron," a young, rich widow, who had decided to marry again, but first attempted to discover what people would say about it. So she tried a curious experiment. She ordered one of her servants to ride through the streets of Rome, mounted on a horse which had been flayed. On the first day, the whole town came out to see the strange sight; on the second, far fewer people – and on the third, hardly anyone at all. Whereupon the widow decided that she might as well get married, "for if indeed people want to talk about me, they will soon get tired of it, and after two or three days, no one will care any more." And so indeed it was.[64]

In all these stories the assumption – as indeed in most monastic teaching to women – was always that temptation, sooner or later, was irresistible. Once, Fra Bernardino related, there was a holy man who, having brought back a woman who had been in a brothel to a virtuous life, began to consider – "since he never had any but good thoughts with regard to her" – how he could best continue to preserve her from temptation. "'We had better build a hermitage,' she said, 'and you will wall me up inside it, so that I cannot fall into sin again; but you will sometimes come to see me and encourage me.' And so they did. . . . He built a hermitage for her and . . . only left a little hole through which they could talk and so live virtuously. . . . But in a short time it happened that the Devil began to wake up and aroused their appetites, so that they tried to see each other through a crack in the wall while they were speaking, and each of them had those thoughts which sometimes come to one. 'Take heed,' one of them said to the other, 'they are saying this and that about us.' In the end the woman took courage and said, 'Well, to stop those people talking, you had better come in.' . . . And so he went in and, looking in each other's faces, they began to laugh. Well, let us not drag it out, soon she was with child. And what did all this come from? From not taking enough care. And this, widow, I say for you!"[65]

71

V

At the end of all these homilies and warnings, we may well ask ourselves what Fra Bernardino's real opinion of women was. It is hardly possible to deny that it still shows traces of a very ancient inconsistency, perhaps inevitable in view of the two contradictory pictures of the female sex which had been offered by the mediaeval teaching of the Church. On the one hand, the Church taught that woman was Mary, the Mother of Our Lord; on the other, that she was Eve, the wife of Adam. In the first aspect, she was to be revered; in the other, to be dreaded as a potential instrument of the Evil One. In all the treatises and homilies addressed to women, this oscillation constantly appears: men never quite made up their minds whether they were much better than themselves, or much worse. And though in daily life men of course well knew that their wives and daughters were neither saints nor devils, the *theory* that they were in some way a race apart, to be kept in seclusion and subjection, was one of the mediaeval ideas that faded slowest, in spite of the fact that, in practice, many women of character came to lead highly active and useful lives. It was the recollection of the evil in them that underlay Fra Bernardino's warnings, while it was the other, higher view that prevailed in his picture of maternal devotion. It was then that he remembered the pattern of perfection to which women might strive to rise, the Mother who was the example for all mothers. "Mary," he told them, "has raised you above shame, sterility and frailty. . . . If some men say, it was woman who made us fall, I say that it is true, but it was also woman who raised us up again. And another man may say, 'If you think it over, it was woman who was the beginning of all evil' – but I reply, 'Woman was the beginning of all good.'"[66]

His respect for women and, in spite of all his strictures, his essential tenderness for them, was founded upon one of his own deepest feelings: the devotion which the Madonna had inspired in him from his early boyhood. In this he was a true citizen of Siena, *vetus civitas Virginis*. He must have heard, as a boy, the tale of how her intervention had saved Siena from a Florentine victory at the battle of Monteaperti, and he must often have seen, too, Duccio's great picture of the Virgin, *La Maestà*, which on its completion had been borne in procession through the whole city before it was placed on the high altar of the Duomo, to watch over her people. "*Tutta vostra città ricoprirà col Suo sacro mantello*". (She will enwrap all your city in her holy cloak). But the picture of her that seems to have caught his imagination most, was the one painted on the wall of the fortified gateway towards Florence, called the Porta Camollia, where she was depicted in glory, surrounded by angels and archangels. It was here that, as a young man, he would come almost daily – gently teasing his aunts, when they asked where he had been, by telling them that he had been with his *bella amica e castissima fidanzata* (my beautiful friend and most chaste betrothed). "I could not sleep at night, without having seen her face."[67]

On the first day of his famous course of sermons in Siena, in 1427, he told his congregation about a vision that he had had on the previous night, in which he had seen Siena with its four gates and "the glorious Virgin Mary standing before her Son, beseeching him with humble prayers to protect the city of Siena, which has taken her for its advocate in every peril and adversity." And in his vision, he said, his prayer was at once granted, and four angels were sent by her to guard the city gates.[68]

All of his sermons devoted to the Virgin are touched by the same breath of poetry – by a freshness and gaiety, a golden radiance, which remind one of Simone Martini's and Vecchietta's *fondi d'oro*, or of Fra Angelico's *Coronation*. "Mary comes, as she was called to do; she passes over the earth and rises through the air, where the clouds are. She goes on higher and reaches the first heaven, the

73

Moon's; and she goes on higher, and reaches Mercury.... She rises yet higher, and reaches the starry sky ... and higher still, to the empyrean, with such rejoicing and delight, with so much glory, with so many dances, that it is a joy even to think of it.... She is called by the angels, and she rises; she is called by the archangels, and she rises. She is called by the choir of thrones, the choir of dominations, the choir of virtues, and she rises higher.... She is called by the cherubim; she is called by the seraphim. All the choirs call to Mary: '*Veni, veni ...* '"[69]

But it was not only in her glory that he depicted her. She was omniscient and all-powerful, she was the personification of beauty and of grace, but she was also "the mother of all the chosen and all the weary" – infinitely tender, infinitely merciful. "She loved all creatures not only as creatures, but because she found in them so great a mystery."[70] Like Dante, Fra Bernardino saw in her the very face of compassion,

> *In te misericordia, in te pietade,*
> *In te magnificenza, in te s'aduna*
> *Quantunque in creatura è di bontade.*[71]

She knew all the ways of common human motherhood. In his babyhood she carried him in her arms, "for they were very poor and he was very small." "She was so poor that she lived by her toil.... When she went to register her Son Jesus, as was their custom, she had no swaddling clothes nor linen for Him, but took a piece of her own garment and a veil, and swaddled Him in it." And she also knew the superhuman suffering of seeing Him upon the Cross: "Her own flesh, with which she had lived in this life for thirty-three years.... And she could not take her eyes away from Him."[72]

Of all her virtues, the one on which Fra Bernardino liked best to dwell, was her humility. "We are told that the Devil fell from

Heaven because of his pride – and so Mary, because of her humility, rose to glory." It was the Church, he said, who later on added the word "Mary" to the angel's greeting, "Hail." "The angel did not say it – and I will tell you the reason. Consider how a young maiden, who is pure and bashful, seems to tremble if you even say her name. That was why the angel did not say it." When the great tidings were given her and she was at first perplexed and troubled, all the saints and angels in Heaven were engaged in prayer that she might accept her great task. "All were watching and crying out, 'Lo, Holy Mother, may it please you to consent!' And the Angel of the Annunciation was beseeching, 'Lo, benign Mother, may it please you to consent! Have pity on this empty Paradise that cannot be filled, unless you consent. Have pity on the Holy Fathers in Limbo, have pity on mankind in the hands of the Devil, who cannot escape from them, unless you consent.' And there stood God and all the angels and the whole choir of Heaven, waiting to see what she would do." Then at last came the Virgin's reply, *Ecce ancilla Domini*. "And when she had said that word the angel sped away with such great joy, considering the delight of the angels of Paradise and of the Fathers in Limbo. The whole of Heaven was upside-down with joy. And at once, as soon as she had pronounced this word, she conceived the Son of God – and He was as very small as a needle's point."[73]

So Fra Bernardino brought the story of the Annunciation within the grasp of every woman of his congregation – and when, from the Bishop's palace at the top of the city hill, the Angelus rang out, he reminded them that this sound, which they heard every day and often failed to heed, was Our Lady's own voice, greeting them. "Consider that when you greet the Virgin Mary, she at once greets you. Do not think that she is like one of those rough country wenches! She greets you every evening when you hear the *Ave Maria* pealing – and will you be such yokels as not to greet her, too?"[74]

75

III. THE WORLD OF TRADE

A fine di riposo sempre affanno
E zappo in acqua, e semino in su rena;
E la speranza mi lusinga e mena
D'oggi in domane, e così passa l'anno.
E son canuto sotto questo inganno
Senza poter ricogliere un dì lena.

BENUCCIO SALIMBENI*

Gli uomini avari dormono con poco sonno.

SAN BERNARDINO**

A GREAT deal of Fra Bernardino's life was spent in a society ruled by values very different from his own, but which he felt bound to try to influence: those of the world of trade. The great merchants of Florence and the lesser merchants of Siena, who had in their hands the reins of the Commune and of the guilds, and the humbler shopkeepers and craftsmen, struggling for a bare living in their little shops, formed, with their wives and daughters, the great majority of his congregation: it was their hearts – beneath the crust of covetousness and competitiveness, of avarice and pride – that he must try to reach.

In laying down the rules that he expected them to follow during that singularly difficult period of transition between the simpler economic life of the Middle Ages and the birth of modern capitalism, he was greatly assisted by the training in both secular and canon law which he had received in his youth. His view of what was licit or not was based on the teachings of St. Thomas Aquinas and of John Duns Scotus, but he was also conscious of the swift changes taking place before his eyes, and he attempted to reconcile them, whenever possible, with the fundamental principles of the Church. He devoted no less than twenty-three of his Latin sermons to the subject of economics[1] and in addition he preached three sermons in Italian on dishonest trade to the Florentines in 1424 and

77

1425, three to the Sienese in the same year on "Restitution,"[2] and a sermon on "Merchants and craftsmen, and how trade should be conducted" in Siena in 1427, which he himself introduced as "one of the most useful sermons you have ever heard from me. . . . For you will see that it is not possible to live well, unless trade is conducted honestly."[3]

In his time Siena, which had been one of the richest towns in Italy, had already entered upon her decline. In the thirteenth century her great merchant families – in particular the Salimbeni, the Cacciaconti, the Malavolti, the Tolomei, and the clan which called itself *la Grande Tavola dei Buonsignori* – had been the bankers of popes and kings. Her traders then went several times a year to the great international fairs of Champagne, to sell their rough cloth and saffron, but above all to deal in money – for Siena had her own mint, and her merchants were great experts in questions of exchange – and to bring back fine Flemish cloth and Eastern spices. Their guilds, though never as important as the Florentine *Arte della Lana* later on (partly owing to the scarcity of water and to the poor quality of the pasture in the Sienese territory) were solidly established. Siena had become almost entirely a city of the merchant bourgeoisie, in which not only the nobles, but also the lawyers and doctors and the whole working class, were excluded from holding any office in the Commune.[4] But with the suicidal step – to which we shall return in Chapter VI – of banishing the rebellious underlings of the wool-guild to Florence, the Sienese had brought about the destruction of their own chief industry and had promoted the rise of their hated rivals. Thenceforth it was the Lamb of the Florentine *Arte della Lana* which predominated in the international wool-trade and the bankers of Florence who furnished loans to the Papal exchequers and to those of England and France – while Siena became, as she has ever since remained, a little provincial town, out of the main current of European affairs. In the second half of the fourteenth century, however, we still find (in the course of thirty years) six thousand names registered as members of the Merchants' guild and some of these, like the Salimbeni and Tolomei, were still rich, even by the standards of Florence and Venice. Above all, though parsimonious in many other matters, they were lavish in everything that contributed to their civic pride: the paving of the Piazza del Campo (completed some years before Fra Bernardino first preached there, and considered one of the finest in Italy), the building of churches and palaces, of towers and fountains.

As for Venice and Florence – the other two places in which Fra Bernardino preached about trade – they were then among the richest merchant-cities in Europe. The great seafaring Republic, governed by a small and stable oligarchy, was at the height of her prosperity: her adventurous commerce with the Far East, her rich colonies of merchants in the Levant, her banks, her well-ordered system of pensions and of charitable institutions, rendered her a model (as Fra Bernardino did not fail to point out) to every other Italian state. But she was also one of the cities most completely devoted to the art of money-making, and which possessed the largest number of money-changers and of dealers in international goods.

Florence, too, after a long period of economic instability and social unrest, following upon the bankruptcy of her three greatest banking houses (between 1343 and 1376) and many of her smaller ones, as well as the decimation of her population brought about by the Black Death, had been ruled for forty years by a small group of merchants of the *Arti Maggiori* and was passing under the beneficent rule of the first of the Medici, Cosimo, under whom the city was to rise to new heights of prosperity. Large portions of the vast sums gained in trade were spent in public works, in the great palaces and churches which still adorn the city, as well as in the collection of paintings and sculptures, manuscripts and codices, while the produce of some of the guilds – such as the *Arte della Seta*, and the guilds of the goldsmiths and leather workers and wood-carvers – were in themselves works of art. There were many institutions for the sick and the old and for foundling children, there were numerous and active schools and a university, many doctors and lawyers and almost too many notaries. There was a great external appearance of order and stability.

But under this fine shell, in Fra Bernardino's opinion, corruption was festering. The chief sins which he denounced in his sermons, in this city of trade – apart from the women's extravagance and the men's addiction to sodomy – were those that follow in the train of successful money-making: cupidity, competitiveness, self-indulgence, pride and avarice. "Three times the angel of the Apocalypse cried, 'Down, down with Babylon!' Three times down for the three great sins: pride, avarice and luxury."

In an attempt to rouse his congregation to a sense of sin, he told them, as usual, a parable. He imagined himself to have climbed to the top of Monte Morello, to the north of Florence, in the company of a man called Gioioso, looking down with him over the city below. "'What do you see?' – 'I see,' Gioioso replied, 'a fine noble house, belonging to a citizen of property and standing, a great merchant. His whole house is full of goods and merchandise. And I see his beautiful wife and fine children, like the organ-pipes of Santa Croce, and his menservants, maids and slaves; much business, letters from every land; and he is honoured in the Commune. I see his full granary and cellars and his great herds of cattle, and the house without any fault, well painted within and without.'" Then, looking in another direction, Gioioso saw, sailing up the Arno, a ship from the port of Pisa, "in full sail, with the wind astern . . . filled with merchandise of wool, silk, wheat and cloth . . . and many merchants sailing home happily, singing and gambling and playing trumpets and castanets, because they are in sight of home." And in yet another direction, Gioioso saw a fine palace where a young man was waiting for his

XI. Fra Bernardino's Siena: *Ambrogio Lorenzetti.*

XII. Merchants of Siena: *Statuti della Mercanzia di Siena.*

bride. "I see the new wife accompanied by two noble knights, riding on a fine horse and dressed in silk and well adorned for her bridegroom."

All this Gioioso watched, and then, unveiling the future, the preacher relentlessly dwelt on what would come to destroy all this joy and prosperity. The great merchant's house was visited by the plague, bearing off first his eldest son and then himself ("I see him dying, his goods dispersed, his factors administering them ill, his wife leaving the house, his debtors claiming to be creditors . . . and all turning into smoke"); the trading-ship was caught up in a storm and the gay, thoughtless company was seized by panic ("I see them confessing their sins to each other and offering up vows to St. James, St. Anthony or St. Nicholas of Bari – the ship striking a rock, the water rising . . . the ship foundering with the whole crew and all the merchandise"). Even in the house where the wedding was taking place ("the best state that you have showed me, my Gioioso, hallowed by the Sacrament of the Holy Church") disaster also struck. "The wife quarrels with her husband and they never know a happy day together . . . they have some wicked children and are overcome with despair at the death of the good ones. You thought it was a house of peace and rest, and it is one of tribulation."[5]

The theme is the one familiar to all preachers, from the days of Ecclesiastes: the vanity of all human joys, and especially of riches. "The man who has the most, desires the most. The older a miser gets, the more his avarice grows, drying up his bones, his heart, his life; his hunger is never fed."

In all Fra Bernardino's sermons on trade and the evils that it fostered, one is conscious that he was simultaneously addressing men of very various kinds, to whom he spoke on different planes. Sometimes he was placing arguments before able, cultivated businessmen, whose commerce was on an international scale and whose

81

moral problems (when they had them) centred on complicated questions of exchange or "usury"; and sometimes merely speaking *alla buona* (familiarly), as he so often did out of the pulpit, too, to the humble tradesmen and craftsmen who lived in the dark little shops round the city square or at the foot of the palaces of the great. How well acquainted he was with these men is quickly made apparent, and soon we come to feel that we know them, too. They are sharp, shrewd little men, always willing to do each other in the eye, always on the lookout for some good chance to get the better of their neighbours; but though the friar scolds them and unveils their little tricks, one cannot feel that he is very angry with them. Beneath his scolding, there is an undertone of both laughter and compassion – and never a touch of condescension or contempt. These are the sins of little folk, elbowing each other out of the way to get some bread for their children, jostling each other to see a good show (even if only a passing funeral, or a criminal on his way to the gallows), coarse and ingenuous in their very craftiness, but working hard for little pay, thrifty and long-suffering, and always grateful for a kind word or a simple joke.

One by one, he paints their portraits in short, incisive sketches – wholly realistic and unsentimental, but never cold. The whole world of dishonest tradesmen passes before us: the cloth-merchant with two rods, "one to buy with and one to sell," "who pulls so hard at his cloth [as he measures it] that he nearly tears it to pieces," the wheat merchant with loaded scales, the butcher who swells up the flesh of his beast with water before selling it, the apothecary who alters the doctor's prescription and the taverner who lets the wine brim over whenever he fills up his drunken client's glass, charging him, too, for all that has fallen on to the ground. He describes the shopkeeper who gives short change to "the poor little woman of little brain, who believes the coins to be what you say they are," by counting "here you are, one, two, three, five, seven,

82

eight, ten, thirteen, fourteen, seventeen, nineteen and twenty! – and it is not until she gets home that she sees that she has been defrauded of three *soldi*!" Then there is the man who, having gone to buy some saffron, sees that the merchant has damped it to make it weigh more, and asks him to bring it to his own house to be weighed, but when he gets there says he must hurry off and persuades the merchant to leave the little sack, to be weighed later. "And hardly is he out of the house, than the other takes the saffron and puts it in the oven to dry, and then puts it back [in the sack]" – and when the seller returns, pays a smaller price for it. But, since it has been dried too much, the saffron goes bad – so both buyer and seller, "thinking to deceive, ended by being deceived themselves."[6]

Fra Bernardino had an especial dislike, too, for the whole process of bargaining, and for the lies and blasphemies that go with it. He described a man going to the cobbler's to buy a pair of shoes, and neither of them being able to open their mouths without perjuring themselves. "'What do you want for those shoes?' – 'I want twenty *soldi*!' – 'By the Gospels, I will not give them.' – 'Come, take them, I swear they are truly perfect' (and he lies in his throat). – 'How much will you take?' – 'I can't take less. By the Gospels, I could get eighteen *soldi* for them' (he is forsworn, for it is not true). 'Will you take fifteen? I will not give more than fifteen' (*he* is lying, too). – 'Well, let's be done with it, give me eighteen *soldi*, as I have often got them before.' – 'By the Gospels, I won't.' – 'By the Gospels, you shall not have them.' And in the end one will give and the other take them for seventeen, when both have forsworn themselves several times."[7]

These were the stories which Fra Bernardino used to catch the attention of the crowd and illustrate his meaning. But when he was addressing men of standing and education, he spoke on a different level, examining the fundamental moral principles on which trade should be based. On the question of property, he followed John Duns Scotus. Before the Fall, all things belonged to all men, but after it, private property became necessary, "*propter exclusione negligentiae, propter exclusione malitiae, propter exclusione inimicitiae*" – in short, to avoid the neglect, injustice and violence that would, to his mind, inevitably be caused by any attempt to hold property in common. But on one of the most vexed questions of the time, that of "the just price," he followed the teachings of St. Thomas Aquinas. St. Thomas based his doctrine on the question of value on St. Augustine's statement in *The City of God*, "that man does not value things according to their rank in the natural order, but according to his own needs." An animate object is superior to an inanimate one, but who would not rather have his pantry full of meat, than of mice? – and sometimes, too, a horse or a gem may be worth more than a slave. St. Thomas concluded that prices are set according to human needs, and that no exchange would take place, if man had no needs. This concept of value as the capacity to fill a need and therefore as the basis for price, was fully accepted, too, by Fra Bernardino, but he elaborated it further, saying that value is made up of three elements: *virtuositas* (usefulness), *raritas* (scarcity), and *complacibilitas* (desirability). "While *virtuositas* was defined as the objective to satisfy human needs, *complacibilitas*, without any hedonistic implication, simply meant the subjective desire for one good in preference to another."[8]

In short, Fra Bernardino entirely agreed with St. Thomas' doctrine that the just price was either the one fixed by law, or the market price, and that this must be accepted by the producer whether it was above or below cost, whether he gained or lost.[9] From this it followed that he should tell the Tuscan merchants that it was not only wrong for them to ask more for their goods than they were really worth, but also to buy something at less than its true value, in the hope of future profit. "For instance, a peasant who has a precious stone which he does not recognize, and you give him what you think best and then sell it for what it is really worth. Do you think you are not sinning? Certainly you are, and are bound to make restitution." "And you, boys, this is your turn! Every time you see a boy steal something at home – you know, little bits of pewter to make *ferlini*[10] – or if he takes a stone from a ring worth a florin, and sells it to someone who knows this, but only gives him fifteen *soldi* – who do you think is sinning? Both the seller and the buyer." It was equally wrong, too, to try to undersell one's competitors (this must have been a common practice in cities in which, as in Eastern *souks* today, merchants of similar goods had their shops next to each other, in the same street). "A man who has bought a bale of goods at fifty florins and sold it again at forty . . . do you know what he has done? He has taken away the profit of someone who could licitly have sold the same goods at fifty florins. I say that this is worse than usury."[11]

And finally, taking his stand on a canon law of the twelfth century, Bernardino emphasized that no one might charge more to foreigners or take advantage of an ignorant "rustic," or a man in urgent need.[12] "You must sell for the same amount to the man who knows [the value of] the goods, and to him who does not." And suddenly, in his disconcerting way, he asked, "Has none of you here ever done such a thing?"[13]

The question of the "just price" involved a fundamental moral principle, since it was closely related to the ideal of moderation, of the avoidance of excess in every field of human life. "In all things," said St. Thomas, "what is just, consists in the due mean."[14] This was a concept entirely in harmony with the Tuscan temperament. "You must know," wrote San Bernardino's contemporary Ser Lapo Mazzei to the rich merchant of Prato, Francesco Datini, "that God loves the mean; and no immoderate thing was ever pleasing to that eternal equity."[15] To Fra Bernardino, too, this sense of moderation was an essential part of the Christian way of life and he consequently considered trade to be licit when it was practised within reasonable limits and "for honest purposes" – such as the maintenance of a man's family, the welfare of his city or the relief of the poor[16] – while it deeply shocked him in men who were already rich and only wanted to become richer still. "If a man does it to support his family or to get out of debt or to marry his daughters, it is licit. But what shall I say of the man who has no such need, yet toils so much? . . . I say that if he is not doing it for the poor, he is sinning." And it was certain, he added, that, however much such a man possessed, he would never be satisfied. "Is there any one of you here," he asked, "who has as much property as he needs? If there is one, let him lift up his hand. Ah – none of you lifts it up, not one!"

It was, he said, in the intention – the desire to get rich for riches' sake, "to pile goods one on the other" – that the sin lay, for this was avarice. "Some ignorant men may say, 'This is my own, I have earned it rightly, and if there is anything left over after caring for the needs of my family I want it for myself.' You are wrong: you are only its dispenser."[17]

It is not difficult to imagine the effect of such remarks upon a congregation almost wholly made up of tradesmen, great and small, for in this summary fashion the saint was placidly destroying (if his hearers had chosen to obey him) the motive power of all the great trading companies on which the city's prosperity was based! And indeed, while he and others of the "Preaching Friars" were still extolling the virtue of poverty and attacking the evils of money-making, a very different current of thought was taking shape. It was just at this time that Poggio Bracciolini was writing his dialogue *On Avarice*, which was not only a defence of the natural human desire for gain, but a virulent attack upon "those rough and hypocritical parasites" (the friars) "who, on the pretext of religion, and without working or toiling, go about preaching poverty and the contempt of riches." "We shall not build our cities," he said, "with such ghosts of men," and he went on to declare that if each man were to content himself with only producing what was necessary for his own needs, "every splendour, beauty and ornament would disappear from our city; no more temples, no more monuments, no more arts. . . . Money is a necessary goad for the State, and men who love money must be considered its basis and foundation."[18]

This indeed is a different world from Fra Bernardino's! It is plain from several references that he was well aware of such theories as Poggio's, but his own attitude remained unchanged. The only kind of trade to which he gave his full approval was that which, in his opinion, was for the common good. He stated its limits very plainly. First, he permitted both the import and export of goods; for instance, he said, "as is plain, here in Siena we have no pepper: it is for the common good to bring it here . . . and so with St. Matthew's wool (i. e. from Africa or Spain) and French and English wool, which are plentiful there and not here. And so, too, with other wares which are lacking elsewhere, it is good that ours should go there. All this is for the common good, and is licit." Secondly, he permitted these wares to be sold, on arrival, wholesale, and agreed that the merchants who had brought them "from far lands, with great trouble and toil and peril," should make some profit on this. He also allowed the man who had bought wholesale, to sell again retail, making some profit, "with discretion." And finally he permitted the manufacture of these goods, the work of the cloth-makers in the *Arte della Lana*, or the leather guilds, etc. "To all of these some profit is permitted."

He was, however, much troubled – not as an economist, but as a moralist – by one consequence of foreign trade: the long absence of husbands from their wives. "You place your wife in danger of great scandal at the least . . . and as she is in danger of falling into sin, so are you . . . and as I see the danger to be very great, do you

87

know, women, what I suggest unto you? Each time that your husband must go far away for a long time, see to it that you go with him."[19] But that this counsel of perfection was often taken, does not appear.

Fra Bernardino then went on to enumerate the numerous times and places in which trade was always wrong – on the feasts of the Church, "in any cloister, church or consecrated cemetery," and in Lent, during the time of the daily sermon, and he also specified the people to whom it was always forbidden, who included "all priests, friars, monks, abbots, prelates, nuns, under pain of mortal sin.... They may sell their crops . . . but not trade in them, no, not on any account." And he added that the prelate who had thus enriched himself was "worse than any pestiferous beast."[20]

Finally, he naturally condemned every form of fraud, from the little tricks of small tradesmen which we have already described, to the dishonesty on a larger and more complicated scale of the international merchants, dealing in foreign exchange (*cambi*) and practising usury.

It is at this point that one must be careful, since these problems are among the most complicated questions of the time. A merchant of the wool or silk guilds often also joined the *Arte del Cambio* (the money-changer's guild) – that is, he became a banker as well. If one year he lost money in trade, he could make it up by his exchange dealings, supplying his clients through his foreign branches with money or goods abroad (without any real transfer taking place, but always taking a commission on the transaction). Bills of exchange, in the shape of an informal letter (as opposed to a formal deed signed by a notary) were already in habitual use, and profits on their purchase and sale were generally recognized to be high, if precarious. "I would rather earn 12% with merchandise," wrote a Tuscan merchant, Domenico di Cambio, to his partner in 1390, "than 18% on exchange dealings."[21]

The man, moreover, who joined the *Arte del Cambio* was likely to lay himself open to the charge of usury which – partly owing to the general confusion of mind upon the subject – often weighed upon the conscience of God-fearing merchants of the time. On this subject, the Church's doctrine was entirely clear and uncompromising: *any* interest on a loan was usury. *Date mutuum nihil inde sperantes*, was the Christian maxim (give a loan, hoping nothing therefrom). By Fra Bernardino's time, however, it was generally accepted that it was permissible for a creditor to receive a *gift* from his debtor (provided it was registered as such) or in some cases to receive a *compensation* for a delay beyond the date established for the return of the loan.[22] This loophole eventually proved to be a very wide one. Fra Bernardino, however, took his stand on a purely moral point: that it was the *intention* that mattered, and that therefore even a faint hope of some future benefit from a loan, rendered it "usurious." "Do not have the intention of being of service to your neighbour, so that he may be of service to you at some other time, for that would be usury.... You may hope for anything that cannot be estimated in money, but if you lend either with a contract or with the intention of getting something out of it – wheat or wine or anything else that can be turned into money, it is a usurious contract."[23] This is the spirit of the Gospels, but not of trade. Fra Bernardino's teaching was based both on the Aristotelian premise that money is, by its nature, sterile,[24] and on the Christian principle that a loan is a deed of charity, of goodwill – and therefore, naturally, gratuitous. "Alexander of Hales says," said Fra Bernardino, "that if even the Apostle St. Peter should return to earth, he could not render it licit to take even 1% – and you say it is licit to take 8 or 10."[25]

So long as these were the principles upheld by the Church, the discrepancy between them and common practice could hardly fail to be considerable – and so indeed it was. In most cities the question of money-changing was solved by giving licences to the

Jews, who were not hampered by Christian scruples, and whom their Christian clients felt free first to make use of, and then to despise. They deposited their money with the Jews, for investment, "without wishing to know" what the Jews would do with it, and then, still "without wishing to know," took the profits. The Commune of Florence, indeed, not only permitted official moneylenders and granted them a licence, but required them to pay a yearly tax.[26] This Fra Bernardino declared to be wholly indefensible. "You are *all* usurers," he told the Florentines. Moreover most merchants, whether they belonged to the *Arte del Cambio* or not, took part in transactions which were at least questionable, in Fra Bernardino's eyes. He included among them the sale of goods, or exchange transactions, with deferred payment (*a termine*, i. e. gambling upon possible fluctuations in exchange between the order and payment of the goods) since in this, he said, there was a concealed loan.[27]

One of the most important questions about which Fra Bernardino had to pronounce an opinion, in view of the large number of people involved, was that of the dealings in government securities of Venice, Florence and Genoa. In these Republics the State often raised forced loans called *prestanze* from their citizens, on which they paid interest (very much like the issue of bonds by a government today), but disguised it by calling it a free gift. The question was, were the State's creditors, who accepted this interest, parties to an usurious contract? Fra Bernardino held that they were not, since the loan was forced; but if a man lent money to the State on his own initiative in the understanding or hope that interest would be paid on it, then he was sinning. He also objected to a very popular institution which had been founded in Florence in 1425, the *Monte delle Doti*, which enabled parents to make provision for their daughters' marriages by lending money to the State, which would be repaid, with interest, fifteen years later, as the girl's dowry. If, however, the child died in the interval (and child mortality was very high), both capital and interest reverted to the State. Fra Bernardino pointed out that this transaction was wrong on two grounds, as being both usurious and a gamble, and Vespasiano da Bisticci describes a heated argument in his bookshop on this subject between the great preacher and a well-known Florentine magistrate, Giannozzo Manetti, in which Fra Bernardino said that this contract was "worse than those of a Jew, lending with his red carpet." "And he [Bernardino] solved all the difficulties," Vespasiano added, "with very strong arguments of great humanity, so that all those who were there were entirely satisfied."[28]

In his whole attitude Fra Bernardino was entirely consistent, and though by his contemporaries, according to Vespasiano, he was thought to be "even stricter than Archbishop Antoninus," by some modern writers he has been considered one of the most clear-sighted economists of the Middle Ages.[29] Certainly his sermons show a remarkably detailed knowledge of the business transactions of his time: he can quote the most recent quotations of the Florentine money-changers, he is thoroughly acquainted with State legislation to prevent the bribing of officials, with the manner in which a money-changer's business is carried out, and, as we have seen, with all the little tricks of both buyers and sellers in the market-square, and he generally speaks of all these things with the same dry clearsightedness, humour and acceptance of the weaknesses of human nature which characterized his approach to most other worldly matters.

He tells, for instance, a story about a priest and a moneylender in a country village, which it is very easy to believe. "There was a country priest, a discreet and perceptive man, who had in his congregation a rich usurer who could neither read nor write, and never went to confession. And the priest began to feel sorry for him, and asked him if he could say the Lord's Prayer. '*Messer no*, I was never able to learn it.' 'What, you are sixty years old and cannot say the Lord's Prayer?' – And the other, 'I have tried to learn it a hundred times and I would gladly pay a large sum to anyone who could teach it me.' – 'Well,' said the priest, 'I will gladly do so.' – Several days passed, and the priest told some poor men of the city to go to the usurer, and he said to him, 'You have much wheat; I want you to lend twenty sacks to these poor men for the love of God and they will give them back to you at harvest-time.' – The usurer said, 'Gladly' – not because he was sorry for the poor men, but because he meant to lend them wheat full of weevils and to get good sound wheat back. – 'Very well,' said the priest, 'I will send for it, but take their names, so that you may know afterwards from whom to get it back.' – And he told the poor men what they must say. When the usurer asked the first one, 'What is your name?' [He replied] 'My name is *Paternoster*,' and the second, '*Quiesincoelis*,' and the third, '*Santificetur*,' and the fourth, '*Nomentuum*' – and so on, all through the Lord's Prayer – and then they took the wheat.... The usurer, who could not write, set down in his mind their names in order from beginning to end, and when harvest-time came, he went to the men, all of whom he knew well [by sight] to ask them to give him back what he had lent them. They said that they could not, and at last said that they had been given it through the priest, at his word...." In the end the matter had to be taken before the *podestà*, who asked what had happened and sent for the priest, who explained the matter. "The usurer replied, 'It is not true that he has taught me [the Lord's Prayer], but I would gladly pay a large sum if he would!' – Said the priest, 'Now say who must give back your wheat.' – The other replied, 'First *Paternoster*, then *Quiesincoelis*, then *Santificetur*, and so on.' Said the *podestà*, 'You silly man, you have just said the Lord's Prayer!' And so the usurer lost his wheat and learned the Pater Noster!"[30]

This is a story in San Bernardino's most characteristic vein. But sometimes his instinctive deep distaste for money in itself, and his memory of the suffering of the poor at the hands of purse-proud merchants and grasping moneylenders, is too much for him, and his tone changes. The truth is that, for all his equanimity, there were two kinds of human beings whom San Bernardino could not abide: witches and money-makers. He found it almost impossible to extend his Christian charity to either. Gradually, piecing together the relevant passages in his sermons, a very clear picture takes shape before our eyes of the rich merchant, the miser, the usurer, as Fra Bernardino saw him – and he is the most miserable wretch on earth.

The friar does, of course, clearly distinguish between the merchant who – however great his avidity – is harming chiefly his own soul, and the usurer, who also causes misery to hundreds of other men. His pictures of merchants dwell chiefly upon the toil and anguish to which, of their own accord, they submit themselves in order to make more money – and the "handful of dust" which in the end is all that is left in their hands. He starts by describing a rich merchant, in the process of making his fortune. "I see vigils, I see anxiety and anguish . . . I have known many of you who pile up riches while suffering hunger, thirst, excessive heat and cold. Sometimes you travel by land and sometimes by sea, in the rain, the snow, the wind, never resting in your own house; you must visit your lands, your vineyards, you must be everywhere, and always with great anxiety. . . . And I ask you all, is there one of you who feels certain of being able to keep all the property he has acquired, that it won't be taken from him?" No one replies. "You see that I speak the truth!"

On another occasion Fra Bernardino described – and it is, perhaps because of the sudden little homely touch at the end, one of his most vivid passages – a proud, successful young merchant talking to himself one night, in his own room. "'My soul,' he says to himself, 'you have so many goods stored up, your granaries are full of wheat, your cellars of wine, you have enough land, you have money, you are young, strong, well-dressed, you lack nothing. What, dying? You will never die!' – And as he is saying these words to himself,

93

suddenly there is a voice that cries, 'You lie in your throat!' (And I think it must have been as he was going to bed, perhaps while he was taking off his shoes.)"[31]

It is, however, when he comes to speak, not of merchants, but of usurers, that Fra Bernardino betrays the unconquerable, blind aversion which he shared with many of his contemporaries. Like Dante, he plainly felt that usury was a direct insult to God's goodness. "*Usura offende la divina bontade*."[32] For over two centuries nothing had been too bad to be believed of the moneylender: he sat all day in the market-place, plain for all to see, with his money-bag and his great ledger on a table before him, demanding an interest of twenty and sometimes forty per cent and, as a pledge, a poor man's last patched tunic, or a widow's cloak or bed.[33] He was, to the poor, the very personification of cruelty and avarice – and, if he was a Jew, an unbeliever besides. In Siena he was forbidden to live "in the most public or beautiful parts of the city" (i. e. "in any house or *palazzo* adjoining the Campo . . . or in the streets adjoining it") because his presence was a direct insult to the Patron of the city, the Virgin Mary;[34] and he was denied, even if he was a Christian, the Sacraments and burial in holy ground[35] – a ruling of which Fra Bernardino approved. He even confessed that though he could make friends, as we have seen, with the ruthless soldiers of fortune and chat with thieves and murderers in prison, he could not bring himself to eat or drink with a Jew, saying that "as to a *general* love, we may love them, but as to a particular love, we cannot."[36]

Fra Bernardino's picture of the usurer is that of a man who, having made an idol of his florins, has betrayed God. "He believes in nothing that lies above his roof." "He learns his evil trade from his evil father, and, knowing no other, practises it all his life and dies in it, and so finds damnation." While he is alive, he is like a barber, "who shaves a man so close that his blood gushes out"; he grinds the bones of the poor, "sleeping and waking, eating and

94

drinking, always making his money work, and grinding his partner's bones"; and when death comes, he is like a swine, "who in all his life has done nothing but damage . . . and when he dies, everyone is glad!"[37]

Traditionally, the miser's last act – if he wished to save himself from the fires of Hell – was to make a clause in his will providing that all that he had earned illicitly should be given back, *pro remedium animae*, to those from whom he had taken it, or if this was not possible, to God's poor. Fra Bernardino preached three sermons on this subject, of which the gist was that such restitutions should be performed as publicly, and above all as soon, as possible. For if the miser waited until the day of his death, his son would probably merely laugh at his wishes, saying, "If my father is now in Paradise, he does not need anything; and if he is in Hell, whatever good I may do on his behalf, it will not avail him."

That "the hot house" was the usurer's most likely resting-place, the preacher did not doubt, and this belief – fully shared by all his hearers – gave rise to terrifying stories about the unrepentant miser's last hours. One of the most macabre was that about "an old man, who died in Lombardy a short time ago, and who had no wife nor child nor close relation. Realizing that he was very ill, he shut himself up in his house with his maidservant and would not confess his sins nor put his soul and his affairs in order, for he thought that he would never die. Then some distant relatives of his, to whom his property would come, entered his house on the pretext of persuading him to make his confession, with six porters, and took all that he had away, before his staring eyes. Little did it avail him to cry out, for his tongue was swollen and he could not be understood. And at the last they took even his shirt away and left him there on the straw. And soon, as they were pulling off him a pair of rose-coloured socks, one pulled and the other cried out, and the Devil came and bore off his soul to Hell."[38]

Stories such as these had become a part of Tuscan folklore, closely connected with the deep mediaeval obsession about death and eternal retribution. The imagery of Dante's *Inferno* and even his actual words had become, to an astonishing degree, a part of common speech and the pictures of Hell frescoed on so many church walls enabled every man to see the torments which already filled his mind. When Fra Bernardino spoke of devils bearing usurers to Hell, his congregation could picture the scene as Vecchietta or Traini had painted it or Dante had described it: the writhing, impotent misers caught up in the merciless claws of monsters and then consigned, with their swollen purses on their bloated bellies, to the flames.[39]

It was at the end of one of these sermons – according to a story told by *l'Anonimo* – that a strange scene took place. A well-known usurer was sitting close beneath the pulpit and it seemed as if, by his glances and gestures, the preacher were pointing straight at him. The congregation began to nudge each other, to whisper, point and laugh, while the usurer, with his head bowed, "eagerly longed for the sermon to be over." At last, *Domine dante* (in God's good time) it came to an end, and the usurer hurried to the door of Fra Bernardino's cell, crying out to the other friars whom he found there, "Truly this is a holy man and God has revealed all my wickedness to him.... Today he has told me all that I have done, said and thought!" The friars explained that the preacher had not meant a personal reference to him, but had been speaking about usury in general. "But I saw him pointing and looking at me all the time!... He has done all this, through the Holy Ghost, for my salvation." Then he went away and made full restitution of all his ill-gotten goods, and went on revering Fra Bernardino for the rest of his life.[40]

It can hardly be denied that – even apart from the question of usury – Fra Bernardino was not always fair to the merchants of his time. It is true that they often oppressed the underlings of their guilds, and that the difference between the way of life of the great

96

merchant in his stone palace, visited by princes and prelates, and that of his workman in his little brick house or dark shop, was very great. But Fra Bernardino makes hardly any mention of the good qualities which these merchants, taken as a class, undoubtedly did possess: enterprise and courage, intellectual curiosity and patronage of the arts, a deep sense of responsibility towards the State, great civic pride, and a religious feeling which, if not wholly free from the self-interest which had become their rule of life, was none the less active and real.

The society in which he preached, indeed, was one in which there was still a singular dichotomy: on the one hand an intense, feverish thirst for money; on the other – perhaps partly in revulsion – an almost mystical cult of poverty. Sometimes a sudden change of heart, like the one in the story we have just told, would bring a man from one of these states of mind to the other, and it was this that Fra Bernardino – by example as well as precept – hoped to achieve. But the main tide was against him: even as he was speaking, the new capitalist world was taking shape.

IV. THE WORLD OF THE POOR

Povertade innamorata
Grand'è la tua signoria!
JACOPONE DA TODI*

THEY stand in the extreme left-hand corner of Orcagna's *Tri-umph of Death* in Santa Croce, four beggars – one blind, one old, one crippled, one merely hungry. They are the personification of poverty. All of them but the blind man, whose head is thrust upwards, eagerly listening to what he cannot see, are watching the figure of Death, descending with her scythe upon mankind. But while, at the other side of the fresco, the rich merchants and priors and pretty women are shrinking from her in terror, the beggars have stretched out their hands towards her: why has she been so slow? They are the men who in Fra Bernardino's time – and indeed for many centuries before and after – were to be found at many street-corners, at every church-door: the derelicts of society, living wholly upon alms – *la poveraglia*.

How large a proportion they formed of the population of the Tuscan cities which Fra Bernardino knew, it would be difficult to say. But certainly in trying to imagine his world, it is necessary to remember the sheer amount of physical suffering that often lay before his eyes, and how many of the people to whom he spoke had never had quite enough to eat.

Impoverished, as we have described elsewhere, by the decrease of her trade and the rise of that of Florence, harassed by the Free Companies, and decimated by the frequent outbreaks of the Black Death – of which three took place during Fra Bernardino's life-time[1] – Siena, a city without a harbour or a river, had one problem which took precedence over all others: how to feed her hungry poor. At the end of the thirteenth century she had attempted to secure bread for her population by annexing both the lands of

99

Monte Amiata and the wide plains of the Maremma on the coast, and by purchasing from the Benedictine monks of Abbadia San Salvatore, the little harbour of Talamone. The priors had seen a vision of the marshes and fallow lands of the Maremma transformed once again into golden wheat-fields, as they had been in the days of the Etruscans and of Rome, and a long procession of laden mules bearing a precious cargo of wheat brought by foreign ships to Siena from Talamone.[2] But these dreams had only partially come true. The importation of wheat from abroad had to be strictly rationed, since there was not enough money to pay for it, and the cultivation of the Maremma met with one unsurmountable obstacle: the lack of men. Every effort had been made to settle the new lands: refuge was granted, in the new little rural communes, to "foreigners," land was granted free for building and for planting new vineyards, and even free labour was provided to help any newcomers to build their houses and plant their fields, "so that the Maremma may be filled with men" and prosperity spring up "for the exaltation, honour and convenience of Siena."[3] But in vain. Not many men felt inclined to cultivate remote fields, of which almost all the produce would disappear within the gates of Siena, and few of the new little rural communes were able to withstand the combined assaults of malaria, of the plague, of the constant raids of "the locusts" (the soldiers of the Free Companies) and above all of the exorbitant taxes and levies imposed upon them. The city, in short, killed her goose before it had even begun to lay its golden eggs. The population of the little country towns, instead of increasing, diminished. In 1370 Grosseto, which at the beginning of the century had numbered 1200 men, was reduced to 100; Magliana had shrunk from 400 hearths to forty, Talamone from fifty to eight. The fields, for lack of hands to till them, lay fallow: where 40.000 *moggia* had grown, now barely 500 were harvested.[4] And the men of these rural communities were as hungry as those of the cities. There is a record in the archives of the Siena

100

XIII. "La Poveraglia": *Andrea Orcagna*.

XIV. A. Driving out the Hungry; B. Feeding the Hungry: "*Maestro del Biadaiolo*".

law courts, which is probably only one of many similar stories: an investigation into the case of a man of Abbadia San Salvatore on Monte Amiata, who was believed to have been killed by witch-craft, but whose death had really been caused by having trudged, when already weakened by starvation, all the way to the coast near Grosseto to find some wheat for his family, and then having walked back to his mountain village with the load on his back – so that, on his return, he took to his bed and died of exhaustion. We hear, too, of the news spreading one year in this same mountain town, as early as February, that the whole year's wheat had already been eaten up, of a bread-riot, and of whole starving families fleeing from their homes, "to beg in other men's lands."[5]

There is a picture in the illustrated chronicle of a Florentine wheat-merchant, Domenico Lenzi, representing a similar scene: only here the starving poor are being driven by force out of Siena, while a companion picture shows, with some smugness, the Flor-entine merchants distributing bread to *their* poor in the market-place. There is, of course, no reason to draw any conclusion from these two pictures, except that the painter was a Florentine – for the territory of Florence was in much the same condition as that of Siena. In spite of all the fine castles and villas that had been built near Florence, there were still not enough men to till the land – as can be deduced from any deed of sale of property at the time, showing the large acreage worked by a single peasant. Many fields still lay fallow and often, even on the cultivated land, the wheat would lie unharvested or unthreshed upon the threshing-floors all the summer, for lack of labour, while at the same time Florence had not enough bread to give her citizens. Moreover the countrymen bitterly resented the exorbitant taxation of the city, and the levies on their produce. "The *contado* was more exhausted and in greater peril than the city," wrote a chronicler in 1376, "and there was no peasant who would not gladly have gone to set fire to Florence."

But the cities, too, were full of hungry and angry men. What an impartial observer thought of the way in which they were treated, we know from Fra Bernardino's own words to the Florentines in his first course of Lenten sermons in their city: "How many are the cries of your poor, oppressed by your officials! They rise up to heaven. If you knew of the oppressions and exactions, drawing out a man's very blood, which they wreak on your underlings, perhaps you would take some measures. Or perhaps you do know of them, and will take no steps, because you want some day to behave in the same way yourselves."[6]

It was a privilege, if you were a townsman, to belong to a guild, but not all those who belonged to one had equal rights. The Consuls of the guild, its treasurer and notary, were the men who controlled its policy and they were chosen from among the entrepreneurs and masters of the workshops; they, with the younger men (generally members of their families) who worked for a while besides them as apprentices and who would eventually rise to similar positions, were the corporation's aristocracy, prosperous and secure; but beneath them were the numerous underlings (*sottoposti*) – humble weavers and spinners, dyers and carders, carriers and messengers – bound by oath to obedience to the Consuls and forbidden to form any associations with each other, and toiling, with many obligations and no rights, for low and precarious wages. Sometimes the price given for their spinning was literally a starvation wage, "and even then," said Fra Bernardino, "they [the spinners] are sometimes paid in kind, so that they lose half the value."[7] But there was no redress. We have seen how, in Siena, their first attempt at rebellion was punished by banishment, and similar insurrections in Florence brought their ringleaders to the gallows. And when at last, in 1376 – after the famous insurrection of *i Ciompi*, the lowest workers of the Florentine *Arte della Lana* – these men did succeed in obtaining leave to form three guilds, which they called "the guilds of God's people," the entrepreneurs closed down the workshops. "The people were mad with hunger," wrote a chronicler, "because the shops were almost closed . . . and the wool-guild would do nothing."[8]

Even in good years the diet of these men consisted almost entirely of bread and cabbages, with a little oil as a condiment – and in bad years, when both bread and oil were scanty, hunger was their daily companion. And lower still there was another, yet hungrier class, that of the unemployed and unemployable: unskilled peasants, who having fled from their barren fields to the city, could not pay the enrolment fee into a guild, slaves recently freed by their masters, soldiers of fortune waiting (though they seldom had to wait long) for the next outbreak of war or civil strife, prostitutes, jugglers and itinerant peddlars, and common criminals. It was a man of this degree of hopeless, shameless poverty, whom San Bernardino describes (without any especial emphasis, as if such things were taken for granted) as stealing flour in the Siena market-place at night, among the six pigs which the city sent there to act as scavengers, and which were known as "St. Anthony's swine." "He had fastened a bag round his thighs and a bell, and crawled on all fours, and when people heard the bell, they thought that he was one of St. Anthony's swine."[9]

It was men as poor as these whom the city rulers rightly feared – men ready to swell any insurrection, to join any bread-riot. Then they would plunder not only the houses of rich private citizens, but also the storehouses of the Commune, sacking the wheat-market and flinging the grain against the windows of the Priors' Palace, while mocking their rulers for their incapacity even to give them bread. It was because of them that the prudent merchant Giovanni Morelli warned any wealthy landowner never to store in his town house more food than was required for his family's own needs, and to bring even that "a little at a time." For, he said, "If the poor see that you have wheat to sell and that you wish to store it to increase its price, they will rail at you and curse you and sack and burn your house and you will be hated – which is most dangerous – by all the *popolo minuto*."[10]

To feed the hungry – that, under circumstances such as these, was the first obligation of every ruler and the first duty of the prosperous, and indeed it was fulfilled (if only in self-protection) both by institutions and by the rich. Both in Florence and Siena, crowds of beggars were to be seen daily at midday at the doors of the hospitals and convents, to whom lay-brothers distributed bowls of soup, and the account-books of most rich landowners show a portion of the produce of their farms set aside for the poor and for religious institutions, while during epidemics wine, too, was distributed free to the sick, and legacies for these purposes were left in every rich man's will.

The other recognized "Works of Mercy," too, were not neglected – to clothe the naked, visit the sick, shelter pilgrims, visit men in prison, and bury the dead. Commended by every preacher, illustrated in innumerable works of art, these duties had become a very real part of daily life. In Florence in 1336 there were, according to Villani, no less than a thousand hospital beds supported by private charity; there were hospices for pilgrims, foundlings and the old, and there was also the newly-founded *Monte de' Paschi* to supply dowries for penniless girls. Many trading-companies even kept, as well as a money-box for each day's small change, which was then distributed to the poor on Thursdays, Saturdays and feast-days, a special account in their ledgers of the portion of the company's profits to be given in alms, and this was called "God's account" – *il conto di Messer Domeneddio*; while in other companies a specified part of the capital was assigned, from the time of their foundation, to charity, the accounts of "God's share" being kept like those of any other partner, and sharing the varying fortunes of the firm.[11]

In Siena, too, long before Fra Bernardino's time, the tradition of almsgiving was already firmly rooted. The great hospital of Santa Maria della Scala, in which Fra Bernardino tended the sick during the plague, had been founded as early as the eleventh century by the canons of the Cathedral and not only contained wards for the sick, but also a foundling hospital, a hospice for pilgrims and a home for orphan girls who, on reaching marriageable age, were dowered by the hospital. It was the custom, indeed, on Easter Day, to hold a banquet for these girls in the Cathedral Square, at which – as they sat at table – they could be seen by their suitors, who could then ask the prior for the hand of the bride he had chosen, while the wedding subsequently took place in the chapel of the hospital.

In Fra Bernardino's time, however, this institution – which, like other similar ones, obtained its income chiefly from the lands which it owned (and to which rich citizens sometimes added by bequests in their wills) – had become less prosperous than in the past, partly because a portion of its income had to be set aside for the defence of its lands against the Free Companies. "It [the hospital] is well off," said Fra Bernardino, "and would be better off still if what belongs to it were not taken away from it." It was the citizens' business, he said, to ensure that alms for it were never lacking. "Citizens, look to that hospital! See that the alms for it are kept up, see that they do not fail."[12]

He appealed to his congregation, too, to support the leper hospital which had only recently been founded outside their gates. Until such hospitals were built, a leper's fate was the worst that could fall upon any man. Banished from his native city and forbidden to return there (in Assisi, in the time of St. Francis, any man who met a leper within the city gates was authorized by the statutes to drive him away with stones and blows), he wandered wretchedly around the countryside, living upon alms, and warning each passer-by to shun him by the ringing of the bell which was tied round his neck.

And indeed, even after the foundation of the leper hospitals, his fate was hardly more fortunate: the sick man, on entering the hospital, was shriven by a priest and sprinkled with Holy Water and with earth from the graveyard, as if he were already dead, with the words, "Die to the world, and be born again to God."[13]

Every rich man felt bound – from self-interest as well as virtue – to contribute to the upkeep of such institutions. No one, according to the teachings of the Church, had a right to keep for himself more than what he required for his daily needs: what was superfluous, was due to God. (The Florentine economists called this part of a man's income *l'avanzo* or *il sopravanzo della vita* – what is left over – and it was on this that a man was also taxed.) And though it was, of course, possible to interpret such a rule with considerable latitude, the *principle* was accepted by everyone: the rich man who gave nothing in alms was endangering both his temporal security and his immortal welfare: he stole from the poor.

All this is constantly repeated or implied in Fra Bernardino's sermons, as in those of other preachers of his time – but was this indeed all that he meant, when he spoke of charity? Very plainly, like his master St. Francis, he meant a great deal more – not only a material gift, but what he called "the alms of the heart." "Compassion," he said, "is a condiment to every virtue that a man can have."[14] And by compassion he meant not only a moment's facile emotion, nor even its relief in the bestowal of alms, but self-identification with the sufferer, and through the sufferer, with God. "There are those who maintain," he said, "that St. Francis had the stigmata only within his soul, and there are others who have said he was only marked by them outwardly. I believe that he had them both within and without. And I say that the man who does not hold Our Lord's wounds within his soul, does not belong to Christ." The *perfection* of love of one's neighbour, he declared, was nothing less than a willingness to change places with him. "Perfection is this, that on seeing a leper, you feel such compassion for him that you would rather bear his sufferings yourself, than that he should."[15]

Deeply imbued with St. Francis' spirit, Fra Bernardino too felt the appeal of the *mystique* which had become attached to the concept of poverty. "*Povertade innamorata, grand'è la tua signoria!*" By those who embraced this belief, the poor were considered, as the rich could never be, "God's friends." "I hear of your banquets," wrote Ser Lapo Mazzei to the rich merchant Francesco Datini, "but do not forget to let the poor, too, sometimes see your fine house and be nourished by your food, lest God reproach you, saying. 'Had you but once asked *my* friends to the house I have given you!'"[16]

Umbria and Tuscany were the regions of Italy in which these doctrines had found the widest echo, and indeed a strong vein of mysticism has always existed in Siena, side by side with the violence, licentiousness and hard commercial shrewdness which also marked its citizens. This was the soil in which Fra Bernardino's spirit had its roots. It was in Siena that, only a few years before, Giovanni Colombini (who in his youth had been as rich and gay as St. Francis himself) had given away all his earthly goods and formed the company of *i Poveri Gesuati*, to beg in the streets for wine and bread for God's Poor, and who, as he wandered about the Val d'Orcia preaching to the peasants, was caught up in a religious fervour "which makes the soul so overcome with joy that the body, too, must cry out . . . not being able to bear the fire of so much charity."

> *Povertà, povertà, il tuo linguaggio non s'intende,*
> *Viva la santa povertà dei nostri cuori.*[17]

Pazzo per Cristo (mad for love of Christ), he not only distributed all his lands to his poor peasants, but told his companions to drag him by a halter through the streets of his native village, San Giovanni d'Asso, beating him and crying to the assembled crowd. "This is the man who wanted to starve you, who lent you old wheat full of weevils every year, requiring you to give back your new good wheat in return, at a florin a bushel! Beat him hard, this enemy of the poor!"[18]

And it was in Siena, too, that St. Catherine, even in the rapture of her celestial visions and the labour of her correspondence with Popes and kings, had never been deflected from a daily round of humble deeds of charity. She tended an old, sick prostitute; she visited the hospitals and prisons and also, in spite of her family's protests, the leper hospital outside the city gates. She asked her father's permission to distribute some of his goods to the poor – and whenever possible, gave them in secret, flitting through the empty streets at night like a gentle ghost, bearing a small sack of wheat or a jar of oil, and, pushing open the door ("for the poor," interpolates her biographer, "keep their doors ajar") left her gifts on the threshold and slipped quietly away. One story, indeed, is told about her, which is reminiscent of the familiar legend about St. Elizabeth of Hungary and the roses. It would appear that although Catherine's father had allowed her to give away many of his possessions, he had in his cellar one special barrel of excellent old wine, which he had forbidden anyone to touch, but that Catherine had drawn many flasks from it (for old wine is the best medicine) for the sick. The day came, however, when her father sent to fetch some of it, only to be told that the barrel was empty – whereupon he lost his temper, accusing each member of the family in turn of having disobeyed his orders. Then Catherine went down to the cellar and knelt beside the barrel, praying God to send a little wine into it – and sure enough, "it soon began to flow and, saying nothing about the miracle, she took it to her father."[19]

This would have been a story after Fra Bernardino's own heart. Men who gave their money openly, "with pomp and show," or "in the square where there are many people to be seen," or who presented churches with golden chalices and rich brocades, or built chapels upon which they had set their arms, waited in vain for his approval. "Why do they place them there?" he asked. "Only so that it should be known that they have given them." Nor did he have much regard for the calculating housewife, who, when she had given alms, was also determined to get something in return. "You give something to a poor woman and then say, 'Just help me to make this bed,' and then you often make her sweep the house and fetch the water and sometimes even spin. And then you say, 'I gave alms.' No, you sold them!"

When such men and women refused to help his poor, he did not hesitate to remind them that St. Francis himself had given up "not only all he had, but all he might have had.... He might perhaps have had a wife, and three or four children and two or three houses. But consider, how many are the children of St. Francis? They are so many that they reach to every part of the world, even to the land of the Saracens.... Those who give up all they have and follow the life of Jesus for love of Him, they are the true lords of the earth. *Viva il Signore del mondo!* (Long live the Lord of the world!) Let those call themselves blessed who can give Him a horse to ride, when He is walking on the roads, or who can ask Him to their house to dine."[20]

On the other hand his shrewd Tuscan clearsightedness kept him from idealizing every beggar and condemning every rich man, merely because he was rich. "Poverty," he said, "is safer (*più sicura*) than riches when it is chosen freely, but to say that all rich men will come to a bad end and all poor ones to a good one, is false, for there are some rich men who will save their souls, and some poor ones who damn themselves."[21] Moreover, for all his Franciscan compassion, he was entirely conventional and orthodox in his conviction that in a sound social structure there was an appointed place for both the rich and the poor. "When God sees that a soul can be saved better through riches than through poverty, God bestows riches ...

God calls each one of us to the state that befits him best."[22] "The rich and the poor are members of the same body. The rich are necessary to the State, and the poor to the rich."

Though in his own life he practised as austere a poverty as St. Francis himself, he did not ask ordinary men and women more than they were capable of giving. "Perhaps you will say, 'God asks of me something that I cannot do.' Now consider a little what God really does ask. He does not ask you to skin yourself." But, on the other hand, poverty is no excuse for lack of charity. "To you who say, 'I have nothing to give,' I reply that even if you are naked you have something that you can and should give, and that you have no excuse before God.... Have you ever considered the dew which you find at dawn, in days of great heat? So it may sometimes occur, as you speak to a poor sick man, that though you can give him nothing of this world's goods, you can yet comfort him with such words, that he is wholly refreshed." Bread given to the sick and to men in prison, he said, was the bread of angels; and a glass of water, a passport to eternal life. "What is it worth, what is it worth, life eternal? I tell you, you may purchase it with a glass of water and even with less – the dregs of the glass will suffice, if given with love."

In all Fra Bernardino's remarks about almsgiving there is an awareness of a beggar's feelings which could perhaps only have arisen in a man who had himself begged in the streets and waited in the cold at a rich man's door – and who once, as we have told, had been hit by a hard loaf flung at him out of the window by an impatient housewife. "It hurt me very much," he said ruefully. "Perhaps she did not give it with a glad heart." And he added: "A poor man would rather have a glass of water given with speed and goodwill, than a bottle of wine bestowed with sourness and re-luctance."[23]

The charity that appealed to him was, above all things, swift and gay – *la compassione cordiale* (cordial compassion). "When you give, give gladly. When a poor man comes to your door and asks for alms in God's name, say, 'Yea, very gladly, I bid you welcome' – with a cheerful face, and swiftly. . . ." And in another sermon, "Know ye why [you must give gladly]? Because *spiritus tristus dissecat ossa* (a sad spirit dries up the bones). This means that if a poor man comes to your door and you give him alms with a lukewarm and unwilling heart, the merit of these alms has gone before you have reached the door." He compared the rich man who waited to give alms until his deathbed to a little boy "who gives his pear to his mother, only when he has bitten it." And he went on to tell the story of a woman who often gave alms, but who was once asked for clothing by a naked beggar in a church, just as the Gospel was beginning, *Sequentia Sancti Vangeli*. "She said to herself, 'What shall I do? Shall I make him wait, or lose the Gospel? If I make him wait, he will die of cold.' So she went quietly to a corner of the church and took off her lining and gave it to him. And lo, a miracle! She went back to the altar, and the priest was still at the selfsame word."[24]

He distinguished, too, between the compassion which merely springs from what he called "an instinct of nature" – a purely physical reaction to the spectacle of pain and poverty, "as a child cries when he sees his mother crying, but knows not why" – and true charity, springing from understanding. "When you see a sick man or one in need . . . at once, before he has asked you for alms or help, you have understood his need. 'I see, you need this or that.' It is brotherly love that makes you see and understand – and therefore did David say, *Beatus qui intellegit*."[25]

Of all the people in need in Siena, perhaps the most unfortunate and certainly those whom Fra Bernardino pitied most, were the "poor prisoners" – and rightly, for the prison system of his time was very harsh and also, like the world outside, had one law for the rich and another for the poor. The prisons were divided into three parts, one for political prisoners, one for common criminals and heretics, and one for poor debtors or men who had committed some minor misdemeanour, but in addition the prisoners of all categories were divided into the privileged – *agevolati* – who were allowed to pay an extra tax for such luxuries as a pallet or another crust of bread, while the *non-agevolati* (unprivileged) were wholly dependent upon alms, or upon such small sums as they could earn by doing the prison's menial services, or acting, if they knew how to write, as scribes. The head-gaoler, who paid the Commune no less than three hundred *lire* a year for the privilege of holding this post, counted on a steady income of a tax of five *soldi* and four pence from every person who entered or left the prison, as well as an additional *soldo* and six pence a day from every privileged prisoner and many tips from their families – the only disadvantage of his position being that, if any of his charges escaped, he was liable to be hanged. But who, indeed, was likely to make this attempt? The city was so small and so full of spies that any fugitive was likely to be caught long before he reached the city gates, while the high city walls were almost unscalable. And even if a man should somehow manage to get out, he well knew what a hunted life awaited him, since the first duty of all the villagers of the territory, if starvation drove him to their doors, was to hand him over at once to the *Signoria* – while to hide him incurred the enormous fine, to the village, of 1,000 florins. The exiled heretic or "traitor" (which often merely meant a man of a different party from the one which happened to be in power) was an *outlaw* – literally outside the law, a man without legal or civic rights, as good as dead.[26] As soon as he was sighted in the district, the hue and cry began: the village bells were rung, the crier blew his horn, the villagers seized their arms, and the man-hunt began.

With such a prospect before them, only very few prisoners attempted to escape. The non-privileged, indeed, were mostly humble

xv. A. Clothing the Naked; B. Tending the Sick: *Domenico di Bartolo.*

XVI. A. Fra Bernardino's Emblem: *Sano di Pietro*.

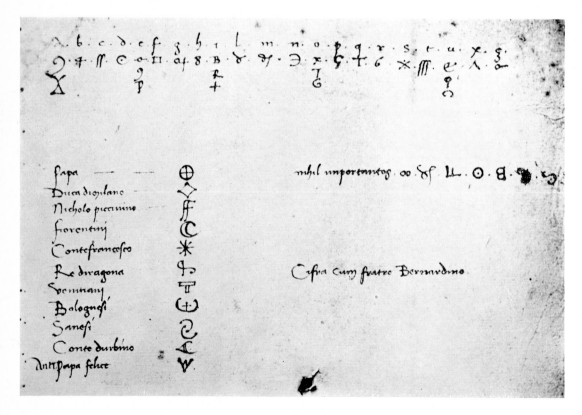

XVI. B. Fra Bernardino's Cypher: *Archivio di Stato, Siena*.

men guilty of little crimes, since the major criminals (whether rob-bers, forgers, heretics or witches) had incurred death by hanging or banishment, or at the very least, the loss of a limb, and the minor offenders who could afford to pay escaped with a fine, so that it was only the political prisoners and the petty criminals and debtors who dragged on, year after year, in their cells. Some of Fra Bernardino's most indignant reproofs are addressed to the men who, from indif-ference or avarice, kept them rotting there. "You who keep a man in prison for the sake of three florins and let him waste away, what is it that you ask of him? Do you want his flesh? For the love of God, have pity on him."[27]

The picture which he painted of the condition of these men – confirmed by other documents of the time – shows an equally com-plete neglect of their bodies and of their souls. "Once," he said "there was a chaplain in the prison, who heard their confessions, gave them the Host, said Mass for them and comforted them in their tribulations; but now they receive no help, no guidance towards a better life, no consolation. They are so completely abandoned that they even lack bread and a bed to sleep on – worse still, I hear that now even their water has been cut off. You have done a fine thing: you have given it to the prostitutes instead!" (The city being short of water, it had been cut off from the prison, though it was still supplied to the brothel next-door.) "If they need bread, it must be brought to them from outside, and so must water, wine and fire-wood. Therefore, you women, I beseech you to have some pity on them: send them some pallets and some mattresses, so that when they have been tortured, they have at least somewhere to rest. And so also I beg you to send them some linen, some pairs of drawers or some shifts. . . . And sometimes send them something from the kitchen, or a little wine – one of you send one thing and one an-other. . . . Be not cruel with them, for if they have done wrong, they are suffering for it."

Above all, he was angered by the hypocrites who excused their own avarice by the sins of the hungry. "How many laws," he cried, "you have made to weigh upon the poor!... Do you think it a greater sin for a man to steal from one who is well off, or for a rich man to give nothing to one whose need is so great that it compels him to steal? Yes, it is God's commandment, 'Thou shalt not steal'! But tell me, if that is a great sin, where are *we* going?"... "Never hold back," he said elsewhere, "because you see a man in need who is wicked and full of vice.... Look not at his sins, but only at his need."[28]

When he spoke to the women of his congregation, he compared God to a woman with her little child. "When he wants something, she gives it to him; when he cries for a fig, she gives it into his hand – not for him to eat it, but to keep him quiet; and when he is quiet again she says, 'My child, give me back that fig, give it me, my sweeting....' And if he will not give it back, she says, 'Go away, you are not my child.' Even so does God to the man to whom he has given abundance.... If you give him nothing for his poor, he will drive you away and say, 'You are no son of mine!'"

Even the beasts and birds, he said, were more compassionate than men. "Look at the pigs, who have so much compassion for each other that when one of them squeals, the others all run to help him, if only they could help.... And you children when you steal the baby swallows, what do the other swallows do? They all gather together and try to help the fledglings.... Man is more evil than the birds."[29]

This is a very Franciscan remark. St. Thomas Aquinas, it is true, had already maintained that, since God is the real object of charity, as he is of faith, charity should be extended to *all* that he has created, even to "the creatures without reason ... the fish and birds, the beasts and plants." But he had added that the *love* which springs from charity – since charity is friendship, an exchange – is only due

114

to our neighbour.[30] St. Francis, however, got round the difficulty by investing all living creatures with human attributes and a human conscience, and thus a human right to redemption and love. Such birds and beasts abound in the Franciscan legend: the fish which he put back into the water, bidding them to "take heed not to let themselves be caught again," the pheasant which would hop after him wherever he went, "holding up his cloak in its beak as if he had been a Bishop," the lamb which, "as soon as it heard the Brothers singing in the choir would kneel before the Altar of the Madonna and baa as if it could reason," the hawk, which would wake the saint every night for his prayers, but once, when he was ill, let him sleep on until the dawn – all these are seen in the light of the charity which is the love of God. "He was compassionate not only with men but with beasts," wrote Fra Bernardino, who delighted in repeating these stories to his congregation, ". . . and in this we see that he was a saint."[31] And once the preacher himself, when disturbed by the crowing and clucking of the barnyard beside which he was preaching, gently bade the cocks and hens to be still – and they, like St. Francis' cicadas, did his bidding and roosted, in motionless and attentive silence, upon the roofs and hedges, until the sermon had come to an end.

Only the rich were deaf – or rather, in Fra Bernardino's image, blind. "There is," he said, "a wrong understanding which brings a blindness to the mind: the man who has eaten well cannot believe the one who has gone hungry, the rich man cannot believe the poor one." "The poor call for alms," he indignantly cried, "and only the dogs reply! . . . You men, who have so much wheat in your granary that your attics are filled and all your shelves laden, so much that you cannot even keep it clean and it goes bad, and the worms eat some of it and even the sparrows have their share, but the poor go hungry – what do you think that God will do to you? Let me tell you that this wheat is not yours, but belongs to the poor man who lacks it. . . . And you women, who have so many garments in your chests and coffers and weighing down your hangers, do you think that God will pay you for them?" The beggars, he said, crouched in rags on the pavement while the fine ladies went by, their trains sweeping the dust and their sleeves "made of as much stuff as would make two cloaks!" ("Nay, laugh not," he interpolated, "for the Devil is laughing too!")[32] "Do you know," he asked in another sermon, "what the moth of the spirit is? It is avarice. All day you shake and hang up your clothes, while that beggar is shivering with cold. Could you but hear, you would hear his shivering cry, 'Vengeance, vengeance!' And so cry your hangers and your coffers. . . . And you see the beggar dying of cold and care not! You do not hear his cries! Do you know why? Because *you* are not cold, because your stomach is filled with good food and good wine, because you have enough clothes and often a fire. Your stomach is filled and your spirit satisfied. . . . And how many shifts have you sent to those poor prisoners? . . . I hear that you have sent two vests, two pairs of drawers and a pair of broken shoes. I think that at the last you will die in all your fine things, and the Devil will bear you away."[33]

He told his congregation – and the story must have been an old one, for it has a flavour of the time when men who had nothing else to give offered themselves or their children to the Church – that there was once a man who all his life long had given alms whenever he was asked for them in God's name, until at last he found himself without a groat. "And then another beggar came to him, asking for alms, and he replied: 'I have given all I had; I have only myself left: *take me.*'"[34]

V. THE CHARGE OF HERESY

Chi mi voleva fritto e chi arrosto.

SAN BERNARDINO*

IN the spring of 1426, when Bernardino was preaching a course
of Lenten Sermons in Viterbo, an unexpected summons reached
him: Pope Martin V required his immediate presence in Rome.[1] He
at once realized why he had been called there. "They say," he told
his congregation, "that I am a heretic and there is a strong report
that I am to be burned with fire – and so I beseech you to pray to
Almighty God for me." Then, shaking off with some difficulty the
most ardent of his admirers, who wished to go with him and defend
him, he set off with his little ass for Rome.[2]

The reason for his summons was an innovation which he had
introduced some years before to his congregation in Bologna and
which had already caused several attacks upon his orthodoxy: an
especial devotion – symbolized in an emblem which he himself had
designed – for the Holy Name of Jesus. Fra Bernardino himself always stoutly denied any intention of introducing a new cult, saying
that it was to be found not only in the writings of St. Paul and of
the "Doctors" (in particular, Duns Scotus), and in the hymn, *Jesu
Dulcis Memoria*, attributed to St. Bernard,[3] but also in the teachings
of St. Francis. He told his congregation in Siena that St. Francis'
devotion to the very name of Jesus was so great that once, when
St. Anthony of Padua was preaching about "Jesus of Nazareth,
King of the Jews," St. Francis suddenly appeared to him in a vision,
giving him his blessing.[4] No doubt, too, Fra Bernardino had read
Tommaso da Celano's two Lives of St. Francis, in which St. Francis' especial devotion to his Saviour was described. "He was always
preoccupied with Jesus," says one passage. "He bore Jesus in his
heart, his mouth, his eyes and ears" – and the biographer added that

if, at meals, St. Francis heard the name of Jesus mentioned, he would sometimes forget to eat, or if he was on the road, would forget his way, "pausing instead to call upon all creatures to praise Him." What was new in Fra Bernardino's teaching was only that he rendered the actual written Name of Jesus (or rather, His initials in a particular design) an especial object of devotion – but this innovation was entirely in accordance with the taste of his times. To the men of the Trecento, as he was well aware, all visible symbols of power had a great and immediate appeal. Noblemen placed their arms and the members of political parties their emblems, not only on their banners and their armour, but on everything they possessed – on their houses and towers, silver and dishes, saddles, headdresses and clothing, and even, to Fra Bernardino's disgust, on the chapels and altars which they built and the chalices and vestments which they gave to the Church. The guilds engraved their emblems on their shops, their altars, their banners and their produce. The *condottieri* of the Free Companies placed them on their standards and lances. And the people made free use of amulets and talismans, of charms and cabalistic seals, all of which they invested with magic powers. For all these emblems of strife, power or superstition, Fra Bernardino now offered a nobler substitute: the letters of Jesus' Name. "It is my intention," he said, "to renew and make clear the Name of Jesus, as in the days of the Early Church."[5]

The monogram he designed consisted of the letter Y H S, standing on a blue ground ("for that colour signifies faith, and without faith we cannot have glory") in the midst of a sun made up of twelve large rays and numerous smaller ones, arranged like organ-pipes, and surrounded by an outer circle bearing the inscription: *In nomine Jesu omne genu flectatur coelestium, terrestrium et infernorum.*[6] "This name, glorious above all others," said Fra Bernardino, "must be set in the most glorious place in the world, namely in the sun."[7]

According to one of the most charming stories told about him by his first biographer, Barnabò da Siena, it was this design that Fra Bernardino himself drew on a rough card for a poor little artisan of Bologna called Valesio, who had come to him in tears after the day on which the Bolognese, at the preacher's behest, had cast into a great bonfire, which they called "the Devil's castle," not only their gaming-boards and dice, but also the beautiful painted playing-cards, called *tarocchi*, which were a speciality of their city.[8] Valesio – so he told the saint – was one of the craftsmen who made their living by painting these cards, and now he and his children must starve. "Well then," said Fra Bernardino, "I must give you something else to sell" – and, taking a piece of cardboard, he drew his emblem on it, telling Valesio to paint and sell this instead. And the little man found so many customers that he never lacked bread again.[9]

The monogram was also sometimes reproduced on a banner, borne before Fra Bernardino when he entered a new city to preach, or on a wooden tablet, which he would place on the small altar on which he celebrated Mass before the sermon. Then, when he had finished speaking, he would hold it up before the congregation, as he gave them his blessing. "Having thus spoken" – the account is given by an eye-witness – "Fra Bernardino would draw out with great fervour a tablet of about an arm's length and breadth. On it was drawn the Name of Jesus on a blue ground, with golden rays and letters around it. And all the people, bare-headed and on their knees, would cry out and shed tears of tenderness and sweetness for the love of Jesus, adoring and revering him with great devotion."[10]

Gradually, wherever Fra Bernardino had been, he left his "sun" behind him – not only on the façade of the Palazzo Pubblico of Siena, in place of the arms of the Visconti, and over church-doors and altars, but over the doors of private houses, at the head of documents and merchants' ledgers, and even on ploughshares and spinning-wheels, on cradles and cooking-pots and, in Florence, upon the swaddling-bands of babies, on the day of their christening. It was worn by soldiers when they went to war, by sailors on the seas, and he even suggested that a godfather might give a baby, for its christening, a little gold or silver tablet engraved with the monogram, "so that the child may wear it for devotion's sake – not because it is of gold or silver, but because of the virtue resting in that Holy Name, and in order that he may understand, as he grows older, the devotion to it. . . . I mean not the carving or the colouring, but the sweetness; not the sign, but the thing signified; for the name of Jesus means for you the Saviour, the Redeemer, the Son of God."[11]

It is hardly possible to speak more plainly, and in almost every passage on the subject he repeated that it was not the emblem in itself that mattered, but the thoughts that it aroused. "Seeing it often, with an inward eye, you will often recall it in reverence, love and faith, and thus form the habit that always, in any event, you have Jesus, Jesus in your heart." But he did not fail also to point out that in this, as in any other devotion, a man only gets what he is capable of receiving. "Take this name, Jesus. . . . Let it be said by a small child in his cradle, whose little mouth is still full of milk – and it will indeed hold sweetness, but very little, for he can understand little. And you, woman, say, 'Jesus': you will receive a different sweetness from the child's, for you know that this name tells you that he is the Redeemer, both God and Man. If a devout man says it with devotion, he receives greater sweetness . . . and if St. Augustine or St. Bernard, greater still. . . . And so it will be, even in Heaven."[12]

The passages referring to this cult are among the most deeply felt in Fra Bernardino's sermons,[13] and some of them show that he, too, was not wholly immune from periods of great spiritual desolation. "It often happens," he says, "that devout souls suddenly feel themselves oppressed by sadness and tedium; they no longer find delight in solitude, reading becomes tedious to them and prayer a weariness." And he goes on to say that this state of "lethargic sleep" is caused by the absence of Jesus. "When he returns, as he did to the house of Lazarus, we come back, as Lazarus did, to life."[14] To look upon the Cross, Fra Bernardino said elsewhere, is to be reminded of Christ's Passion; but to hear his name is to recollect *every* aspect of his Life: the poverty of the crib, the humility of the carpenter's shop, the penance in the desert, the miracles of the divine charity, the suffering on Calvary, the triumph of the Resurrection and the Ascension. "This Name reveals to you God in Man."[15] "May I be imbued," he prayed, "with Our Lord Jesus Christ, as cloth is with colour, or the air with light."[16]

How effective his sermons on this subject were, together with the emblem he displayed, is shown in the letters written in 1424 by a Tuscan merchant, Sandro di Marco di Sandro Marcovaldi, to his brother (who was trading in Ragusa), after Fra Bernardino's sermons in Prato. Sandro described how a miracle had taken place, after one of these sermons, before his own eyes: a woman possessed of a devil had broken out into loud cries as the holy tablet was held up, and then, as everyone fell on their knees, imploring God's mercy, the preacher, descending from the pulpit with the tablet in his hand, exorcized her – "and the demon came out of her and all those who were there, in their adoration and amazement, burst into laments, as if someone had beaten them.... It has pleased Jesus," he added, "to send us a prophet.... He seems a St. Paul in his doctrine and his teaching, for never in our life have we heard such eloquence. And even if the hearts of sinners are as hard as stone or steel, he tears them open and breaks them ... and makes them come back to salvation in the Name of Jesus." And his letter ended by advising his brother to wear the emblem always upon his person, "for you travel in peril from the world, the sea and the Devil, and therefore I desire you to do this."[17]

One might think that such a cult could hardly have aroused censure, even from the most orthodox, but instead it swiftly gave rise to charges of both heresy and idolatry. Fra Bernardino's chief accusers were the members of the rival preaching Orders, the Augustinians and the Dominicans, and among the latter there was a fervent and fanatical friar, Manfredi of Vercelli, whom Fra Bernardino himself, on entirely different grounds, had once accused of heresy. It was he who, supported by the Dominicans, spread charges against the Franciscan's orthodoxy in both Bologna and Florence, and even gained the ear of the Florentine Archbishop, St. Antoninus. At first Fra Bernardino was inclined to attribute these accusations chiefly to envy, merely saying, "I must defend this truth" – but when, in 1425, he realized how fast they were spreading, he was more explicit: "Because I was reproved and calumniated last year for what I said about the Name of Jesus, this year . . . I will say a great deal more in reply to those who speak as they should not: for I did not say they should adore the colours or the gold and silver, but the essence of that name, Jesus, God and man." "Not the letters," he repeated, "not the colours, not the adornments: God, God, God."[18]

Nevertheless public opinion in Florence gradually hardened so much against him that the Archbishop spoke of his doctrine as "superstitious, dangerous and likely to cause scandal,"[19] while the humanist Poggio Bracciolini – already no friend to the Observants – was delighted by this opportunity to refer to "the impudence of those men who, calling only upon the name of Jesus, are starting a new heretical sect, seeking popularity by giving resonance to that name from the coarse populace, whose rewards they desire."[20] Even Fra Bernardino's friend, the mild, learned Camaldolese monk Ambrogio Traversari, thought it wiser to write to Fra Alberto da Sarteano, advising the Observants to abstain for a while from preaching in Florence.

A more specific attack was launched against Fra Bernardino by the Augustinian Fra Andrea de' Bigli, a theologian and historian of some renown, who, while declaring his personal admiration for the Franciscan's goodness and eloquence, yet published a pamphlet emphasizing the dangers of his newfangled doctrines and devices, and referring to him and his disciples as "spreaders of superstition and scandal."[21] He inquired why it had been necessary to invent a new symbol to arouse popular devotion, when true Christians already had the Cross, declared himself shocked to see the name of Jesus inscribed at every street-corner and over the doors of taverns and even of brothels, and ended by suggesting that Fra Bernardino should look into his heart and ask himself whether, in making use of the Holy Name to increase his eloquence, he had not also been feeding his own vanity. Finally he pointed out how easy it was to confuse the minds of the simple and thus stir up discord, instead of bringing peace. In Sicily, he said – thanks to one of Fra Bernardino's disciples, Fra Matteo of Messina – there were men who refused to give alms for the love of God, and would only do so if they were asked in the name of Jesus; there were others who, in making the sign of the Cross, said "In the name of the Father and of the Son and of the Holy Ghost *e del buon Gesù*"; and in one place a preacher's sermon had been interrupted by the cry, "Unless God is Jesus, talk no more about God!" And he added that, according to a report which had reached him, Fra Bernardino had once told in the pulpit the story of a man who, when his soul was freed from Purgatory, had asked for admission to Heaven in the name of the Trinity, but had only been admitted when he mentioned the name of Jesus. Such doctrines, Fra Andrea said, came dangerously close to Arianism.[22]

It was the cumulative weight of such protests as these that at last caused the Pope to summon Fra Bernardino to Rome, and it was with a full awareness of the strength of the charges against him, that the Franciscan obeyed. The Pope, indeed, received him with great severity – telling him that his case would be fully investigated in a public trial, but that in the interval he must remain in Rome at the Curia's disposal, refrain from preaching, hand over his sermons and cease from displaying the tablets of the Holy Name. Fra Bernardino received these orders in silence upon his knees, and then, saying no word to defend himself, made his way back to his cell in the Convent of the Observants on the Aracoeli.[23]

Then came a period of waiting, which must have been one of great distress. On the last occasion that he had been in Rome, only three years before, he had displayed his tablet on the Campidoglio to a reverent and fervent congregation. Now, as he walked about the town, he saw that the monogram had been chiselled away over the doorways or hidden by a veil upon the altars, and if one of his brother friars knocked at a door in search of alms, he was turned away with the cry, "*Fora i Gesú!*" (Away with the Jesuses).[24]

Sometimes an old friend would draw away from him as he passed, fearing to be seen with a suspected heretic; sometimes a rough crowd would jeer at him, foretelling the penalty that awaited him. "Some wanted me roasted and some fried!" he said with a smile on his return to Siena. He was even told that in some cities, priests had denied absolution to anyone who still kept one of his tablets.

But his peace of mind, even now, was not troubled. "Those who blame me, are kinder to me," he once said in a sermon, "than those who praise me; for those who blame are helping me to rise, and those who praise, to fall."[25] His days were spent in study and when the other friars asked him how he could find enough inner quiet to concentrate, he replied: "Whenever I enter my cell, all the wrongs and insults inflicted upon me stay outside the door."[26]

Meanwhile, however, his friends were gathering in his defence, and foremost amongst them a Franciscan Observant who was an expert in canon law and whom Pope Martin himself had recently

XVII. Fra Bernardino before the Pope: *Giacomo da Lodi*.

XVIII. The Peacemaker: *Sebastiano di Cola.*

appointed as Inquisitor against those unruly offspring of the Franciscan Order, the *Fraticelli*. This was Giovanni da Capistrano, the son of a woman from the Abruzzi and a German baron, whose fair hair had earned him the nickname of "Giantudesco" – a man whose eloquence, piety and austerity of life were only second to Bernardino's own and who, like him, had vowed a special devotion to the Holy Name of Jesus. His conversion, when he was already a magistrate of Perugia and engaged to a noble young lady of that city, had occurred after a vision which appeared to him when, as prisoner of war, he was lying in a cell in one of the city towers. "As I slept," he wrote, "I thought I heard a great noise, owing to which I woke up and saw a ray of light illuminating all the tower, and lifting up my head to thank God, I saw standing above me a friar whose feet were pierced – but, as I lifted up my hands to clutch him, he disappeared. And when I lowered my head, I found it as you see it now [i. e. with the tonsure of the Minorites] and so I realized that this friar had been our father, St. Francis, and knew it to be God's will that I should leave this world and serve Him."[27]

Fra Giovanni had first met Fra Bernardino when they both were still young, in the convent at Fiesole, and they had become close friends, so that, as soon as he heard of his brother's plight, "Giantudesco" at once interrupted the course of sermons he was giving in Naples, rode to Aquila to collect some papers which he thought might be useful for the defence, and hurried on to Rome. Here, ignoring the Pope's prohibition, he entered the city at the head of a group of friends, bearing a banner on which the sacred emblem was displayed – and so, with a large crowd gradually gathering behind him, he triumphantly entered St. Peter's square.

When at last the day of the trial came – after a lengthy examination of the charges by a commission appointed by the Pope – Fra Giovanni and Fra Matteo of Girgenti were the only two friars who followed Fra Bernardino into the Pope's presence, to find themselves confronting fifty-two doctors of divinity and all the chief Cardinals and prelates of the Curia. The debate began with their charges – expressed, according to Barnabò da Siena, "with the greatest magniloquence and in complicated syllogisms" (*magna cum pompa et implicatis sillogismis*). "Oh, how they did maul him!"[28]

When they had finished, Fra Bernardino rose and spoke in his own defence. Whether the text of his speech that has come down to us is authentic or not, is still disputed, but it is certain that he spoke simply and firmly, basing his defence upon the words of the Gospels and the traditions of the Fathers of the Church, "who knew a great deal more than I do," and reiterating that what was essential in the new object of devotion was not any of its accessories of shape or colour, but the actual letters (whether abbreviated or not, and whether written in Greek or Latin) of Jesus' Name, and their significance.[29] Perhaps, too, Fra Bernardino's transparent sincerity and humility pleaded for him as much as any argument, for when he had finished a unanimous ovation greeted him and – almost without waiting to hear what Fra Giovanni da Capistrano had to add – the Pope pronounced him innocent of any heresy, gave him his blessing, and permitted him to preach again.

On the following day a solemn procession took place, in which Fra Giovanni bore the banner with the sacred monogram, followed by the clergy and by the fickle Romans, singing hymns in honour of the Saviour. Fra Bernardino was presented with a small oratory – on the site on which the great church of the Gesú now stands – and, at the Pope's request, stayed on in Rome to preach for eighty days in St. Peter's. On each occasion the great church was packed, not only with the whole of the Curia (including sometimes the Pope himself), but with the Roman nobles and fine ladies, the scholars and the populace – many of them men who, a few weeks before, would gladly have hurried to see him burned alive as a heretic on the Capitol. "Now they want me alive and only a short time ago they wanted me dead," he commented dryly – adding that the only true satisfaction he had obtained from this change of heart was the gift of enough money to purchase the freedom of thirty poor men imprisoned for debt.[30]

For even now, the battle was not over. Although, after the Pope's pronouncement, the friars of Santa Croce in Florence promptly carved Fra Bernardino's emblem on the façade of their church and his fellow-citizens in Siena received him with great honour, there was still a small minority which went on murmuring against his doctrine, both in private and in the pulpit. It was even said that some peasants in Umbria had become sun-worshippers, because it was a sun that Fra Bernardino had shown them.[31] To all these attacks the preacher swiftly and publicly replied, saying that any attack upon his private life was a matter between the speaker and himself, "but if a man calumniates me in something that affects God's honour, and does so in public, it is in public that he must be refuted.... If such a thing concerned myself alone, I would gladly be patient. But this concerns God.... And you know that Jesus Christ himself did not show patience, when he saw what had been done in the temple to God's dishonour."[32]

But still the charges continued. In 1431 Fra Bernardino was obliged to return to Siena to preach in his own defence, and he was also attacked in Perugia and Rimini, while in Bologna the Inquisitor Lodovico Tosi of Pisa, who had found a picture of the holy emblem on the High Altar of San Petronio, ordered it to be removed and replaced by a Cross.[33] Finally, in November 1431 – availing themselves of a provision decreed by the Council of Constance, that a secret process might be instituted against Religious suspected of heresy – Fra Bernardino's enemies persuaded the "Promoter of the Faith" in Rome to summon Bernardino and some of his friars, to appear for trial before the Dominican Cardinal Giovanni di Casanova. It was on this occasion that the Dominicans wrote two pamphlets, repeating and summarizing all the accusations against Fra Bernardino's orthodoxy and maintaining that his new cult was suspect of a) diabolic influence, b) idolatry, c) Hussism, d) Jewish depravity and e) the doctrine of Anti-Christ.[34] Meanwhile Pope Martin V had died, and his successor, Pope Eugenius IV, knew nothing of the matter – but as soon as he discovered what was going on, he indignantly put an end to it and issued, on January 5, 1432, the Bull *Sedis Apostolicae*, in which he declared that the trial had been instituted without his knowledge or consent, and stated – in terms of such high praise as has seldom been awarded to a Religious during his lifetime – that he considered Fra Bernardino to be "the most illustrious preacher and unerring teacher of all who are preaching the Gospel in Italy or abroad."[35]

So at last Fra Bernardino's doctrines were fully approved, by the highest authority on earth. To understand what this must have meant to him, it is necessary to realize how deeply orthodox a man he was. All his fire had always gone into fighting against sin; none, into rebelling against authority.

Always he had warned both friars and laymen against one of the most popular heresies of the day, which had first been held by the Cathars and which was still preached by some of the *Fraticelli* – that the unworthiness of a priest can hinder the effect of a Sacrament – quoting to them the saying of St. Francis, "If he should meet in the street an angel and a priest, it would be to the priest that he would show greater reverence." And he told them, too, the legend about the day when St. Francis came to a place where there was "a priest of such evil life that another man who lived there said that one should not go to his Mass, for his sins were such that he was not worthy to perform the act of consecration. . . . Without making any answer, he flung himself on to the ground at that priest's feet and kissed his hands."[36]

Martin V and Eugenius IV were good and upright Popes, but

even if they had not been, Fra Bernardino would have accepted from them with the same humility the long, painful delay while his doctrines were being tested, the ordeal of the trial, and the humiliation of being ordered to put away the emblem by means of which he had hoped to bring the simple, bewildered men of his congregation a little nearer to God. It was the doubt of his intention that distressed him, not the pinpricks of his accusers; but he seems to have accepted his vindication as quietly and steadily as he had borne previous discipline. "This concerns God."

The last episode of the long controversy took place during the Council of Basle in 1438, when one of Fra Bernardino's adversaries asked the Council to re-examine the whole case, pointing out that though Pope Martin V had absolved Fra Bernardino of heresy, he had forbidden the public exhibition of the tablets.[37] According to the *Anonimo*, the President of the Council then wrote to the Duke of Milan, asking him to send the dangerous preacher to appear before it – but Visconti, having taken the advice of some theological experts, at once replied to the Council (which he did not hesitate to call *concilium malignantium*) defending Fra Bernardino with great energy[38] – whereupon the whole matter seems to have been allowed to lapse. That in Rome the whole episode was considered of little importance, is suggested by the fact that it was in this same year that Fra Bernardino was appointed Vicar General of the Italian Observants. It is, however, noticeable that – perhaps in order to avoid entering upon the ground of such recent and heated controversy – the thirty-three articles presented as causes for his canonization contain no mention of his devotion to the Holy Name.[39] It was not until 1530, under Pope Clement VII, that this cult was officially included in the Church's liturgy, and under Innocent XIII that its celebration was set for a definite date, the second Sunday after the Epiphany.

Wherever, in the last five centuries, Fra Bernardino's followers have been, they have taken his emblem with them. Already in his lifetime it had spread to every Italian town and village, from Friuli to Sicily, and immediately after his death, Fra Giovanni da Capistrano bore it to Hungary and Fra Giacomo della Marca to the Balkans. Sainte Colette and Joan of Arc – who died with the name of "Jesus" upon her lips – spread the devotion in France,[40] and the friars of the Observance took it with them to Spain and Portugal, to Mexico and to the Levant – and later still, to India, China and Japan. Wherever, in the most remote regions of the world, Fra Bernardino's emblem is carved over a doorway, or painted on a church wall, we may know that one of his followers has been – bearing with him "the sun, which is Charity."

VI. STRIFE, CRIME AND PEACEMAKING

I' vo gridando: pace, pace, pace.

PETRARCA*

I

"THE reasons why God hates you," said Fra Bernardino one day to his congregation in Siena, "are called vanity, curiosity and self-indulgence," and to this list he added, on another occasion, the sins of avarice, sodomy, blasphemy, vindictiveness, fickleness, factiousness and arrogance, as well as the sharp eye for his own interest which is a Tuscan trait to this day. "Whether a Tuscan has given his word or not," he said, "he will never fail to do what suits his own interests best!"[1] He deplored the softness and inconstancy of purpose, too, which caused the Sienese to change their mind with every breath that blew. "*Sangue senese, sangue dolce*" (Sienese blood is soft blood), he quoted, adding, "But I would rather see in you one firm feeling, and not watch you veer about in every matter as you do, for you veer as rapidly towards evil as towards the good." And finally, he told them that they had acquired a universal reputation for treachery. "Hark to the fine name we bear! If a Frenchman or another foreigner comes here, he is always in dread lest an Italian should betray him."[2]

These remarks were undoubtedly sincere: Fra Bernardino had few illusions about his fellow-citizens, and did not hesitate to say so. But the reason why his words aroused no resentment was that, whatever fault he might find, he never forgot that he was a *Senese* himself: "O my Sienese citizens," he cried, "I too belong to you, and I speak to you in great love." This, surely, is why his congregation put up with his upbraidings; they knew that his anger was a father's anger; his fear, a brother's fear. "You are better off than any city in Italy. Alas, I am so much afraid that something is brewing under so much good fortune, that it is wasting me away. When I have left you, I shall always keep my ears pricked whenever I hear Siena mentioned, on account of my fears for you. I shall bear with me a great breastful of sorrows and sighs, in my dread that evil will come upon you.... For I fear that another preacher will come to preach to you – do you know his name? He is called Brother Staff, Brother Rod ... and his preachings bear such fruit, as you here in Siena will hardly believe."

The occasion for these remarks was the course of sermons held by Fra Bernardino in Siena in the summer of 1427, immediately after he had been absolved from the charge of heresy – a course delivered by the Pope's own request, to quieten the party strife which seemed likely to burst out again in Siena. "What do you suppose," he asked, "was the reason for my coming here now? It was because I had heard that there was a great division amongst you ... and I said to myself, 'If I can do good to others, am I not the more bound to do so to my fellow-citizens?'"[3]

He was well aware, as he spoke, that, with the possible exception of the Florentines, no other Italian was as passionately and persistently addicted to party politics as the Sienese. "This city," wrote the French chronicler Philippe de Commines a few years later, "is at all times divided into factions, and rules itself more foolishly than any other in Italy." Month by month, year by year, the strong civic spirit which had originally brought about the rise of the Commune of Siena and had fostered the development of its trade, and which still inspired its citizens to adorn their town with magnificent works of art, was being sapped by the violence of the various rival factions. Throughout the second half of the fourteenth century, the struggles between Guelph and Ghibelline, or between the parties of the nobles, the merchants and the people, had kept the town in a perpetual turmoil. In one year (1368) the Magistrates of the Commune were changed four times in four months. First, the city was ruled by a Council of nine merchants known as *i Signori Nove*;

then by "the Twelve," who were set up jointly by the nobles and the people; then by "the Fifteen," the representatives of the wool-workers' guild; and finally, these too were thrown out by a revolt fomented by some of the nobles, with the support of the poorest class of all, the *popolo minuto* (the "little folk"), who appointed as their representatives another group, "the Reformers." But how far from secure the members of any of these parties felt, even when they were in office, is told by a chronicler of the times, who describes "the Twelve," when they had been appointed, as being afraid "even of the air," and as appointing police captains with troops in every quarter of the city, with orders to behead whoever should even "cough against them."[4]

The various factions were called *monti* – the *monte* of the Nobles, the Nine, the Twelve, the Fifteen, the Reformers, the People. You could see to which party a man belonged by every gesture he made and every word he spoke, and even, according to Fra Bernardino, by the way he ate his garlic. And how they all lived with one another, in the dark, narrow little streets of Siena, is described by one of their own chroniclers: "No man understood or kept faith; the Nobles kept it neither among themselves nor with other men; and the Reformers, that is, those now in power, neither with themselves nor with other people at all perfectly. And so the world is all one darkness."[5]

So strong was the violence of party feeling, that even self-interest could not restrain it. When, in 1371 – nine years before Bernardino's birth – the starving underlings of the wool-guild organized a strike, the ruling merchant family, the Salimbeni, not only mercilessly suppressed the insurrection, but banished from the city no less than four thousand of the wool-workers, who promptly took themselves and their skill to Florence. A few years later the party responsible for this suicidal folly, "the Reformers," was overthrown and yet another *monte*, that of "the People," came into power. But it was

133

too late: the wool-trade of Siena had already received its death-blow.

At that time both Milan and Florence were struggling to obtain supremacy over Northern and Central Italy, and the Free Companies fighting on either side were laying waste the country round Siena. After Florence had seized Arezzo and fomented a revolt in Montepulciano, Siena declared war upon her, and appealed for protection to the tyrant of Milan, Gian Galeazzo Visconti, who had already declared that "Tuscany and Lombardy should be one and inseparable" and was glad to gain this foothold in Tuscany. For ten years Siena was held to Milan by a treaty of alliance and in 1399 the Duke Gian Galeazzo Visconti (who in the interval had also added the territories of Bologna, Pisa, Perugia and Assisi to his dominions) was also offered the sovereignty of Siena, which he held until his death three years later. But the first use that the Sienese made of the independence that they had got back, was to return to their old quarrels. In 1403 the Twelve formed a conspiracy with some of the nobles to overthrow the government, and, on being discovered, were excluded from the city council, while the rule passed into the hands of a coalition government of three parties – the Nine, the Reformers and the People – and remained with them for forty years. Thus, during most of the time in which Fra Bernardino was preaching, Siena appeared to have a stable government, but he well knew how precarious this stability was. The two excluded parties, the Nobles and the Twelve, were constantly plotting to return to power, and at the slightest sign of an uprising, their leaders were sent into banishment; while if for a year or two comparative quiet reigned, the young men of the city found it so unbearably tedious that they formed two bands with the significant names of *Chiasso* and *Graffio* (Shout and Scratch), so that they might again indulge in the pleasures of street fighting.[6]

It is with such a background as this in mind, that Fra Bernardino's diatribes against party politics must be read. He had watched them destroying, day by day, the peace of mind of his fellow-citizens and the prosperity of his city, and it is hardly surprising that he should have attacked them with a vehemence such as he hardly showed towards any other sin or folly. Political hatred, he said, when not controlled in its early stages, grows like a thistle in the fields, "which at first has such tender spikes that you can put your foot on it without being pricked," but by August has become "strong and hard."[7] In his eyes the rift between Guelph and Ghibelline was merely a symbol of every other form of discord – in the family, the city, the State, the Church itself.

His remarks, moreover, must also be read against a wider background – that of the political and religious climate of the whole of Europe. From the year of Fra Bernardino's birth to 1417, Christianity had been cut in two by the Great Schism; for nearly forty years there had been two and sometimes three Popes on the papal throne, and two or three Bishops in the same diocese; two or three Superiors had sometimes been appointed in a single monastery, and two or three rival priests in the same parish. Within Fra Bernardino's own Order, the Franciscan Conventuals and the Spirituals were still at strife. In the cities, the Pope's Guelphs were fighting against the Emperor's Ghibellines; in the country, fields were laid bare and farms and abbeys burned down by the mercenary Free Companies. Can one wonder that to Fra Bernardino party feeling had come to signify not only a human weakness, but a sin against God's love?

"Now tell me," he cried, "what is a party? Do you know what it is? It is a division: this sundered from that. And tell me what charity is? It is the union of one man with another." An apocalyptic vision came to him of "a red horse, bathed in blood, like its riders, to whom strength was given to destroy the world's peace . . . and he was given a very long sword." It was, he said, a sword bigger than Roland's, longer than the Campo, longer than the street from

135

the Campo to the city walls, longer than Tuscany, longer than Italy itself. "It was greater than the whole of Christendom. I tell you, it was as great as the whole of the earth and sea."

"Do you not see," he cried, "that you have turned every man, woman and child into either a Guelph or a Ghibelline? The only things that you have not turned into either Guelph or Ghibelline are bread and wine." Even the saints and angels in Paradise were believed to take sides. "Some say that St. John is a Guelph and some that he is a Ghibelline, and so they say even about the angels." Men set up their arms and their party emblems even in the churches, "and I have seen them even above the head of the Cross. Then said I, 'O Lord God, the Devil is above you, and is pissing on your head.'"[8]

It is interesting to note that he saw no whit of difference between Guelph and Ghibelline; these names had now become nothing but battle-cries. "Some foolish men," he said, "believe the Church to be Guelph – but experience has shown us that, to gain their own ends, the Guelphs will fight against the Church and the Ghibellines against the Empire, seven times a day."

A sin so deeply rooted, he considered, could only spring from Lucifer himself, the Prince of Darkness. The "man possessed of a devil" was, to his mind, a party man. "Has none of you, women, a husband belonging to a party? Is none of you, men, at the head of a party? If he has one man under him, he has a devil at his back; if he has fifty men, fifty devils; if a thousand, a thousand devils are upon him."[9]

As to the confessors who absolved men who still belonged to a faction, he told them that they would be sent to Hell, bound to their own penitents. "Do you want to absolve a man? First make him give up any faction to which he belongs and [promise] that he will not do so again.... But if he does not, I tell you that he will go to the Devil's house, and you with him!" "*Assolvere non si può chi non si pente.*"[10]

136

So Fra Bernardino preached – but he himself well knew that, however easily he could sway his congregation's feelings in other matters, in this respect public opinion was against him. "A man came to me," he said, "and brought his son with him, and for all I could say in the pulpit and in private, I could not make them understand . . . how great a sin it is, to belong to a party. . . . They were good men, but I could not get that cursed idea out of their heads. Now one of them is dead, and I think he has gone to the Devil's house."[11]

The truth was that the whole question of party strife was closely connected with one of the most deeply-rooted mediaeval traditions: the belief in the righteousness of private vendettas. When Fra Bernardino was preaching, the Commune of Siena had recently revived the old custom of keeping an official record (in a book called *Il Balzano*) of any offence committed against the city,[12] while the private avengement of an insult or injury by bloodshed was not considered a crime by the law, but merely an act of justice. Such deeds, indeed, were quite frankly admitted to be not only a sacred duty, but a pleasure. "The greatest grief," wrote the Florentine merchant Paolo da Certaldo in enumerating the joys and griefs of life, "is to receive an injury; the greatest pleasure, to wreak vengeance."[13] Moreover, this was a duty which was considered to extend even to the most remote members of a clan, and to children yet unborn when the original injury had taken place. "Many men say to me," Fra Bernardino admitted, "'It is shameful to forgive'; and others, 'My house was never wont to forgive.'" And elsewhere he added, "I have heard of women so fanatical that they will themselves put a lance in their little boy's hand, so that he may wreak vengeance by murder." "How many crimes," he cried, "have taken place in these regions, how many women have been murdered in their own cities and their own homes, how many men have had their guts torn out! How many children have been slain, to avenge

137

their fathers – babies torn from their mothers' wombs and trodden underfoot, children whose heads have been beaten against a wall – enemies' flesh sent to the butcher's like any other meat, and the heart torn from the body and eaten raw! Some men have been thrown down from high towers, some cast into the water from bridges – women have been raped and murdered before the eyes of their husbands and fathers. . . . O women, what say you to all this?"[14]

While life in the cities was thus rendered precarious both by the brawls between the factions and the menace of private vendettas, that of the countryside was made almost equally unsafe by the passage of the mercenary Free Companies whom the various cities and tyrants hired to fight on their behalf, and who frequently went over from one side to another, following the highest bidder. The records of the passage of these troops are as brutal as they are monotonous. Wherever they went – and sometimes they would camp in the same region for many months – they left devastation behind them: a world of stunned, destitute peasants or villagers, who cared nothing for the reasons for which either side was fighting, but only knew that they were left to starve among their ravaged fields and vineyards, with their women raped, their cattle stolen or slaughtered, and their farms in ashes. Not even the convents and abbeys were spared: they too, if they happened to be on the Companies' path, were taken and sacked. Indeed such raids had become so much of a commonplace that Fra Filippo degli Agazzari, who was the prior of the Augustinian convent at Lecceto, about seven miles from Siena, remarks in passing – as if he were speaking of some hurricane or other natural disaster – how inconvenient it is for a prior to have to move everything out of his monastery "once or twice and sometimes even thrice a year," to take refuge in a walled city, "for fear of the Companies."[15]

The larger cities, such as Siena, sometimes saved themselves by bribery. The German Company of Werner von Urslingen, the

Provençal troops of Fra Moreale, the English soldiers of Sir John Hawkwood, the Breton Company of the Hat, the Italian one of the Star, each in turn, within the short space of fifty years, collected thousands of gold florins from the exchequer of Siena – and there was even an occasion when, to conciliate one of these brigands, the *Signori* sent to him, in addition to the money, "beautiful and rich gifts – to wit, a magnificent horse with hangings and much wax and sweets and well-ripened wine."[16]

Fra Bernardino called these troops "locusts, who leap here and there," and described an incident which he knew would also shock the natural thrift of his fellow-citizens. "I myself have been in a city wherein these executioners of God entered, and in the houses where there was some wine, do you know what use they made of it? They let it run for washing their horses' hoofs!"

Yet – since it was always the leaders whom Fra Bernardino blamed, reserving his compassion for the men whose sins were rooted in ignorance or hunger – it is pleasant to read that sometimes, when he met these brigands upon the highways, he would stop and talk to them, telling them that, to his mind, they had a better excuse than the prosperous city tradesmen to pass from one side to another, since they depended on their pay for their daily bread. And sometimes – grateful for so much understanding from such a holy man – they would ask for his blessing and call out, when they met the little grey friar upon the roads: "Fra Bernardino, remember the poor free-lancers!"[17]

Moreover, there were some occasions – and it was with deep satisfaction that he himself described them – on which Fra Bernardino's words did indeed bring about a change of heart and restore peace to a whole region. Once, when he had been preaching in Crema in Lombardy – a little town which had recently sent ninety of its chief citizens into banishment, after the defeat of their faction – he was so successful in softening the heart of the new seigneur, Giorgio

139

Benzoni, that he said he would allow every man who had been banished to come home again. Fra Bernardino went on his way and a few days later came to a village where one of these men was living – in penury as well as exile, since he had also been despoiled of forty thousand florins. He hurried out to ask for news from home, whereupon the preacher replied, "'In God's name you may go home again.'... And his joy was so great, that he could neither eat nor drink nor sleep." A few days later the banished man gathered up his courage and went home – and, sure enough, his chief enemy met him in the square and took him out to supper with him. "And while he was supping another fellow-citizen, who in his absence had taken possession of his house, hastily moved out of it," and everyone else who had stolen something of his sent it back – "his bed and his chests, his shifts, his tablecloths, his basins, his wine-barrels and his silver, so that on that same night he slept in his own house, among his own possessions.... And on the following days, anyone who had stolen his cattle or his chattels, would come up to him: 'Here are your oxen, your asses and your sheep' – and thus nearly all that he had was given back to him.... And think you not," Fra Bernardino added, "that all this was pleasing to God?"[18]

In several other cities, too, his words were equally effective. In Vicenza, where he preached on Easter Day, 1423, a young man whose father had been murdered and who had vowed vengeance on his assassin, was so ashamed "that he sought out his enemy, with the intention of embracing and forgiving him. And on the way he met the murderer – for each one of them was looking for the other – and at once he [the son] went towards the other and embraced him, saying, 'Forgive me, for I have forgiven you!' And there was such tenderness between them, that there was not a man who saw this sweet action, who did not weep."[19]

He "pacified" the cities of Casal Monferrato and Treviglio, whose inhabitants were about to massacre each other, and the field in which the reconciliation took place is still called "the field of peace." In Pavia, which had been sacked by the *condottiere* Facino Cane, his words were so effective that, though the raid had taken place eight years before, a large part of the booty then stolen was restored to its owners, placed secretly upon their doorsteps at night. Furthermore, in several instances, Fra Bernardino took some extremely practical steps to try to forestall fresh occasions of strife. In Belluno, where the Guelphs and the Ghibellines ruled the city in turn, each of them undoing whatever had been done by their predecessors, he not only succeeded in altering the statutes which had decreed this undesirable arrangement, but persuaded all the citizens to substitute for the party emblems on their houses his own monogram of Jesus' Name. And in Rome – when he went there in 1427 – he succeeded in putting an end to a custom which had been a frequent cause of bloodshed. This was a rule that any murderer who could take refuge behind the iron gates or fences of his own *palazzo*, was immune from punishment by the laws, so that often the relatives of a murdered man would lay a veritable siege to his enemy's house, to avenge their kinsman themselves. During Fra Bernardino's visit, almost all these gates and fences were removed.[20]

Fra Bernardino was not, of course, the first or only preacher of his time to try to bring about Christian brotherhood and peace. He was merely following the example of his master, St. Francis, whose greeting to every man he met had been the words, "God grant you peace!," and whose friars, after his death, had often acted as peacemakers and arbitrators of quarrels, while the popular preachers of other Orders, too – in particular the Spanish Dominican, St. Vincent Ferrer, whom Fra Bernardino had heard in his youth – had often caused their sermons to be followed, before the emotions of the crowd had died down, by spectacular "peacemakings." Similar scenes, too, often followed the passage of the companies of Penitents or Flagellants which sprang up all over Europe throughout the fourteenth and fifteenth centuries, impelled both by a deep sense of guilt and by an intense nostalgia, in a world of such widespread violence, injustice and social unrest, for the peace and concord which neither the State nor the Church had been able to give them. Barefoot and hooded, clothed in long pilgrims' robes, and bearing a Crucifix at their head, they wandered across Europe from city to city, from shrine to shrine, scourging themselves in penance for their sins, preaching the Gospel of "a holy Communism." The most recent of these movements, in Fra Bernardino's time, was one which had started in Lombardy. Its members were called *i Bianchi* from the white robes they wore, and declared that Christ Himself had appeared in a field to a starving peasant and filled his sack with bread, revealing to him that peace would be brought back to the world, not by the rich and powerful, but the humble. "For since neither prelates nor wise men will bestir themselves, the Divine Mercy has elected to show its power through coarse working-men."[21]

Soon the movement spread throughout Northern and Central Italy, intensified by a renewed outbreak of the Black Death. Great companies of penitents followed the *Bianchi* wherever they went, scourging themselves and singing hymns in which they implored God to grant them "peace and mercy," and wherever they went, their passage, too, was often followed by sensational "peacemakings."

Such forms of enthusiasm, however, were regarded by Fra Bernardino with some distrust. Not only did he dread – in common with most Churchmen and rulers – the social unrest which they often aroused and the spiritual discontent of which they were a token and which was undermining the Church's absolute authority, but he was also well aware of the dangers of such excessive and undirected manifestations of religious fervour. "The ignorant and inexperienced in ways of the Spirit," he wrote, "and as a rule any layman, are edified by the spectacle of chastisements and of things that torture and afflict and the like, even though they are per-

142

formed without discretion; and on the contrary, they are scandalized by things that give pleasure, even although sometimes they are not even venial sins."[22]

Moreover, as an experienced preacher, he knew only too well how seldom such sudden waves of emotion were followed by any durable change in behaviour. After the passage of the *Bianchi*, or during epidemics of the plague, spectacular "peacemakings" did indeed often take place. Men who had been fighting against each other all their lives or carrying out a family vendetta, suddenly sealed their reconciliation with a formal and public embrace. But often these reconciliations ended as swiftly as they had taken place. When the penitents passed on, or the plague had abated, civil war and private vengeance began again.

It need hardly be said, in view of Fra Bernardino's opinion of party politics, that he took no part in them himself – but there were at least two occasions on which, without playing an official part, he did bring his influence to bear in favour of the welfare of his city and of peace in Italy. One of these occasions was when, in his old age, he acted as an unofficial envoy from Siena to Visconti of Milan; the other when, in 1432, the Emperor Sigismund of Germany spent several months in Siena. The friar's friendship, indeed, with this handsome, ambitious and pleasure-loving ruler – a Teutonic François I – and the influence which he exerted over him, are a further tribute to the strength of his personality, which at once charmed the Emperor, even though, on arriving in Siena, he was told that Fra Bernardino had been accusing him of heresy, or at least of an inclination to support the schismatic Bishops of the Council of Basle. This accusation, however, was not true, and as soon as the two men had met, the Emperor fell under Fra Bernardino's spell. "He went to visit him or to hear his sermon every day," says a biographer, "for he reckoned the day lost, on which he did not see him."[23]

The circumstances of the Emperor's long visit to Siena were very

143

curious. The preponderant part which he had played, twenty years before, in the Council of Constance to bring about the end of the Great Schism and the election of Martin V as the single true Pope, had rendered the Church greatly indebted to him, and now – perhaps seeing himself as a second Constantine – he had crossed the Alps to obtain the only reward he desired: the sanction of his election as Emperor by a formal coronation in St. Peter's. This, however, the Pope – suspicious both of the Emperor's friendship with Visconti and of his role as "Protector" of the Council of Basle – showed no inclination to grant. Visconti, on whose alliance Sigismund had counted, permitted him to crown himself in Milan with the Iron Crown of Lombardy, but offered no other support; the Florentines – jealous of his friendship with both Milan and Siena – would not let him cross the Arno, and so the Emperor found himself stranded in Siena, and, though he was received with all suitable honours by the priors and smiled upon by the beautiful Sienese ladies, he considerably outstayed his welcome. The Sienese sent off envoys, including their own Bishop, to the Pope to implore him to remove this expensive and inconvenient guest, but it would appear that the most effective arguments were set forth, more privately, by Fra Bernardino (on whose opinion Eugenius IV set great store) and were re-enforced by him when, after nine months' delay, a meeting at last took place in Viterbo, after which Sigismund bound himself, in a letter to the members of the Council of Basle, never to agree to any decision that might prove damaging to the Papacy. Then, and only then, did the Pope agree to a date for the coronation – Whitsunday 1433 – and when the great day approached, it was Fra Bernardino, riding on his little grey donkey beside the Emperor's great steed, who accompanied Sigismund to Rome. Then – having seen, as he believed, a ceremony which would help to consolidate the peace of Europe – he went back again to Siena.[24]

144

During the whole of Fra Bernardino's life he never ceased to promote the cause of peace, not only condemning, as we have seen, any form of political dissension, but also every other custom which led to brawling and bloodshed – in particular, the wide diffusion of the vice of sodomy, the official encouragement by the State of spies and talebearers, the universal passion for gambling, and the lax and unjust administration of justice.

In his time sodomy – against which he preached, in this course, one of his most effective sermons, as well as several in Florence – was considered to be more prevalent in Tuscany than in any other part of Italy. "There are some Italian cities," he said, "in which no Tuscan is allowed to live and in which no schoolmaster may be a Tuscan, for fear that he will corrupt the boys." "Were I a Sienese," he cried, "(as I am) and had I sons (which I have not) I would send them abroad as soon as they were three years old, and not let them return until they were at least forty. . . . Woe is me, what have you come to, city of Siena! What safety is there in you, if one cannot send a little boy out into the street, without his being seized by force and corrupted! . . . O women, do not let your boys go out; send rather your girls, for there is no danger at all for them, if you send them among such people."

One night, he related, he had been awakened by hearing a cry of "'Fire! fire! fire!' Lord God, what can this mean? And then I heard another cry, which I thought came from the shops: 'Fire! fire! fire!' Fear and terror came over me; I stood and hearkened, and I heard cries from all over the city, even from within the beds: 'Fire, fire, fire!' . . . and so I heard the whole city crying out. Woe is me, I know not whether you have understood me, but I vow unto you that God will punish you!"

In addition, he said, to being a sin against nature and against God, sodomy led to the destruction of all peace of mind, both in the family and the State. "It turns a wise and gentle man into one who is always uneasy.... When he comes home, he is troubled by the fear in his mind ... he is always filled with irritation and agitation, always afraid of being disgraced by an evil boy." All his gifts are wasted away, both in private and public life. "He may be a young man of rare talents and of great intelligence, fit to perform marvels, but once he has been corrupted by sodomy, he turns into the Devil's creature. He rejects all natural good things, all thoughts of God, of the State, of his family, his business, his honour, his very soul ... he thinks only about evil matters and is constantly complaining – about his father and his mother, his brothers and his brothers-in-law.... He lives in discontent, he talks angrily, he contradicts his father and his mother; and as to his wife, she knows not a single happy day.... Appoint him *podestà* (Mayor) and you will see in him a demon of ambition and of hardness of heart. Woe to the man who does not take off his cap or hood to him!"[25]

The sodomist, in Fra Bernardino's opinion, was not only unusually prone to jealousy and envy, but also to all forms of gossip and talebearing – a tendency which, at the time, also received encouragement from the State, since the Council of Siena appointed official spies and reporters to bring to their notice any infringements of the law, as well as any faint rumour of discontent or treachery, the reporter receiving in return a quarter of the consequent fine. Such a system was well calculated both to increase the general sense of uneasiness and to afford opportunities for the satisfaction of private spite, and Fra Bernardino considered it so pernicious that he devoted no less than four sermons in Siena and two in Florence to the evil effects of calumny. "Oh, the tip of the tongue! It is the worst part of a man!" Calumny, he said, sprang from three sources, malice, pride and cruelty; those who spread it had three-forked poisonous tongues, like snakes, and a stinging tail, like a scorpion,

146

and their mouths stank like the open mouth of a sewer. "So as soon as you hear one of them speaking ill of another, pinch your nose and cry, 'He stinks!'" The slanderer was worse than a thief, for what he stole, "more swiftly than a bird can fly," was a man's good name – even sometimes at the very moment in which he was performing a good deed, by hinting at an unworthy motive for it. "If a man fasts, [the slanderer] will say to another, 'Please God, he may be fasting for a *good* intention'... or else, as a man gives alms, 'May it please God, that they are not bestowed hypocritically!' ... And so gradually, like a dung-beetle, the slanderer puts together his little round ball of dung. 'O children, when you hear a man speak ill of another, call him a dung-beetle!'"[26]

Finally, some of Fra Bernardino's most eloquent diatribes were directed against what was then an almost universal vice, shared by men of all ages and every class: the passion for gambling. A boy, he said, would begin to play with dice when he was a mere child, with a few groats given him by his parents ("and there are even some bad fathers who teach their sons how to play ... so that they may not be cheated"), and when he reached old age, he was still at it, "old and toothless, with his spectacles on his nose and his dice in his hand, and still happy to lose eight or ten florins – though if he had to pay a single one of them for a tax or for the needs of the Commune, his cries would shake the world!"[27] Many addicts spent the whole of their lives in the gambling-booths erected in their city's main square (in Siena, they stood in the Piazza del Campo, in Florence, in the Mercato Vecchio), and the owners of these booths, the *barattieri* (often represented in art with the conical cap that was also worn by Jews and usurers), were not only licensed by the Commune, but sometimes also employed in minor unpleasant jobs such as street-cleaning, tax-collecting and the flogging of criminals, which could not be given to men of better standing.[28] In addition, there were professional swindlers, whom Fra Bernardino called *bari e berti*, who waited in taverns for unwary travellers, to entice them into a game. The *baro* wore a wide, hollow belt, in which he concealed false dice; the *berto* enticed the traveller into the game, while pretending that he did not know the *baro* – "and they do not cease until they have pleasantly removed all the money from his purse and hand."[29]

The games most in vogue – apart from cards and chess, which was mostly played at home, but also for money – were of two kinds, those played with a board and men as well as dice (like backgammon) and those with dice alone, of which the most popular was *zara* (from which the word *azzardo* = hazard, originated): a game played with three dice on a counter, with the *barattiere* shaking the dice and the players shouting their numbers and their bets, and calling out *zara*, when certain combinations occurred.[30] The noise apparently was deafening, since, in addition to the normal shouts of the players, the piazza also re-echoed with the curses and blows of the losers.

> *E vedesi chi perde con gran soffi*
> *Bestemmiar colla mano alla mascella*
> *E ricevere e dare molti ingoffi,*
> *Ed allor vi si fa colle coltella*
> *Ed uccide l'un l'altro, e tutta quanta*
> *Si turba allora quella piazza bella.*[31]

What Fra Bernardino deplored, indeed, was not so much the playing of games of chance in itself (nor even the sheer waste of time, though he called it "the dearest thing that God has lent us"), as the violence to which it often gave rise. The rage and despair of defeated gamblers seems often to have expressed itself, not only in curses – since they felt that God had abandoned them to the blind power of fate – but in actual deeds of violence. Sometimes the loser would take his adversary by the throat to choke the breath out of

XIX. The Gamblers: *Lippo Memmi.*

xx. The Bribe: *Privilegi delle Famiglie Bresciane*.

him, or lie in wait for him later that night with a dagger; sometimes he would attack the owner of the gambling-booth, or even
the man who had made the dice – like Sacchetti's Messer Giovanni
da Negroponte, who left the booth *"caldo caldo, con l'ira e l'impeto
del giuoco"* (Boiling, boiling with rage and with the zest of the
game) to kill the dice-maker with his knife. Sometimes the defeated
gambler's despair would express itself in suicide (perhaps even
causing his family to perish with him) or, in the hope of recovering
his losses, in the sale of his soul to the Devil. One such man, said
Fra Bernardino, was standing guard upon the ramparts one night,
when he felt a great claw clutching at his shoulder, and looking
round, saw the Devil in the form of a griffin, standing beside him to
claim his own. He cried upon God to help him and made the sign
of the Cross, and then, as the griffin disappeared, hurried to the
nearest church, where the priest dressed his stinking wound. But
within a few days he was dead, and presumably the griffin came to
fetch his soul – and, Fra Bernardino added, "the good and holy
priest, Jacopo of Modena, told me this tale a short time ago."[32]
　　Sometimes, too, the despairing gambler would even vent his rage
upon some holy image or upon God himself. The Sienese chronicler
Paolo di Montale told the story of a man who, having lost at *zara*,
flung a stone at a fresco of the Annunciation, "as if the Virgin Mary
had been the cause of his defeat," while in Bologna another angry
man threw one of the round pieces of wood with which he was
playing il *giuoco dei zoni* at an image of the Madonna, but then –
according to the story – was transfixed where he stood, motionless and gaping, until a prayer restored the use of his limbs to him
again.[33] And Fra Bernardino also repeated to his congregation the
familiar mediaeval legend about the gambler who, in his fury, shot
an arrow into the air against God himself, and the shaft returned
dripping with blood – but whereas in the original version the
blasphemer then repented and became a hermit, Fra Bernardino said

149

that the earth opened to swallow him up, and the Devil bore him off to Hell.

The preacher went on to compare, in a somewhat cumbrous simile, the Devil's institutions with those of the Church. The Devil himself, he said, was the gamblers' Pope and the gambling-booths his cathedrals, the taverns his churches, the playing-board his altars and the dice his missals; while in his Mass, the Introit was the players' shouts, the Kyrie their quarrels, the Gloria their blasphemies. Everyone who shared in this vice was condemned by Fra Bernardino to "the house of fire" – not only the gamblers themselves, but their wives and children, who shared the ill-gotten gains, the men who kept the gambling-booths, the craftsmen who made the boards, cards and dice, and even the shopkeepers who sold the bone the dice were made of, and "yes, even the men who stand looking on and call the score and watch the cheating and hear the lies and curses." But if a man wished to mend his ways, he had only to bring his boards, dice and cards to Fra Bernardino, "and I promise that, for the rest of my life, I will mention him in my Mass."[34]

That Fra Bernardino's sermons against gambling were singularly effective, is indisputable. In almost every city in which he attacked this vice – in Modena and Treviso, in Bologna, Florence and Siena – he succeeded in inducing his hearers to bring their boards, dice and cards to be consumed in the flames of "the Devil's castle," promising to give up their favourite occupation for ever. But whether indeed the temper of these cities was more peaceful afterwards, I should not like to say.

Fra Bernardino himself, indeed, plainly said that any temporary changes of heart, in such matters, that he might bring about, were of little value unless they were also supported by stable laws, justly and fairly applied. "Justice," he said, "can be understood in many and various ways, but among others, it is a constant and unswerving will... unfaltering, giving each man his due."[35] We now encounter a very different man from the gentle, compassionate little friar who tended the sick and played with little boys in the street. When he speaks of the crimes of violence and corruption he is as harsh and uncompromising as any of the Early Fathers: he believes not in forgiveness, but retribution. The statutes of Siena in his time were still based, like those of most other Italian cities, on a mixture of Roman law, Germanic law and "the law of custom" – and they were not mild. Witches and heretics were burned at the stake, the corpses of thieves and murderers were left hanging for days, as a warning, on the gallows at the city gates, poisoners and traitors were driven in an open cart to execution, while their flesh was torn from them, piece by piece, with red-hot pincers; harlots were flogged naked down the street. None of this aroused Fra Bernardino's squeamishness in the slightest degree. The murderer, the sodomist, the usurer, the witch – these were the corrupters and oppressors of mankind. "As refuse is taken out of the house so as not to infect it, so wicked men should be removed from human commerce by prison or by death."[36] Moreover (this was an argument used also by the Inquisition), it was for the criminal's own good to be made to realize how wicked his crimes were considered, for only thus would his heart become contrite, only thus would he die – after confession and absolution – "in the belief that God would pardon him and grant him eternal life." "One day," Fra Bernardino said in Siena, "I will preach to you about how justice should be understood – as retribution to the body and mercy to the soul." "Our Lord," he said elsewhere, "has two palaces and two law courts – one of justice and one of mercy," and "if His mercy is very great, His justice is no less." To those who asked him to pray for a captured criminal, that he might he spared the gallows, he replied that this was not mercy, but hypocrisy. "He has either been captured justly or un-justly. If justly, never say a word; if unjustly, then you are bound to help the truth. . . . One cannot pray that justice should perish, for neither the city, castle or province, nor even one's own house can flourish, unless one lives there justly. Justice is bread and wine."[37]

What aroused his indignation was not the brutality of some of the laws of his time, but the laxity and unfairness with which they were applied. "A governor," he said, "will issue a decree, ordering that no one may blaspheme or go about the town at night or gamble or bear arms or insult other men.... And sometimes then the police will find men [doing these things] and will take them to the *Signoria*, to pay a fine. And then one of them will appear before the governor, 'Sir, I pray you to pardon me,' or 'You have captured such a man for going about at night, I pray you for my sake to set him free.' 'Well,' says the governor, 'did he not hear the decree? Did he not know our customs?' And the other replies, 'Oh, it is the custom to issue such a decree, and it is also the custom to grant such favours.' And he (the governor) cannot deny it, and sets the man free."[38] Few crimes were so grave that a rich man could not escape punishment by means of a large bribe or fine, while a poor one might lose his hand or languish in prison for years, for stealing a faggot of wood. The only remedy, to Fra Bernardino's mind, lay in an unswerving application of stricter laws, and when, in 1425, both Siena and Perugia asked him to help them to reform their statutes – the new ones, which were called the *Riformagioni di Fra Bernardino*, were even more severe than those which had preceded them. The sodomist was heavily fined and banished or, if he persisted in his offence, sent to the stake. The blasphemer lost his tongue or, if he had injured a holy image, his right hand. Usurers were excluded from public office and any loan on interest was punished, in the case of a Christian, by the confiscation of both capital and interest, and in that of a Jew, by the amputation of his right foot. Heavy fines were decreed against gamblers or breakers of the new sumptuary laws, as well as against men who visited convents without permission (a frequent occasion for sin), or who took part in the dancing in churches which often ended in pagan bacchanals. It was forbidden to hold the *litomachie* or sham battles which took place in Perugia on some feast-days, during which the upper and lower city fought against each other "for the sole desire of glory," but in which fifteen or twenty men would often be killed or wounded in a single day.[39] And finally, in the belief that many of the gravest evils sprang from idleness and from the general conviction that "only those men are gentlemen who sit all day polishing a bench or stroll about with a hawk on their wrist," all citizens under fifty, irrespective of their rank, were compelled to exercise some trade, profession or art, and those who refused to work were excluded from public office.[40]

That the *Riformagioni di Fra Bernardino* were considered too severe, even by the men who had asked him to draw them up, is shown by the fact that they were mitigated almost immediately in Perugia by the city's Governor, the Cardinal of Crete, and were revoked in Siena two years later – providing Fra Bernardino with a theme for a sermon: "On those who begin to behave well, and then draw back."[41]

But the truth was, that it was not only difficult to convince the populations of these cities of the need for such reforms, but also to find rulers upright and courageous enough to rise to Fra Bernardino's standards.

The officials of a city, to his mind, were responsible not only for the actions, but for the characters, of those set under them. "As waters flow or are directed according to the way they are guided, so men take on the shape given to them by those who guide or rule them." There were, he said, some rare rulers who were natural lovers of justice, men who "walk straight on the path of righteousness with a good conscience and a pure mind – and for these no laws or statutes are needful, for God has laid his mark upon their minds, so that they no longer know how to do what is not right."[42]

But where could such men be found? How many were the officials entirely free from the corrupting sins of power – tyranny, credulousness, simony, pride, negligence, ignorance, arrogance and indifference? Many of the *Signori* spent all their days with their hawks and hounds and their nights in the taverns, paying no heed to their duties, except in so far as they could extract some profit from them. "They devour and grind [the poor], those bad rulers," said Fra Bernardino, "with teeth of iron" – and he proceeded to describe a few of the things that he himself had seen. Some governors, he said, on coming into office, were supplied with many servants, pages and horses, but "after a few days, out of avarice, had only kept half of them, while retaining the full salary for themselves." There was one of them who even stole his peasants' spades and hoes when his period of rule was over, and another, "who burned more than four thousand loads of wood in six months, to sell the charcoal in Florence."[43] And there were hardly any who would not take bribes. "It is said that a bad ruler steals for himself, and his notary also steals on his behalf, and between them they eat up their subjects. . . . The Venetians, to their honour, do not behave like this, and have a very different reputation. If an official in their territory accepted a single gift, he would be so discredited that he would never be able to hold office again." And worst of all, there were hardly any rulers strong or firm enough to punish criminals. "You call your land," he said to the Florentines, "a land of liberty! If you mean that it is free never to punish a criminal, you are right, but I would rather call it a free tyranny."

In the hope of shaming these weak and powerless officials, he told them a parable: the story of a monkey and a bear at the court of the King of France. The bear, he said, being the stronger of the two, stole one of the baby monkeys from its mother and ate it. Then the poor monkey wandered all over the house, running from one person to another and looking up into their faces, "as if asking for justice." But no one paid any heed. So one day the monkey went to the place where the bear slept, in the hay-loft. "And she took the hay and piled it around the bear and finally set fire to it and burned him alive. And thus she carried out justice herself!"[44]

Of all the Italian governments, the one he most approved of was that of Venice, which was then in the hands of a strong oligarchy. "It is the firmest men who rule over her, and therefore does God grant her such great prosperity. All pull together for the common good." It was to his memories, too, of the Venetian lagoon, that he turned for an illustration of his meaning. "If you have been there," he said to his congregation, "you will know that there are many vessels in its waters . . . galleys and galleons, cargo-ships and boats and gondolas and little skiffs. . . . And some of them go here and some there, and some men have one occupation and some another: one man is rowing, another mending the ropes, another sailing, and they are never idle. . . . All these ships, galleys, cargo-boats and gondolas, when they are united, can never know defeat. But if they are divided, none of them is so strong as not to be defeated."[45]

Thus Fra Bernardino's sermons on good government came back in the end to their starting-point: an appeal for unity and peace. All his admonishments, all his harsh laws, aimed at the fulfilment of this dream. "So needful a thing it is, this peace. And even its name – peace, *pace* – so sweet it is, that it leaves a sweetness on the lips. Try saying the opposite – war, *guerra!* It is so harsh a thing, so rough, that it sours the mouth." One can almost hear the preacher lingering over the words – savouring the broad vowel of *pace*, accentuating the harsh initial consonant and the double *r* of *guerra* – and see the crowd, agape, nodding in agreement. "*Dice bene, dice bene.*" And then, turning to the Palazzo Pubblico behind him, he reminded his hearers that there, in the Sala della Pace, one of their own painters had depicted the effects of a wise and strong government, which bent all its efforts towards peace, and those of a weak one, which abandoned its city to lawlessness and strife. "To see Peace depicted is a delight and so it is a shame to see War painted on the other wall.... Turning towards Peace I see merchandise journeying and houses being built, and dancing; I see ploughing in the fields and vineyards and sowing, and men on horseback riding to the baths, and girls to a wedding, and flocks of sheep. And I see a man being hanged, to protect the law – and because of all this, all men are living in holy peace and unity.... But turning to the other side [where war was depicted] I see no merchandise, no dancers, but only men killing each other; no fields are ploughed, no vines pruned, no seed is sown.... I see a murdered man and a raped woman; I see no herds, except for some that are being stolen; men are traitorously murdering each other, and Justice has fallen to the ground with her scales broken, and her hands and feet are bound. And all she does, is done in fear and trembling."[46]

This course of sermons was drawing to an end, and soon Fra Bernardino would be leaving Siena again, and bidding farewell to his fellow-citizens. But before leaving, he asked one last thing of them. "O my brothers and fathers, love and embrace each other, and if any wrong was done to you in the past, for the love of God forgive those injuries and keep no more hatred in your hearts.... And you too, women, I beseech you for God's love to assist me; give your aid to this toil which I have undertaken so gladly, to bring about love and peace among you." Let them at once hasten to a church, he asked, even if only for a moment, while his words were still fresh in their memories. "O women, when you leave this sermon, go to San Martino, and let your entering that church be a sign to all men that you wish to make peace and to offer up your reconciliation within the church – and then, when you meet the people whom you have hated again, you will make peace with each other.... And to you, men, I say the same: go and offer peace to the Virgin Mary in the Bishop's Palace – so that she may keep you in peace and preserve you from the perils which lurk about you, while you still have hatred in your hearts."[47]

So Fra Bernardino preached to his *Senesi*, but though they obeyed him in most matters, to live in peace with each other and with their neighbours was beyond them – as it still is. He had no illusion about this, and it never ceased to grieve him. There is a legend that, several days after his death in Aquila, when his body was still lying unburied in the church of San Francesco, an insurrection broke out in the city, in consequence of which several innocent persons were about to be beheaded. Then suddenly a voice was heard, bidding everyone to cease fighting, and to hasten to the church of San Francesco, where they would find blood enough; and when they got there, they found blood flowing from the corpse's nostrils, and fell on their knees, praying for forgiveness. Thus the first recorded miracle of Fra Bernardino after his death was a final plea for "Peace, that most needful of all things." "I would give a pound of my blood," he had said, "to bring about peace."[48]

VII. THE PRETERNATURAL
AND SUPERNATURAL WORLDS

Lume v'è dato a bene ed a malizia,
E libero voler...

DANTE*

"LO," said Fra Bernardino suddenly, interrupting himself in the midst of one of his sermons, "the Campo is full of angels!"[1] He was not speaking in terms of metaphor, but as a man stating a plain fact. And indeed it is not possible to read either his works or those of the historians of his time, without becoming aware of how very thin the veil then seemed between this world and the supernatural one. This was not only true of the uneducated. To read the Chronicles of Philippe de Commines or of Giovanni Villani is to realize how large a part, in the interpretation of any unusual occurrence, was attributed to supernatural intervention, and sometimes to the direct action of the Evil One. Villani, for instance, records as a historical fact that, on the night before the great flood of the whole Arno valley in 1333, "a holy hermit praying in his solitary cell above Vallombrosa, heard a sound of demons, as if a company of armed knights were riding by furiously." He asked them where they were going, and received the reply: "We go to drown the city of Florence, on account of her sins."[2]

A belief in such stories naturally implied a view of the whole course of history as part of God's plan for mankind – a vision not necessarily incompatible with a full awareness, on another plane, of what is caused by the vagaries of human character, and the vices and virtues of individuals. This view of history, far from being exclusively mediaeval, was accepted by most of the historians of the Renaissance. In 1499 the Neapolitan humanist Giovanni Pontano, as he laid down the principles by which a historian should be guided, declared that in writing about war (which he assumed to be the

159

main subject of history) he should report not only events naturally affected by chance (such as weather, pestilence, treachery and the spreading of false rumours), but also those entirely outside the normal course of nature, such as oracles, prophecies and visions.[3] The great Florentine historian, Francesco Guicciardini, was of a similar opinion; he repeatedly affirmed that the intellect alone cannot enable a man to understand the processes of history; behind his conscious actions, there are forces beyond his ken: there is always room for a miracle. It is for this reason that so much importance was given, both by him and by other historians of his time, to signs and portents. In Guicciardini's *Storia d'Italia*, for instance, there is a long account of the terrifying portents that preceded the French invasion of Florence in 1494 – "things beyond the course of nature and the heavens." "In Apulia by night three suns were seen in the skies, but clouded in their centre and accompanied by horrible thunder and lightning. In Arezzo for many days there passed through the air great numbers of armed men riding on huge horses, with a terrible sound of trumpets and drums. In many places in Italy the images and sacred statues were seen to break into a sweat. Many monsters were born among men and animals."[4]

It was hardly strange that, in a world so full of wonders, men also accepted without question, and often believed that they saw with their own eyes, the angels and devils which their poets and preachers had described so vividly and of which the appearance had also become so familiar to them in art. In the Augustinian convent of Lecceto, for instance, near Siena – the community which Bernardino had considered joining before he had the vision which called him to the Franciscan Order – the loggia before the church was entirely frescoed with pictures of activities inspired and fostered by the Evil One. In one scene, a gambler was clutching his victorious rival by the throat, while a demon with raised talons stood at his back ready to seize the dying victim's soul: in another, a chariot

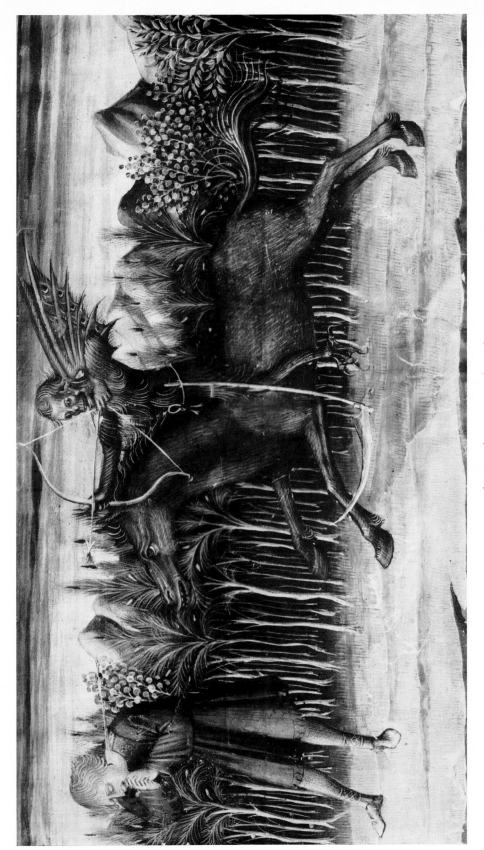

XXI. The Devil: *Giovanni di Paolo.*

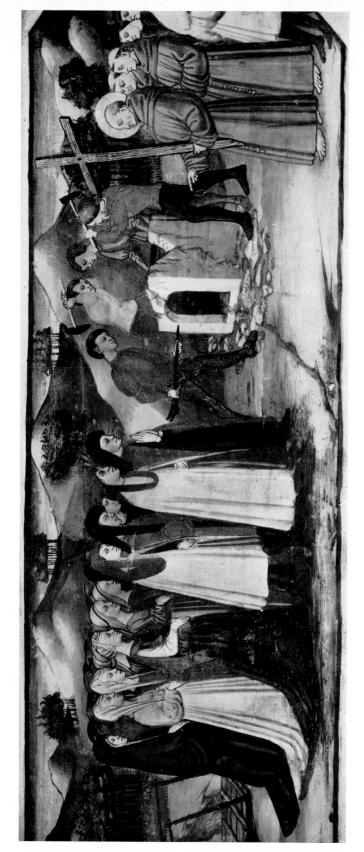

xxii. The Destruction of Fonte Tecta: *Neri di Bicci*.

of merry-makers was drawn by two white horses on which two devils sat; a devil stood at a money-lender's elbow and another lurked behind a tree, watching the huntsmen in the forest, while yet others flew above all those who were waging war, whether by land or sea.

More terrifying still were the various representations – such as those by Traini in the Camposanto of Pisa or by Orcagna in Santa Croce in Florence – of *The Triumph of Death*. In these, while Death with her great scythe hovered over mankind, grotesque and monstrous demons with horns and hoofs, or with bats' wings and the faces of grimacing apes, swooped down over the dying, to bear off their souls to the flames of Hell.

Yet in these pictures, at least, unlike those at Lecceto, the vision was not wholly dark: there were also angels in the sky, bearing with them the souls of the just, and sometimes actually snatching one from a devil's clutches. And in the frescoes on the walls of the Sienese Palazzo Pubblico, in front of which Fra Bernardino was preaching, it was angels who, in this world too, were deputed as the symbols of "distributive and commutative justice," and who took on the shapes of Faith, Hope and Charity.

Fra Bernardino had a very special affection for the angelic host and devoted two of his Latin sermons to them, as well as his forty-third Italian sermon in Siena.[5] They were "the glorious company of Heaven," forever living in God's love. "All the angels worship God in love, through love they desire and carry out his will, in love they possess his immense goodness." But they were also God's deputies on earth, entrusted with the guardianship of men's souls. "He shall send his angels unto you," he quoted, "that they may guard you in all your ways." "The angels," he told his congregation in Siena, "have dominion over the soul; they inspire, encourage and illuminate us in all that we ought to do. It is they who have brought you to this Campo, and who make you take heed to the words which I

161

am saying to God's glory." Looking round the square, he asked his congregation to consider their own great good fortune. "Here we are in such great comfort and prosperity, without suspicion and without fear, standing in this square in so orderly a fashion, with our souls at peace, and all listening with good will to God's word. . . . This is half a Paradise, a glorious ark to which – with the consent of our own free will – our angels have led us." The number of these angelic visitors, he said, was infinite. "How many do you think there are here at this moment? You will reply 'As many as there are persons present,' and you will be right, for each one has his guardian angel. But beside these, there are many million others."[6] It is they, he declared, who show us "a ray of light, so that we may distinguish right from wrong," and in return men owe them (in St. Bernard's well-known phrase) "reverence in their presence, devotion for their kindness and trust in their protection." It is for the angels' sake that women must be veiled in church, lest – by showing that even in God's house they wish to display their vanity – they make their angels weep.

Fra Bernardino's description of the battle in Heaven between the good and evil angels was entirely orthodox, but coloured by Dantesque phraseology and by the images of the other Sienese preachers of his time. His devils were Dante's *angeli neri, neri cherubini* (black angels, black cherubim), whose greatest torment was, in the words of Fra Filippo Agazzari, "to look at each other and see each other's darkness," but who were also extremely busy in the world of men.

It was he, the Devil, "*Cappelluccio maledetto*," who interrupted Bernardino's sermon by causing a heavy downpour, and who slept with a woman for a whole year, before she realized, by seeing the scales under his belly, who he really was.[7] And it was he, too, who (according to a well-known story which Fra Bernardino repeated) during the war between Florence and Gian Galeazzo Visconti, car-

162

ried off a gambler and blasphemer from his gambling-table and bore him off through the air – his boots, hose and other garments dropping off him one by one, as he was borne away to Hell.[8]

In a sermon, too, on "the nobility of the soul," Fra Bernardino related a dialogue between God and the Devil, in which God offered the Evil One, in return for a promise to leave mankind in peace, silver and gold, air and water, the earth and the constellations, and the Devil replied, in the words of Genesis, "Give me the soul and keep all else." Whereupon, of course, God refused: "I want the soul for myself!" So the Devil continued to roam the earth, sowing evil on his path in small things and great.[9]

So often, indeed, was the Devil in and out of Bernardino's sermons, that a girl who was reproved by her mother for pronouncing the name of the Evil One, replied, "Why may I not do at home what Bernardino is always doing in the pulpit?"[10]

In the popular traditions of Siena the Devil was not only depicted as the tusked and horned, winged or muzzled monster of the eighth Canto of the *Inferno*, or as the foul and grotesque creature of the Lecceto frescoes, but also – more dangerously and subtly – as "a dark knight or an Ethiopian."[11] In Lorenzetti's fresco in the Palazzo Pubblico it was he, in human form, who personified "Bad Government" and Fra Bernardino, too, often gave him a human aspect – and moreover sometimes an attractive one. "*Il diavolo è gentilissimo.*"[12] He even appears, in one tale, as a harmless hobgoblin – "*uno spirito folletto*" – who, having fallen in love with a human girl named Margherita, was continually touching her hand and cheek and even placing himself in her bed (though always invisible). Her father at last turned to Fra Bernardino, and was told to sprinkle the house and bed with holy water – "and some days later he came and told me that he had done this, and had delivered himself of the inconvenience."[13]

The Evil One, Fra Bernardino said, is flexible both in his essence and his mind – able to pass through a stone or wall as easily as through an open window and also to enter a man's body, and always swift to perceive his victim's weakest spot, in order to tempt him just there. He is malignant, he is swift as the mind itself ("consider that your mind can reach Paris or Florence in a single instant, and so can the Devil"), and he is also extremely expert and persistent. If one method fails, in leading a man into temptation, he will try another and yet another, until at last he succeeds. And he is especially gifted in bewildering men, "so that they can no longer distinguish good from evil." It was thus, Fra Bernardino said, that human beings became subject to the powers of darkness; and indeed, as one reads his sermons, one cannot fail to become aware of the pervasiveness of a shadowy borderland of superstitious practices and fears, on the fringe of the life of even the most practising Christians. "If a man has five *soldi* stolen from him, he goes to a sorcerer or a magician. Do you know what he is doing? He is offending God and adoring the Devil."[14]

Did a child seem ailing? Its mother's first thought was that it must have been bewitched, and she would at once hasten to procure for it, from a witch or sorcerer, one of the charms called *brevi*, written out on parchment scrolls ("*carta d'anticristo*," was Fra Bernardino's name for them) and sometimes even inscribed with the name of Jesus, or else with "words which cannot be understood." These were worn round the neck, "on a hair from a virgin's head," and sometimes they were also tied to the big toe of a woman in labour, to draw the child down more easily. ("But it is the Devil dragging you down to the accursed house.") Very popular, too, was "the prayer of St. Cyprian," which was also worn on one's person and which protected the wearer from any sorcerer's spell – "by iron, pewter or lead, by wool or linen, by dice or bones, by earth, water or fire, in tombs or bridges, trees or caves, roads or doorways."[15] Yet other spells shielded the wearer from sudden death "by steel or fire, in water or in earth." ("You will die in the air instead," Fra Bernardino sardonically commented, "hanged by your neck!")

Fra Bernardino's sermons frequently refer not only to love potions, death potions and evil charms, but also to minor superstitious practices which were plainly in such common use as to require no explanation – for instance, "placing juniper at one's door for the witches' sake," "using a hog's bristle for a charm," "eating elder-leaves in order to have a child," "placing a naked sword on a bed," "opening one's purse when one sees the new moon," and ("I say this for the goldsmiths") "making a ring for Good Friday." (This was a ring which a person put on his finger while the Gospel of the Passion was being read.) As for love philtres, the saint declared that "something very different is needed [to obtain true love] from spells and paint or dead men's hair or cork or cotton-wool." "And you who have had such a charm made, so that your daughter's husband may love her, do you know what God will do to you as a judgment? He will see to it that the love does not last."[16]

Avoidance, too, of the *giorni egiziachi* – the unpropitious days – was obviously widely practised, and must have been extremely inconvenient. On these (and there were at least two of them in every month) it was inauspicious to do any work, to begin a journey, or to do any buying or selling, "and a child born on one of these [days] will not live, or if he lives, will always be poor. And if he takes a wife, he will lose her soon or she will be unfaithful to him, and never will they have peace together."[17]

It was, of course, the pagan element in these practices which disturbed Fra Bernardino so much, and which he also deprecated in the primitive popular customs which had gradually become incorporated in some of the feasts of the Church. "The very feast-days," he said, "on which our spirit should turn to God are obscured by pagan ceremonies."[18] One of the most popular of these, in Tuscany,

165

was the ceremony of the Yuletide log or *ceppo*, which was placed on the hearth on Christmas Eve by the head of the family and decorated with gifts and coins. "Give it to drink! Give it to eat!" The *ceppo* was then anointed with oil and blessed, and sometimes some other smaller logs, representing the children of the family, were placed beside it in the fire. Sparks were drawn by striking the logs with a flint or other metal and omens were drawn from them, while the number of the sparks that had been drawn was supposed to show the number of years that the head of the household would still remain alive. All this was probably a survival of fire-worship at the winter solstice, when the fire's aid was called upon, on the shortest day of the year, to promote the growth of the new sun."[19]

Another superstition which was presumably also connected in its origin with fire-worship, was that it would bring ill luck to light a fire on New Year's Day, or "to lend fire" to a neighbour on the first day of the week, while other traditions connected with the feasts of the Church included a belief that bread "stored away on New Year's Day" would bring fertility and prosperity, and that good luck was brought "by putting a piece of iron in one's mouth" on Holy Saturday, by opening one's purse on seeing the new moon, by picking ferns on St. John's Day, or by eating fresh eggs on Ascension Day. (This last action was supposed to preserve the eater from fire.) And on St. Bartholomew's Eve those who suffered from epilepsy used to "dance and sing all night, drinking and feasting, in the belief that thus they will be preserved from another attack for a whole year."[20]

The real evil inherent in these practices, as Fra Bernardino pointed out, was that by employing them you placed yourself, "through your own bestial imagination," in the Devil's power. "If you believe the cackle of a hen or the caw of a crow or an encounter with a weasel or snake or wolf or hare or partridge, to be a good or an evil omen, or if you observe the unlucky days . . . you are adoring the

Devil." Besides, you were likely to bring upon yourself the very evils that you most dreaded. "All the diabolic fancies that you have put into your head, whether in evil dreams or forecastings, the Devil will indeed send to you, and with God's permission."

Moreover, a belief that good or evil charms were efficacious was not only an error, but a deliberate denial of both the natural and the supernatural remedies bestowed by God. "God has given us two ways of recovering from infirmities: the first is the natural one, by means of doctors and medicines, and the second, through the grace of the name of Jesus." We must note that the preacher did not for a moment deny that a sick person might be bewitched; he was merely told to turn to God, and not to the Devil, for healing. "If an evil spell is laid upon you or any of your children are bewitched, see to it that you be not in a state of mortal sin – and then you can mock at any spell, any evil, any sorcery. For if you are not in mortal sin, then you are in God's grace and need have no fear, for the shadows cannot live in the light."[21]

With these remarks, Fra Bernardino was admitting the value of *certain* types of incantations – those which made use of the name of Jesus or of symbols of the Faith. "In the name of Jesus you will heal the sick and the poisoned, and avert storms or pestilence." And indeed such incantations were often used not only by friars, but by eminent doctors of the time. As early as the eleventh century Avicenna – the great Arab doctor and philosopher whose influence on the thought of the later Middle Ages and Early Renaissance can hardly be overestimated – had expressed his conviction that it was possible to effect physical cures by influencing the patient's state of mind through magic formulas or rites – "natural events brought to pass through spiritual means" – thus becoming one of the earliest practitioners of psycho-somatic medicine.[22] And as late as the days of Savonarola we still find such methods being used by one of his companions, Fra Domenico da Pescia, who healed a crippled knee of

Roberto Salviati's, after first praying with the patient, by "making the Sign of the Cross upon the naked flesh, and saying 'Let it be according to my faith'" – whereupon the knee was instantly healed.

Avicenna's opinion with regard to such matters was not that the ordinary practices of medicine should be disregarded, but that the physician must not close any door in his mind to mysterious powers of which he might not yet fully understand the nature. "Beware of taking pride in a critical spirit.... It is no less superficial to deny what is not yet evident, than to affirm what is not yet adequately proved.... Remember that nature is full of marvels, and that active forces may unite with a passive disposition of mind to produce extraordinary effects."[23]

In these opinions, Avicenna was a forerunner of the Renaissance scholar, who differed from the mediaeval one not in his practice of the magic arts (in which indeed he had learned almost all he knew from his mediaeval predecessors), but in his attitude. In the Middle Ages the magician was a man who was disturbing the appointed order of nature, which followed the will of God; his arts were considered to belong to the daemonic world, "the powers of darkness," outside the rational order, and it was as such that Fra Bernardino still condemned them. But to the humanist, the magician was a man who was attempting to overcome the barriers which until then had limited man's knowledge, and to become better acquainted with the infinite variety of the universe. The astrologer who could predict the future from the course of the stars, the alchemist who could cause the elements to do his bidding, were unifying thought and raising man to the power which the Lord himself, according to Genesis, had awarded to him. "He has given him dominion over *all* his creatures."

Of all the magic arts, the one which carried with it the greatest prestige was that of astrology. Avicenna, indeed, attached no value to it and in the full flowering of the Renaissance Pico della Mirandola attacked it in his treatise *Contra astrologos* (in which, however, he showed a considerable belief in other forms of magic). But the extent of the influence of its practitioners throughout the Middle Ages and the Renaissance on both the simple and the learned can hardly be overestimated. There were chairs of astrology in the universities of Siena, Padua and Bologna and few of the courts of the Renaissance princes lacked their private astrologer (in Florence it was the pious and learned Marsilio Ficino) – while the Church maintained an uncertain position, declaring that though the stars might indicate the destiny of a man, they could not determine it, and only condemning to the stake such astrologers, like Cecco d'Ascoli, whose views also appeared suspect of heresy. As to Fra Bernardino, he did not consider astrology *wrong*, but merely extremely liable to error. "The practice of the astrological science," he said, "is permitted by Holy Church, but if they [the astrologers] make an error in the smallest point, they achieve nothing."

He added that while astrologers could foresee *general* events from the course of the stars – such as war, pestilence or famine – they could not predict particular ones, such as the death or life of an individual, and he entertained his congregation with the story – very mediaeval in its robust humour – of a great seigneur who, having been told by an astrologer that he would die within the year, had immediately taken to his bed and developed a high fever, weeping and wailing and finding no rest. But one of his barons, "who had a broader mind," went to the astrologer and asked him how he knew what he had foretold, and when the other replied that he had seen it in the stars, asked him whether he also knew when his own death would take place? The astrologer replied, that he would live for another twenty years. "Then the baron took out his knife and said, 'I will seek proof of this,' and gave him so many stabs that he killed him" – and, returning to his seigneur, pointed out that, as one prediction had been shown to be false, so might the other. "The seigneur began to laugh with great gusto, and got up and lived for many more years."[24]

Of all the magic-makers, the most industrious and popular were the witches, since it seemed natural that the daughters of Eve, the temptress, should continue to be the link between the Evil One and superstitious men. The witch provided the ignorant and the frightened with what they most needed: hope. She promised health to the sick, love to the deserted mistress, marriage to the husbandless, children to the barren, vengeance to the injured: she provided waxen images and she practised abortions. Her magical potions were brewed at night, often in the presence of virgin children, and appear to have contained, besides herbs, marmot fat and beavers' skins, many other loathsome ingredients such as human hair, bones and teeth, and dead men's eyes and skin – all cooked in boiling oil stolen from church-lamps. One charm for summoning a reluctant lover was to make a heart of glowing ashes, and pierce it, while singing:

> *Prima che 'l fuoco spenghi*
> *Fa ch'a mia porta venghi;*
> *Tal ti punga mio amore*
> *Quale io fo questo cuore.*[25]

Even so sceptical and level-headed a Pontiff as Pius II, when asked by a Saxon scholar whether it was true that in Italy there was a Mount of Venus where witches and magicians taught the magic arts, replied that though he himself had not actually been there, he had heard of it. "In Umbria, near the town of Nursia [Norcia] there is a cave beneath a steep rock, in which water flows. There there are witches, demons and nightly shades, and he that is brave enough can see and speak to the spirits, and learn the magic arts."[26]

About witches, too, Fra Bernardino had a great deal to say. One of his stories is slightly reminiscent of the tale of Kilmeny. A Cardinal's servant, he said, while riding to Benevento by night, saw many young people dancing upon a threshing-floor, and after a while, although much afraid, was persuaded to dance with them. But as the morning Angelus rang out, they suddenly vanished – except for one girl, whom he held by the hand. "And she pulled and he pulled – and so he held her until it was broad daylight and then, when he saw how young she was, he took her home with him . . . and he kept her there for three years, and she never spoke a word. And it was discovered that she came from Slavonia. Do you think it was right that a young girl should have been taken away like that from her father and mother?"[27]

Yet another of the preacher's stories – plainly told in order to show that witches worked at the Devil's behest – was that of a man in Lucca who, having lost sixteen florins, had hastened to consult "a friend who was a witch" about his loss. She told him to come back the next day, but he, being curious, decided to hide instead in a wood close by, to see what she would do – and sure enough, when nightfall came, "she went naked to the wood and called the Devil." The Evil One agreed to tell her where the money was, "but only on condition that some scandal should come of it," and then informed her that the lost coins had really been eaten by a pig, but she must instead tell their owner "that his wife has stolen them, to give them to the priest, whom she loves." . . . The man went home, killed the pig and found the coins in its belly, and on the following morning went back to the witch, who repeated to him what the Devil had told her to say. "'You lie in your throat!' he cried, 'for I heard last night what you promised the Devil, and I have found my money and you deserve to be burned.' And the story spread through Lucca, and had she not escaped to the territory of Pisa, she certainly would have been burned."[28]

The episode, however, which most clearly shows the extent of Fra Bernardino's abhorrence of witchcraft, is that of the trial and death at the stake, in 1427, of two witches in Rome. On his return to Siena, he described the trial very fully, making no secret of his pleasure at having been partly instrumental in bringing about their sentence, and even expressing a wish that "a little incense of the same kind could also be offered up in Siena." (We must remember his conviction that one of the witches, named Finicella, had confessed, "without torture," to murdering thirty children by sucking their blood.) The trial of this wretched, half-crazed woman, which is also described by the chronicler Stefano Infessura, took place during Fra Bernardino's first visit to Rome in 1424. The course of sermons which he then held, denouncing the evils of party strife, gambling and sorcery, had been so successful that many "reconciliations" had taken place between mortal enemies, a great bonfire had been kindled on the Capitol "of gambling-tables, charms, spells, and women's hair," and finally, at the end of the course, two witches had been denounced to the Inquisition.

The story of their trial is so characteristic of the time and gives so vivid a picture of the confusion of mind of everyone concerned as to be worth relating. According to Fra Bernardino, Finicella confessed that, in addition to the children she had murdered, she had "delivered" sixty more – an expression which he interpreted as meaning that she had freed them from sickness "by foolish and utterly false incantations," in which she believed herself "to be invoking the Lord's name, while really invoking the Devil's." Finicella added that "every time that she delivered one of them [the children], she was obliged to offer up a limb to the Devil in sacrifice, and she gave him the limb of a beast . . . and moreover she confessed that she had killed her own son and had made powder out of him, which she gave people to eat. . . . And since it seemed incredible that a creature should do so many evil deeds, proof was sought. . . . She was asked whom she had killed . . . and men were sent to obtain the parents' evidence. And they asked, 'Did you ever have a little son, who wasted away at such and such a time, and died?' And the father answered, 'Yes.'" She also said that she used to go before dawn to the hill above Piazza San Pietro and she had some jars full of ointments made from herbs that she had gathered there, on the days of St. John and the Ascension. Fra Bernardino added that he held these ointments to his nose, and "they stank so much that they seemed to be things of the Devil, as they were." And his account continued: "The witches said that they anointed themselves with these ointments, and when they were anointed, they thought they had turned into cats. But it was not true, for their bodies did not change and take another shape, though they thought they did." The preacher made it clear that he did not himself believe that the women had taken on this shape, but that their imagination had been acted upon by the Devil, so that they themselves believed that they had been turned into cats and had then sucked the dead children's blood – while in reality it was the Evil One who had done so. "And there are people who have seen it, when he does such things, and sometimes, having something in their hands, they have thrown it at the cat" – but if they succeeded in hitting the animal, it was the witch's body that was bruised. "And in the end the witch was condemned to the flames and was burned, so that nothing remained of her but ashes." "And the whole of Rome," wrote the chronicler Stefano Infessura, "went to see the sight."

Fra Bernardino went on to say that another witch who was tried at the same time, also confessed, and that she, too, was condemned to the stake, "but in another fashion, for when she was put in the *capannuccia* (a straw hut soaked in oil) she was not strangled, but burned while she was still alive.... And as it was done to her, so should it be done wherever one of them is to be found. And therefore I admonish you, wherever one of them may be, or if any man knows where she is to be found . . . let him denounce her to the Inquisition. Whether she be in the city or the territory, denounce her: every witch and wizard, every sorcerer and sorceress or caster of spells. Do this, so that you be not called to account on the Day of Judgement."[29]

This trial is of especial interest because, though it took place nearly sixty years before the Bull by which, in 1480, Pope Innocent VIII sent two Dominican friars, Heinrich Kramer and James Sprenger, to act as the official Inquisitors of witchcraft in Northern Germany, it clearly foreshadows, even in its details, the pattern subsequently taken all over Europe by these relentless persecutions. Kramer and Sprenger's manual, the *Malleus Maleficarum* (which became the undisputed authority referred to by all subsequent inquisitors and magistrates) contains several passages describing cases extremely similar to Finicella's, and interprets them very much as San Bernardino did. The *Malleus* told, for instance, the story of a workman in Strasbourg who, as he was chopping some firewood, was suddenly attacked by three large cats and defended himself by belabouring them with a stick – and was subsequently cast into prison for having beaten "three respected matrons of the town, so that they lie in their beds unable to rise or move." The poor man at last succeeded in proving his innocence to the magistrate, who, "understanding that it was the Devil's work, released him, telling him not to speak of the matter to anyone." The author's conclusion was that this was possible "because of a former pact made between the women and the Devil, which enabled him to turn them into cats."

The essence, in short, of these practices was supposed to consist in the witch's or sorcerer's previous pact with the Devil. "For the Devil receives blows in the form of an animal and transfers them to someone who is bound to him by a pact, when it is with such a one's consent that he acts in this manner and in such a shape. Therefore he can in this way hurt only the guilty who are bound to him by a pact, and never the innocent."[30]

This book, as we have said, was written more than half a century after Finicella's death, but the spiritual climate revealed is remarkably similar. Witchcraft, paganism, heresy – all these were the devious paths by which the Devil made his way into the hearts of men. For the past two hundred years the Inquisition had been combating, in Tuscany and Umbria, the form of Catharism which had taken root there and which, in its later depraved form, sometimes lent itself to the popular belief that heresy and sorcery were closely allied. The Cathars – who in Milan and in Central Italy called themselves *Patarini* – believed in a dualistic universe, containing both a heavenly world created by a God of Good and peopled by spiritual beings created by him (of whom Jesus Christ was one), and an earthly one, created by a God of Evil – Satan or Lucifer, the Prince of this world. Many *Patarini*, moreover, in addition to denying (as a consequence of their conviction that everything made of matter was evil) such fundamental Christian dogmas as the Incarnation and the validity of the Sacraments, believed in a modified form of metempsychosis. It is not difficult to see how the grosser forms of such doctrines, especially with regard to the dualistic nature of the world, could be twisted by the accusers of this sect into devil-worship, and their secret rites into something very like the Black Mass. Fra Bernardino may well have heard in his youth (for these were stories that passed from mouth to mouth) of the lonely castle in the Sienese territory, Rugomagno, in which, according to a letter sent by an Inquisitor to the *Concistoro* of Siena in 1385, witchcraft had been practised for years with the help of a book in which Satan and Beelzebub were invoked. "In [the castle] idols are worshipped and all the princes of darkness are summoned . . . so that by means of certain invocations of demons a man may gradually be caused to die . . . or to follow any woman." The Inquisitor's letter asked that the book's owner should be punished, not only by a fine, "as is the custom," but, after consultation with the Bishop's Vicar and "with all the doctors learned in theology," more

175

severely – presumably at the stake. "For where incense and the sacrifice of idolatry have been offered up to Lucifer, even there would I offer up to God the sacrifice of justice. . . . For I would extirpate idolatry and diabolic powers from this land."[31]

Fra Bernardino himself, in such matters, was no less severe. He, too, told his congregation that it was the duty of every believer to capture and hand over any heretic, or even any man whom they suspected of such beliefs, and he himself took extremely prompt action when he smelled even the faintest whiff of black magic or neo-Paganism. When first he went to Arezzo, for instance, in 1425, he was told that near-by, close to a spring called the Fonte Tecta, there was a grove which had once been sacred to Apollo and which had now become the resort of witches and magicians – *malefici et incantatores* – who plunged ailing babies into the waters of the spring and declared it to have healing properties. He at once preached a vehement sermon against "those pestilent men and women," but so great was the attachment of the Aretini to their miracle-working waters (which were also a source of some profit) that there was an insurrection against him, and the incident ended in his being expelled from the territory of Arezzo. About fifteen years later, however – when the Rectors of the city had been changed – he returned to the charge. After delivering a course of Lenten sermons, he adjured all true Christians to follow him and, with a Cross borne before him, led his congregation to the Fonte Tecta, where he lost no time in hewing down a tree with his own hands and throwing some earth and stones into the spring. For a while the crowd watched him, trembling and convinced that some terrible calamity would fall upon him – but as they saw that nothing happened, some of them began to help him. The Cross was set firmly in the ground beside the spring, some men were sent to drain off the remaining water, and later on a small church was built nearby and dedicated to Santa Maria delle Grazie. The miraculous cures continued, and it gradually became one of the most popular sanctuaries in Tuscany.[32]

Nor was it only the practitioners of the magic arts who confused the minds of the simple. They were also exposed to the frauds of impostors who, in the name of the true faith, claimed that they could perform miracles and offered sham relics for sale. Fra Bernardino said that he himself had met such a man, "who went about begging with a nun, painting angels and saying that she was with child by the Holy Ghost," and even offering for sale the milk which he drew from her breast. "God does not like such things," he mildly commented, "because they are not reasonable" – nor does he like, he added, the folly of people who are ready to believe any object to be holy, as soon as they are shown it. "If all the pieces of wood that are shown as belonging to Christ's Cross were put together," he cried, "six yoke of oxen could not draw them!" And as to one of the most popular "relics" sold by itinerant friars, some drops of the Virgin Mary's milk, he declared that "All the buffalo cows of Lombardy would not have as much milk as is shown about the world! . . . You must know that she had just as much as was needed for the little mouth of her blessed Son, Jesus, and no more."[33]

Idle dreams, too, were often accepted as visions by the foolish and the vain. "How many there are who say to me, 'I had a fine vision last night . . . the Virgin Mary herself appeared to me!' – And another, 'An angel appeared to me' – and another, 'I saw the moon' – and another, 'the sun' – and another, 'my whole room was lit up by a star.' I tell you, this is just madness that has entered your heads."[34]

Then there was the complicated question of miracles. A miracle is "an object of wonder" – and it is indisputable that to Fra Bernardino's congregations wonder came easily – and indeed, up to a point, to himself. But he was always careful to remind the faithful that they must distinguish between true miracles and false, between God's and the Devil's. It was easy, he said, to do so, since the Devil's are performed only within the course of nature, while God's are

177

supernatural – and above all because all Christian miracles have a spiritual purpose: they are the signs and mysteries through which God conveys a spiritual truth. *Numquam aliquod miraculum fecit sine magno misterio.*[35]

And finally, he bade his hearers remember that some so-called "miracles" were the fruit of nothing more than their own lively imagination – and as an example of this, he told them one of his most delightful stories: that of a miracle-working dog.

This animal, whose name was Bonino, belonged to a seigneur who left him alone in the house with his small son, a baby only a few months old. While he was away, a great snake glided into the room and, in attempting to get at the baby, overturned the cradle, but was killed by the dog before the child could be harmed. On the master's return, Bonino came bounding towards him, with blood-covered jaws; the man saw the overturned cradle and, concluding that the dog had killed his child, took up a skewer and killed him on the spot – only to discover the baby safe and sound beneath the cradle. Whereupon, "to testify to his remorse, he built a tomb for the dog in the square and wrote upon it the name Boninforte [the strong Bonino]. And soon many women, seeing the inscription Boninforte, believed that a human body lay there, and knelt down before it – and soon it came to pass that he was called San Boninforte and performed miracles. And he was a dog!"[36]

As to the miracles attributed to himself, there was no subject that Fra Bernardino avoided more carefully. Many of them, as related by his earliest biographers, should perhaps rather be considered as fortunate coincidences – such as the tales of the day at Corneto on which, soon after he had begun to preach, a heavy shower began to fall upon him and his congregation, but at once ceased in response to his prayers, of the numerous occasions on which his protection saved ripening wheat-fields or vineyards from hailstorms, and of the day on which, on the contrary, it was a violent storm which came

178

to save him from being pursued and killed by some brigands, who feared that he would reveal their hiding-place.[37] Other legends, too, of which the tradition persisted in country places for centuries after his death, have a childlike simplicity very reminiscent of *I Fioretti*, and are probably equally apocryphal. In one of these stories, some flasks of wine, which a lady had given to the poor, mysteriously returned of their own accord to their giver; in another, a fall of Fra Bernardino's caused five little springs to bubble out of the ground at the points where his fingers had rested. There is also a charming legend in the Marches about the wild winter's night on which Fra Bernardino and Fra Giovanni da Capistrano knocked at the door of a country house to ask "for a night's lodging for two poor pilgrims" – and were turned away by the owner, in his fear of robbers. But a compassionate maidservant led them to a cellar, to sleep under a stone tub containing some dry vine-shoots, and when, the next morning, she went to unlock the door, she found that the shoots had burst into bud, and the pilgrims departed.[38] And finally there is the story, in Montefranco near Terni, of how a kind old woman was rewarded by the saint. At the end of a long day's march, the tired little friar had sunk down on a stone outside her house and begged for a crust of bread. "But Father," said she, "the cupboard holds nothing but spiders' webs." "Look and see," advised the saint. She obeyed and found it full of fresh white loaves. Then he asked for a glass of wine. "Father, there are only mice dancing in the barrel." But when she went to look, she found it full of good wine. Later on, after preaching in the city, the saint showed his hearers a site where he wished to build a small convent. "But there is no water there." "God will provide" – and a fresh spring suddenly gushed out of the rocks. The story is still told at Montefranco, and the spring and the convent may still be seen.[39]

And finally, there were the miracles of healing – testified to by numerous eye-witnesses and later on accepted by the ecclesiastical commission which examined the cause for his canonization – as well as the other miracles of the same nature which took place after the saint's death. Many of these episodes were later on depicted in works of art, in particular in several pictures by Sano di Pietro and Neroccio di Bartolomeo, in the fine series of paintings by Perugino, Pinturicchio and their school in Perugia, by Pinturicchio in a chapel of the Aracoeli in Rome, and by Giangiacomo da Lodi in the church of San Francesco in Lodi. The favourite subjects are almost always the same: the saint is healing a little boy gored by a bull (this incident happened in Prato), rescuing a drowning girl from a stream, setting an innocent prisoner free, bringing back to life a dead child, causing a blind man to see and a cripple to walk, freeing a bewitched woman from a devil or healing a Spanish leper outside the walls of Massa Marittima, by taking off his leggings and placing them upon the sick man. Sometimes, too, he is depicted, as a large congregation saw him in Aquila, with a great star shining, as he spoke, above his head. And perhaps the most popular legend of all was that of the day on which – finding no boat to take him across the Mincio to his expectant congregation in Mantua – he floated across the river upon his cloak.

This last is the only "miracle" to which Fra Bernardino himself perhaps indirectly referred – and only to say that he did not perform it. "You know," he told his hearers in Siena, "that St. Peter walked on the water, as others do on the ground. I would never attempt such a thing."[40] And he bound his daily companion, Fra Vincenzo, by a solemn vow never to talk about any such incident that he might have seen or imagined. "There is a great danger here," he said. "There are many who have thought they could reach eternal life in a skip and a hop – and many of them have gone mad."[41] But Fra Vincenzo was not of the same opinion. On his death-bed he was seen to be weeping bitterly – not, he said, because of any fear of "Sister Death," but because he could not bear to enter

XXIII. San Bernardino heals a Wounded Man: *School of Pinturicchio*.

xxiv. The School of Law: *Antonio Rossellino*.

eternity without having told all the instances of his companion's saintliness, which he had vowed never to reveal while Fra Bernardino was still alive.[42]

One is left with the impression that, whatever miracles San Bernardino may indeed have performed during his lifetime, it was – as some have entertained angels – unawares.

Of his theological ideas on these subjects – since they are expounded in his Latin sermons rather than his Italian ones and have been very fully treated by various eminent Franciscans – I shall not attempt to write. He himself – coming, as he did, at the end of the age of the great Schoolmen – did not claim for them any great originality, merely saying with his customary humility that he had "clung to the sleeve of the Doctors, who knew a great deal more than I do." In speaking to the people, his object was a very simple one: not to dwell on subtleties which they could not follow, but rather gently to draw them away from the powers of darkness towards the other, higher world, which to himself, since childhood, had always seemed so very near. "The stairs of Paradise have very high steps, but if you wish to climb them, God will help you, as you help your little child to climb up on to a bench." Heaven is as near to him, its skies as clear, as they were to Fra Angelico; and if the men and women kneeling in the foreground are often as earthy and ribald, as superstitious and sensual, as those in Boccaccio's or Sacchetti's tales, and the Devil is often lurking in a corner, the angels are also always hovering, too, very close above. "As in the springtime the earth is full of flowers and scented things, so Mary is surrounded in every season by angels.... They are all around her, bestowing on her sweet and harmonious scents and songs ... rejoicing, singing, dancing, encircling her, as you see them painted on the Porta Camollia."[43] That world and this – the only barrier, to his mind, was our imperfect sight.

VIII. THE WORLD OF LETTERS

Niuna impresa, per minima che sia, può
avere cominciamento o fine senza queste
tre cose, cioè: senza potere e senza sapere
e senza con amore volere.

STATUTES OF THE
PAINTERS' GUILD OF SIENA*

"ITALY," said Fra Bernardino, during his first course of sermons in Florence in 1424, "is the most intelligent country in Europe, Tuscany the most intelligent region in Italy, and Florence the most intelligent town in Tuscany" – but he went on to say that she was also the most corrupt, "for where noble gifts are allied to malice, you get the most evil men."[1] In his own terms, he was right. Since the Athens of Pericles, there had not been another town holding within its walls so many active minds, so much knowledge and taste and talent, so lively a curiosity for what was both old and new – and also, to the eyes of a man like Fra Bernardino, so much that was deplorable.

What can have been the effect of this busy, seething little town, so full of new riches, new treasures, and new ideas, upon the mind of a man dedicated since his early youth to the monastic life? It is, of course, quite impossible to describe the society he saw in the compass of one short chapter; all one can attempt is to catch a glimpse of a few facets which seemed important to him, and which affected his teaching. It was a world in which changes of outlook were rapidly taking place in almost every field, but custom had not yet quite caught up with them; in which his congregation was made up of men who were by temperament both sceptical and ironic, and in whose minds the new ideas of the Renaissance were already taking root, but who were mostly still closely bound to Christian tradition and practice. It was a society in which, as we have seen, a mystical cult of poverty could exist side by side, not only with an extremely flourishing trade but with a deliberate cultivation of the love of money as the basis of civilized life, in which a pagan sensuality and gaiety flourished beside extremes of austerity and asceticism, the senseless violence of party strife beside a deep nostalgia for peace, and a widespread moral corruption beside a high awareness of "the dignity of man." And it was also a society in which the cult of man-made beauty – whether in art or letters – had reached an unequalled intensity.[2] "*Graecus est*," wrote Poggio Bracciolini, of a marble head which had just been unearthed, "*Donatellus vidit et summe laudavit*"[3] – and one feels that never has an inanimate object been given greater praise.

These were the years in which Luca della Robbia was sculpting all day and drawing all night, "putting his feet into a basket of wood-shavings when they were numb with cold, rather than interrupt his work,"[4] in which Ghiberti, Jacopo della Quercia and Donatello were creating, for the Florentine Baptistery, the "doors of Paradise," Brunelleschi designing the dome of Santa Maria del Fiore, and Fra Angelico painting in his cell in San Marco – some said, upon his knees – his clear, cool visions of Paradise. Undoubtedly a man as sensitive to beauty as Fra Bernardino was not unaware of all this, and indeed, his asceticism held no trace of either the denial of beauty or the fanatical mortification of the body of many mediaeval monastics, including his own favourite poet, Jacopone da Todi. But no works of man could equal, to his eyes, those of God himself. "Consider," he said, "how many [flowers] there are, varied in so many forms and colours, and consider that all the artists in the world cannot make a single violet!"[5] The only pictures which, in his sermons, he singled out for his approval, were those which had, like the Sienese *fondi d'oro* depicting the Madonna, a religious intention, or, like Lorenzetti's fresco of Good Government, an allegorical significance.

While he was a young novice at Il Colombaio, the controversy had broken out which was still one of the vital topics of the day: was it possible for a fervent humanist to remain a good Christian? Fra Giovanni Dominici, the famous Dominican preacher, had emphatically declared that it was not. Children who had become familiar with the names of Venus, Jupiter and Saturn before they knew those of the Father, the Son and the Holy Ghost, young men nurtured on Plato and Aristotle instead of on the Bible and the Early Fathers, would always, he maintained, be brought back by the voluptuous wanderings of their mind – *voluptuosa vagatio mentis* – to the ideas first implanted there in their youth. Nothing could come of these pagan myths, but a *falsum et vetustissimum chaos*. A man, he said, "becomes what he knows."[6] Coluccio Salutati, the chancellor of Florence and the most renowned classical scholar of his time, had held the opposite opinion. The man with a well-trained mind, he said, was better equipped than another in maturity to choose between the ideas that had been imparted to him: a good humanist need not lose his faith.

In this controversy, which increased in violence and acerbity as time went on, Fra Bernardino took no active part. He would often see the celebrated Florentine scholars of the day in the bookshop at the corner of the Piazza della Signoria of the garrulous and kindly Vespasiano da Bisticci, the friend and biographer of all the men of letters. Vespasiano not only collected and sold the ancient codices which had been brought back by scholars from Athens and Constantinople or had recently been unearthed in the monasteries of France and Germany, but also set forty-five scribes to transcribing them, for the libraries of Cosimo de' Medici and Federigo da Montefeltro. In his shop Fra Bernardino met the learned, wise old Camaldolese humanist, Fra Ambrogio Traversari, who translated from the Greek faster than a scribe could follow him, the poor young priest who had been a tutor in Casa Strozzi, Tommaso Parentucelli – who used to say that "if ever he became rich, he would do two things, build walls and buy books,"[7] and later on, when he became Pope, fulfilled both desires by founding the Vatican Library – the famous collector of codices and works of art, Niccolò Niccoli,[8] the eloquent Leonardo Bruni, chancellor of Florence,[9] the silent and melancholy atheist, Carlo Marsuppini,[10] the devout Hebrew scholar, Giannozzo Manetti, to whom the truths taught by the Church were as evident as the properties of a geometrical figure,[11] and the irascible, violent Poggio Bracciolini, whose invectives against the scholars who differed with him were so violent "that there was no man who was not afraid of him."[12] Fra Bernardino knew them all, and, standing in the shadows at the back of the shop turning over the pages of the codices, could hardly fail to hear their acrimonious disputes,[13] but, unless he was drawn into the talk by a direct question, he would take no part in it. "He was neither for humanism nor against it," wrote Bontempelli rightly. "He travelled by a different path."[14]

One should, however, be careful not to draw clear-cut lines of demarcation which were not perceptible to the people concerned. There is always a temptation to overemphasize, in describing times of transition, the traits which differentiated one phase of civilization from the one before it, rather than the characteristics which they both still possessed in common, but in reality there is almost always a period during which the new doctrines are merely superimposed upon the old, without destroying them. We find, at the end of the Trecento and the beginning of the Quattrocento, some of the finest works of art of the Gothic world in decline, side by side with the new realism and concreteness of the Renaissance, and the same thing is also true in the world of letters. Moreover, the Italian humanists were very conscious of the link which the classical studies of the Early Fathers of the Church had formed between them and the great writers of antiquity.[15] The "modern" Christian of Fra Bernardino's day found a sanction for his love of the classics in St. Jerome, St. Augustine and St. Basil, and freely quoted them in his defence. In a letter written in 1450 by the celebrated humanist Guarino Veronese to Fra Giovanni da Prato, who (according to his correspondent) "not only rejected but detested and spat upon" the classical authors whom he considered pernicious for the young, Guarino pointed out that St. Basil himself had gone to Athens to perfect his knowledge of Greek, that St. Jerome had approved the reading of Terence and St. Augustine of Juvenal. How, he inquired, could the young learn to distinguish between the pagan authors and the Christian, unless they were first allowed to read them? "The doctrines of the Gentiles," he quoted from St. Augustine, "do not only contain false and superstitious fictions... which each one of us, under Christ's guidance, should hate and combat. They also hold all the liberal arts . . . and even some truths with regard to the only God, which Christians, too, should acquire."[16]

The first and most authoritative holder of such opinions as these had been, in Fra Bernardino's youth, Messer Coluccio Salutati (whom he mentions in the same breath as Dante and Petrarch, and who had been the friend and master of his own teacher of rhetoric and philosophy, Giovanni da Spoleto) – a man deeply imbued with the ideas of Duns Scotus, as opposed to the strict Thomism of the Dominicans. The controversy, indeed, between Salutati and Fra Giovanni Dominici was largely based upon one of the principal points which separated the Dominican from the Franciscan way of thought – the question of the primacy of the will in the conduct of human life, as opposed to the Aristotelian theory of the primacy of the intellect. To the Dominicans it was above all important to know and to understand; to the Franciscans, to make one's own life bear witness, through the exercise of one's will, to one's knowledge of the truth. "The will," wrote Fra Bernardino, "is the empress of all the powers [of the soul] and of all our emotions; the will rules over our mind . . . Good will is the empress of the whole universe."[17] This was a view of life which Coluccio Salutati, too, accepted. He, and the humanists who agreed with him, considered the study of philosophy to be not merely an intellectual process, but one which led to the strengthening of the will and of "virtue." To his mind philosophy – as he wrote in a celebrated letter on the occasion of the death of Petrarch – was not only the empty dialectic of the sophists, but a school of life and character, an approach to God. "I do not refer to [the philosophy] which the modern sophists, with empty vanity and foolish and impudent frivolity, exalt in the schools, but to a wisdom which shapes the souls of men, forms virtue, wipes out vice, and illuminates, apart from all dialectic subtleties, the truth."[18] The purpose of the study of letters was to form, not only learned scholars, but civilized human beings. "They are called *studia humanitatis*," wrote Leonardo Bruni, "because they form a complete man."[19]

It was for similar reasons, too, that many of the humanists were so strongly opposed to a sterile asceticism and to the monastic ideal of solitude. Man, they held, is essentially a social animal; if he isolates himself from his fellows, his virtue will become "frozen, solitary, sterile." The true virtue, fit for a "complete" man, is that which lives and strives in society.

This, too, was an attitude which was in harmony with the Franciscan tradition and what personally appealed to Fra Bernardino. Sociable by temperament and firmly convinced that it was only by frequent contact with one's fellow-creatures that one can learn anything about them, he was also fortified in his instinctive distrust of monastic solitude by the excesses to which it had been carried by some of the *Fraticelli*. Though he sometimes felt bound to defend the life of the contemplative, it was the active life of *charitas* to which, both by temperament and conviction, he himself was drawn. "The man who loves, understands more than the one who does not love."

Above all, he perfectly agreed with the humanist emphasis upon the dignity of man, made in God's own image, and capable of perfecting himself by the exercise of his own free will. This was an idea which lay at the very heart of humanist philosophy and which was expounded, in Fra Bernardino's time, by his friend Giannozzo Manetti in his treatise *De dignitate et excellentia hominis*, by Alberti in his *Iciarchia*, and above all, a few years later, by the great Platonist Pico della Mirandola, who considered the very essence of man's nobility to lie in his ability to shape his own destiny. "If he cultivates sensual things, he will become a brute . . . if those of the mind, he will become an angel, and the son of God."[20]

This view of man's infinite perfectibility was often expounded, too, by Fra Bernardino – as deriving, in addition to his own reason and will, from divine Grace. He saw, like St. Augustine, in the union of the body and the soul a synthesis of the whole of creation. Man is in himself "a little world." At his birth, he is weaker and more defenceless than any animal. "Look at a chick: as soon as it is born, it recognizes the grain and pecks at it, and the newborn lamb recognizes his mother and her teat . . . but the child, at his birth, knows neither where he is nor who his father and mother are. . . . Every creature is born with some protection: skin or feathers, claws or hoofs – except man, who has no armour and no strength." But "so great is the dignity of intellectual light, that it penetrates and transcends every bodily virtue." Fra Bernardino did not believe, like Fra Giovanni Dominici, that "a man becomes what he knows"; he believed that "he becomes what he loves."[21]

It was on such opinions as these that Fra Bernardino founded his theories of education, which were – up to a point – very much in harmony with those which were then being practised in the famous schools of Guarino in Verona and of Vittorino da Feltre in Mantua. Guarino – the son of a blacksmith of Verona – had been stirred by such enthusiasm for the Greek language in his youth by the Greek scholar Manuele Chrysoloras (whom he had met in

Venice, in the train of the Emperor Palaeologus) that he had followed him to Constantinople, to study with him there for five years – after which he had taught Greek himself in the universities of Florence and Venice and finally had opened his own school in Verona, which Fra Bernardino, when preaching there, sometimes attended. It seems probable that he did so, not so much in the hope of perfecting his slight knowledge of Greek (since he was never in Verona for more than a few weeks) – as owing to the unfailing curiosity about different ways of life which had also led him to the armourers' shops of Milan and the fishermen's boats of the Venetian lagoon. But certainly in Guarino's school he must have found an atmosphere extremely sympathetic to him. Guarino was not only a learned but a humane teacher, and the society he had formed with his pupils had become, according to a contemporary, a true "republic of the spirit," in which a genuine and deep culture directed the "urbane conversation," and the study of "letters" was also a lesson in the art of living. "Some men," Guarino wrote to a friend, "expend their diligence and care in taming birds and little beasts; and shall we hesitate to shape boys who are well disposed, that is, to instil humanity into man?"[22] In the dedication of his translation of Plutarch's Life of Themistocles, he wrote that the value of this Life lay not only in its portrait of a wise citizen and able general, but in its description of "the variety of the times, the changes in human matters, the vicissitudes of fortune, the uncertainties of events, the wonders, fears, hope, joy and sorrow manifested in the life of a single man."[23] It was by such teachers as this that the "universal man" of the Renaissance was shaped.

It was in Guarino's school that Fra Bernardino met the young Franciscan scholar, Fra Alberto da Sarteano, who was one of Guarino's most able pupils, but who, after meeting Fra Bernardino, devoted the rest of his life to preaching and to the strengthening of the Observant Order.[24] And it must have been here, too, that

Fra Bernardino first heard of the famous school in Mantua, La Giocosa, founded by another of Guarino's pupils, Vittorino da Feltre, which became, in the words of Vespasiano da Bisticci, "a temple of good customs, words and deeds," and one of the most delightful experiments in education that there has ever been. At La Giocosa the pupils, both boys and girls, were given the rigorous physical training of the Greek gymnasium and instruction in music, dancing and jousting, as well as a thorough classical education, but the development of what Vittorino called "the heart" and we should call character, was still based upon reverence and devotion, a daily attendance at Mass, and the cultivation of those Christian virtues which they could daily observe in their own master: self-restraint, humility, truthfulness and kindness. It should always be remembered that Vittorino considered humanist education to be essentially a *practical* preparation for life. His aim was not the formation of scholars, but of "complete citizens." "Not everyone is obliged to excel in philosophy or the law, nor are all equally favoured by nature; but all are destined to live in society and to practise virtue."[25]

This was an education remarkably similar to the one that Fra Bernardino believed in. He, too, considered that while "learning adorns a man, as a jewel does a ring," it was the formation of character that was essential. There is, indeed, one sermon of his, on "the qualities which constitute true nobility," which might almost have been drawn up by Vittorino da Feltre himself for the formation of young men who would one day rule over a State, and which incidentally reminds one that (however seldom he might remember it) this was the class into which Fra Bernardino himself had been born. The virtues he enumerates are "liberality, gratitude, mildness, virility, magnanimity, modesty and activity." Liberality, he says, is a noble virtue, because it is what is most unlike the behaviour of a thief: "the most villainous thing on earth is to steal, and so the most noble is to give." Mildness is defined as a manifestation both of Christian kindness and of aristocratic self-control ("a serf in power will be rough and harsh...capable only of cruelty"). Gratitude is opposed to the serf's inborn ingratitude. "It is noble to be grateful." Virility and activity are to be cultivated by means of all the knightly sports, so that a man may become "vigorous and brave, when it is needful to defend his city, or widows and orphans. And therefore are knights given a sword." Modesty is "a gentleness of the soul." And finally, magnanimity is defined as a contempt for all that is vile and an admiraton of what is fine, thus bringing a man close to God. "The closer you draw to God, the more you will be courteous and noble."[26] Here, in the fusion of the ideals of the mediaeval knight and of the humanist gentleman, Fra Bernardino is standing on the threshold of two worlds, taking what is best from each.

Fra Bernardino preached four sermons in the vulgar on the benefits of education: two in Florence, one in Siena and one in 1442 in Padua, before the assembled teachers and students of the great university. In all of them, one is made aware that, like Vittorino, he expected a good school not only to form the minds of its pupils, but to prepare them for life. "Ignorance," he said, "the Devil's best assistant," brings about "the ruin both of peoples and of individuals"; while "young men who acquire knowledge bring first honour and praise to their city, and then gain."[27] He implored his fellow-citizens in Siena to realize that their university was no less useful to them than their wool or leather-guilds, and to remember how much of her reputation Bologna owed to the scholars she had nurtured. "The money you spend best, is that which you spend on your university." Every young nobleman, who had no need to work or trade, should study rhetoric and science; they should "learn to live like men, so that, if their country needs it, they can serve as ambassadors for the Republic.... A man who has studied will always cut a fine figure in the world, but of what use is one who cannot even speak correctly?"[28]

For all four of his sermons on education, he chose the same text (from the 118th Psalm): "*Bonitatem, et disciplinam, et scientiam doce me, quia mandatis tuis credidi*" (teach me goodness and discipline and knowledge, for I have believed thy commandments.) Discipline and knowledge are necessary, but first comes *bonitas*, which he translates in these sermons as "good will," a right intention – for it is by the will that the soul is ruled. It is only through good will, too, that a student may attain the unquestioning faith which alone will enable him to learn. "It is needful, in order to learn anything whatever – whether Greek and Latin and the liberal arts, or to sew and cut out and spin, or to make cloth or silk . . . to have faith. . . . For if you do not have faith in the man who teaches you, you will never learn that art."[29]

As to discipline, his requirements may be summed up in a single word, single-mindedness. "When our soul is still, it is like clear water, but when it is moved, it becomes turbid."

> *Quattro venti escon dal mare – che la mente fan turbare:*
> *El dolore e il gaudiare – el temere e lo sperare.*[30]

Joy and sorrow, fear and hope – these are all, he said, attributes of the soul, but they will only bring harm to us unless, by the determination of our will, they lead us back to God. The student, who is a man attempting to draw nearer to Him by acquiring knowledge and virtue, will gain little profit if he wastes his energies in dancing, jousting or gambling, or even (this is very Franciscan) in melancholy moods. "Be as merry as you can." Over-anxiety and over-self-confidence are equally undesirable, and a steady physical self-discipline is also necessary: "To eat neither too little nor too much . . . for one will bring you to consumption and the other coarsen the mind. . . . To sleep neither too little nor too much –

either going to bed early and rising early to study, or else working late, but also getting up later, according to each man's nature.... All extremes are dangerous, the middle way is best." And finally: "Life is a spiritual order. The soul should be ruled by the fear of God – hearing Mass and the sermon, fasting on the specified days, observing chastity according to the decrees of the Church – and, with due order, also taking delight." For in this, too, Fra Bernardino showed his usual moderation, answering the boys who asked him whether it was necessary to study *all* the time, with an emphatic, "Certainly not! But you must take the pleasures of this world with due measure, having first clothed yourself in those of the spirit."

He had much to say that was sensible, too, about the actual method of planning one's studies. "Do not put the cart before the ox: begin with a good foundation.... Esteem one doctor more than another, and attribute a different value to the ancient masters from the modern; but do not despise any.... And do not go, following your fancy, from one book to another. Take one master, put him before you, and ruminate every sentence well ... without going all the way to Paris to study, learn from the animal with the cloven hoof."[31]

To all this, no exception could be taken in any age. It is only when he comes to the choice of subject-matter that one realizes how much Fra Bernardino still deliberately restricted his students' range. Both Guarino and Vittorino da Feltre – following Vergerius' theory that liberal studies should include *all* subjects "worthy of being studied by free men" – included in their pupils' curriculum, as well as philosophy and history, mathematics and natural history (in a rather rudimentary form) and all the great classical authors then available: beginning with Homer and Virgil, Demosthenes and Cicero, and passing on to Lucan and Ovid ("to form an elegiac taste") – while the older boys, whose characters were considered to have been formed, were also allowed to read Aeschylus, Euripides and Sophocles and some parts of Aristophanes, as well as Terence, Plautus and Juvenal. Fra Bernardino was considerably less liberal. Though in his own sermons he quoted freely from classical authors,[32] for the young he only specifically advised the study of Cicero – "Young men who study Cicero do well, in order to learn how to speak" – and he at once added, "For your delighted contemplation, take the Epistles of St. Jerome, who was so well-grounded a master – you know, the one with the grey beard – and learn from him. . . . Would you not be glad," he asked, "if you could hear Jesus preaching, or St. Paul, St. Gregory, St. Jerome and St. Ambrose? Well, go, read their books, whichever one you like . . . and you will converse with them, and they with you. . . . Do you know," he went on to inquire, "how young oxen are tamed? I know it well, though I am a friar! Haven't you seen how one always puts an old ox beside the young one . . . and then he goes steadily and straight? And when the young ox wants to follow his own will . . . the old ox turns round and gives him a thrust with his horn, and makes him come back to the harrow. And so should you do; take your master St. Jerome, the greybeard, and when you are going off the track . . . read him, and he will thrust away your erring thoughts."[33]

As to the poets, he admitted that he himself, in his youth, had "delighted in their sweet sounds"; but he added: "Then, as God willed, the Epistles of St. Jerome came into my hands and took me away from all poetic fantasies to Holy Writ, which has a sweeter savour. . . . It holds in itself the glory of Paradise."[34] Poetry, he said, has "a sweet rind . . . but Holy Writ, the marrow." Among the modern authors, he himself was plainly well acquainted with Dante, for he not only often quoted from him, but also sometimes – perhaps half-unconsciously – used sentences of which the rhythm or content have a vague Dantesque echo,[35] and he referred to both him and Petrarch as writers "who did most notable things, which should greatly be commended." But of Boccaccio he could only say that "with due respect, he produced books which he had better not have written. An able man he would have been, had he not made those bestial errors, and perhaps in his old age he regretted them."[36] And he went on to warn his listeners to refrain from the poets, especially Ovid – "for under their honey poison lurks" – and from "all other books about falling in love," even advising parents who had sent their son to a university in another city, to stop his allowance if they heard that he was in love. "Make him come home again, for he will learn nothing but songs and sonnets, and will pawn his books."[37]

In all this, Fra Bernardino was laying himself open to the accusations of obscurantism which the Renaissance scholars freely aimed at the "Preaching Friars." But we must remember that, when he was speaking, the books most widely read and quoted in Florence did indeed contain a great deal that even a less strict moralist than he might have considered undesirable for the young – not only the tales of Boccaccio, Sacchetti and Sermini, and, more recently, Aeneus Silvius Piccolomini's *Storia di due amanti*, but also the scurrilous anecdotes about monks, nuns and impostors in Poggio Bracciolini's *Facezie*, and the obscene and cynical epigrams of Antonio Beccadelli's *Hermaphroditus*.[38] Moreover, if many of the men whom he met in Vespasiano's bookshop were good Christians as well as ardent humanists – scholars like the gentle old Camaldolese monk, Fra Ambrogio Traversari, the devout and learned Giannozzo Manetti or the historian Leonardo Bruni, to whom the revival of classical studies signified also a renewal of the life of the spirit – there were also others who openly proclaimed their allegiance to Stoicism or Epicureanism, and who did not hesitate to denounce (with a violence and plainness of speech unsurpassed by any subsequent reformers) the follies and vices of the monks and priests. Among the most formidable of these were Poggio Bracciolini (to whose diatribes against the Observants we shall return in the next chapter), and

xxv. Boys of Florence: *Tuscan School, XV century.*

XXVI. San Bernardino: *Andrea della Robbia*.

Lorenzo Valla, whose most famous work – the treatise *De voluptate* – was an attack upon every form of asceticism, whether Stoic or monastic, and whose later dialogue, *De professione religiosorum* (which was probably directed against Fra Bernardino himself) was written to disprove the assumption that a man who had taken monastic vows was in any way better than a good layman.[39]

It was hardly strange that Fra Bernardino should have wished to shield the young from such works as these, and that he should have attributed to their influence, at least in part, the general decline of Christian practice and the relaxation of morals which, as he walked about Florence, he could hardly fail to observe. Even the little boys in the street reflected the general contempt for the Church and for all it taught, as they sang the latest doggerel about the Pope: "*Papa Martino – non vale un lupino!*" (Pope Martin isn't worth a bean!) The solemn religious processions which used to mark every feast-day now drew lesser crowds than the brilliant secular *trionfi*, in which masked actors paraded on foot or in fantastic chariots, representing the gods and goddesses of Olympus or figures of classical mythology, while wine flowed and music and dancing filled the streets. The pagan superstitions which had never lost their hold upon the simple were now both defended and practised, as we have seen, by educated men. The rich adorned their houses with classical statuary and erotic pictures; they dressed their women in rich, low-necked dresses and their boys in unseemly short tunics and tight hose; and they also imported Greek and Circassian slaves, whose offspring, if not suppressed at birth, grew up in their own households as little bastards, or filled the beds of the foundling hospitals.

All this greatly dismayed Fra Bernardino. A single word might sum up his exhortations to the Florentines: "Beware!" Beware of pagan superstition, beware of a weakening of the faith, beware of lust and sodomy. Florence, he cried, "was never so beautiful and well-adorned, she never sailed so far upon the seas, she was never

197

more powerful nor noble . . . but her people are the most wretched upon earth, owing to sodomy and women's extravagance."[40] If a man chose to listen, he could hear, beneath the music in her streets, "cries that would cause amazement both on earth and in heaven." "Go to the Ponte Vecchio," he cried, "there by the Arno, and put your ear to the ground and listen: you will hear a great lament. Go to the privies, the stables, the gardens, both in the country and in Florence itself; go to the barbers' and apothecaries' shops and the doctors' houses. . . . Listen, and you will hear voices rising to heaven, crying, 'Vengeance! Vengeance! O God!' . . . What are these cries? They are the voices of the innocent babies thrown into your Arno and your privies or buried alive in your gardens and your stables, to avoid the world's shame, and sometimes without baptism; the cries of babies killed in their mothers' bellies by the drugs of the barbers, apothecaries and doctors. . . . The cries of souls who might have been born, but were not, on account of the cursed vice of sodomy." And he went on to say that, for this very reason, the Florentines were only half as many as they had been fifteen years before, "and if you continue in this fashion, in another fifteen years you will be half as many again."[41]

Whether Fra Bernardino was right in attributing the prevalence of sodomy in Tuscany to the influence of neo-paganism must remain uncertain, but he also did not fail to blame the weakness and cupidity of the boys' own parents. "I have heard of some boys," he said, "who paint their cheeks and go about boasting of their sodomy and practise it for gain. . . . It is largely the mothers' and fathers' fault for not punishing them, but especially the mothers', who empty their purses without asking where the money came from. And it is a grave sin to make them a doublet that only reaches to the numbril, and hose with one small patch in front and one behind, so that they show enough flesh to the sodomites. You spare the cloth and expend the flesh! . . . And what of the contamination which they bring to those who see them at home, their sisters and sisters-in-law? . . . How many souls, do you think, are damned by those dishonest doublets and hose?"[42]

Such plain speaking was – as it often is – extremely effective. "You have sent us all to damnation!" said Giannozzo Manetti one evening in Vespasiano's bookshop, after a particularly fiery sermon. "No," Fra Bernardino replied with his thin smile, "I have damned no one. Man's sin and wickedness damn themselves."[43] Some of his hearers, of course, disregarded his warnings or scoffed, and a few (as we have already seen) muttered accusations of heresy. Yet that, even in the first flowering of the new ideas of the Renaissance, there were still many men in Florence of his way of thinking, is shown by the fact that, during his two long courses of sermons, the great church of Santa Croce was packed every day, while many of his hearers were moved by his words to return to the religious practices of their youth, and that, when the course of sermons was over, the chancellor of Florence, Leonardo Bruni, wrote to beg him to return to preach again in the following year.[44] "He modified and changed the minds of men most marvellously," wrote Vespasiano da Bisticci, "and many who, on account of their blindness, had not been to confession for a long time, were led by him not only to confess, but to restore to others both their goods and their reputation. And in many mortal quarrels, he brought peace."[45]

When, at the end of his first course of sermons, a great bonfire was held in Piazza Santa Croce, in which the gambling-boards, dice and cards of the Florentines and the wigs and cosmetics of their women perished in the flames, the enthusiasm of the crowd was no less fervent than it had been in Bologna and Siena. "The crowd was great," an eye-witness wrote, "the people quivering." The whole church and square of Santa Croce was filled with citizens and countrymen, numbering several thousand. The shouts of the boys and men were so loud that Fra Bernardino was obliged to stop preaching and to come out of the church into the square with several friars, and start the blaze. . . . It flared right up into the sky, to the confusion of the Devil, God's enemy, and to the glory, honour, praise and reverence of our Lord Jesus Christ." And the writer added that many of the people watching, both men and women, were in tears, "and the shouts echoed like thunder."[46]

Fra Bernardino returned again to Florence in 1439, to take part, as the Vicar General of the Observants, in the Council which was taking place there, to bring about the union of the Greek and Latin Churches, a union rendered urgent by a new political factor, the menace of the Turks to Constantinople, since it was only to Western Christendom that the Emperor of the East could turn for aid. Already in 1418, at the conclusion of the Council of Constance, the Emperor had sent ambassadors to congratulate Pope Martin V upon his election and to negotiate for a reunion of the Greek and Latin Churches, but it was only Pope Martin's successor, Pope Eugenius IV, who convoked a general Council to discuss the points which still divided them. The Council – transferred from Basle to Ferrara – opened on April 9, 1438, and was attended, under the leadership of the Emperor John Palaeologus and of his octogenarian brother, Joseph, Patriarch of Constantinople, by no less than seven hundred Greek prelates, monks, courtiers and attendants. The beginning was an unfortunate one, since the Greek Patriarch refused to pay the Pope the customary homage of kissing his toe, saying that if the Pope was older than he, he would embrace him as a father, if of the same age, as a brother, and if younger, as a son; but this obstacle was overcome by causing their first meeting to take place in private, and a further dispute, about the position of the seats of the Pope, Patriarch and Emperor, also found an ingenious solution.[47] The Emperor, moreover – in the hope of the arrival of some of the Western princes who would give him military aid – had stipulated that no doctrinal discussions should take place for the first four months. The princes did not arrive, the summer came, the plague broke out; the troops of the hostile Milanese *condottiere*, Niccolò Piccinino, were much too close for safety, and the seigneur of Ferrara, Niccolò d'Este, showed his eminent but too numerous guests a somewhat parsimonious hospitality, only offering them hard beds and scanty food, while the Pope, on his side, felt disinclined to pay for them himself. In the autumn the first doctrinal discussions began, but by the end of the year it was evident that they would drag on for some time longer and that it was necessary to move the Council elsewhere. Florence – a city for which the Pope felt an especial attachment – extended a more cordial invitation, offering to lend the Pope (from Cosimo de' Medici's bank) 1300 florins a month for the maintenance of the Greeks, provided that their stay should not be longer than eight months, and also voting 4000 florins from the treasury of the *Signoria* for their entertainment.[48] So, in January 1439, the Council was transferred to Florence and the little grey Franciscan, too, returned there once again – both to observe a scene of great splendour and to listen to the views of very numerous and various kinds of men.

The sessions were held in the church of Santa Maria Novella (next to the great Dominican convent where the Pope was lodged) and here, "on a very fine structure of benches and seats," the Fathers of the East and the West faced each other for six months. The chief figure of the Greek Church was of course the venerable Patriarch, Joseph of Constantinople, and with him had come the celebrated Platonist, Bessarion of Trebizond, Bishop of Nicea, the uncompromising Mark Eugenicus, Archishop of Ephesus, the philosopher Gemistos of Plethon – who persuaded Cosimo de' Medici to found the Florentine Academy – the Greek grammarian Theodore of Gaza, and a vast train of bearded and long-haired priests and monks, whose strange appearance, "untidy and towsled," somewhat disconcerted the Florentines. They were, however, much impressed by the long heavy robes of brocade and gold (preserved for us in Benozzo's paintings) of the Emperor and the high prelates, noting that "the fashion of their garments seems more dignified and fit than that of the Latin prelates."[49] But for sheer dignity of presence, no one could surpass the Pope himself. "Tall in stature, most handsome in features, the sight of him awakes great reverence," wrote Vespasiano da Bisticci, adding that the austerity of his life and the authority of his glance were so great that, when he bestowed the Papal blessing, "the people felt as if they were seeing not only Christ's Vicar on earth, but something of his divinity".[50] With him had come several of the Latin cardinals and many other eminent members of the Roman Curia, and each of them had brought with him a little court of secretaries, notaries and men of letters.

Day after day, the sessions in Santa Maria Novella continued. The main point at issue, in the mind of the Greeks, was "the Procession of the Holy Spirit" – i. e. the addition by the Latins of the word *filioque* to the Nicene Creed, thus declaring the Holy Spirit to proceed, not from the Father alone, but from the Father *and* the Son – since the Eastern Church maintained, through the mouth of the Bishop of Ephesus, both that the Latin doctrine was erroneous and that the interpolation into the Creed was not legitimate. There were also three other points of divergence: that of the primacy of the Pope, that of the use of unleavened bread by the Latin Church in the Eucharist, and that of the incomplete acceptance by the Greek Church of the Latin doctrine regarding Purgatory. But from March to May the sessions in Santa Maria Novella were wholly given up to the "Procession of the Holy Spirit", with Mark of Ephesus as the chief speaker for the Greeks and the Dominican Giovanni da Montenero for the Latins. After three months of debate, the Greeks determined to have no more of it. "Disputation," they said, "produces nothing but irritation. If we say anything, you are never at loss for an answer, and that at great length. . . . Who can go on listening and answering for ever?"[51]

Nor were these disputations the only ones to be heard in Florence during these months. While the members of the Council were busy in Santa Maria Novella, other and no less lively debates were taking place in the convents and palaces, the gardens and the squares of Florence. Men of diverse nationalities and shades of belief, of varying races and cultures – theologians and statesmen, monks and humanists, philosophers and poets – "tired the sun with talking"; they spoke of philosophy, philology, astrology, history, music, science. And was Julius Caesar really greater than Scipio? And what was the Platonic conception of the soul?

Within Santa Maria Novella an agreement was reached at last – just at the point when any hope of doing so seemed to have disappeared. At the end of May, the Greeks told the Latins that they would hear no more arguments: it was up to them to find some other approach to union, and if they could not, the Greeks would go home again. But an address from the Pope himself, speaking to both the Greeks and the Latins and taking his stand, not upon any doctrinal point, but upon the fundamental principle of charity and a deeply-felt appeal for unity, made a profound impression, and finally, upon the point of the Procession of the Holy Spirit, an acceptable formula was found. Of all the speeches made at the Council, this must have been the only one which was entirely to Fra Bernardino's liking. Of his own part – though we know that, with Fra Giovanni da Capistrano and Fra Alberto da Sarteano, he attended many of the meetings – only one record has come down to us, and this story may well be apocryphal. According to Wadding, he was overcome one day by so great a desire to see the union at last effected, that he prayed to God to make his speech intelligible to the Greeks and was granted, like the Apostles, the gift of tongues – becoming suddenly able to address the Council in fluent Greek, but "thereafter remaining as ignorant [of that language] as he had been before."[52]

The agreement which he so ardently desired – but which unfortunately proved to be only a temporary one[53] – was at last reached. The Patriarch of Constantinople died suddenly in June, but before dying, signed a document in which he unequivocally declared that he recognized the Roman Pontiff as Christ's Vicar on earth.[54] A solution was found, too, for the other two points still under debate – the doctrine concerning Purgatory and the use of unleavened bread in the Eucharist – and thus on July 5, 1439, it was possible to issue, in the name of "Eugenius, Bishop of the Universal Church," and with 117 signatures on the Latin side, but only 33 on the Greek, and with the abstention of Mark of Ephesus, the decree announcing the union of the two churches. "Let the heavens rejoice," the decree began, "and the earth exult, for the wall is fallen which divided the Western Church from the Eastern, and peace and concord have returned."[55] A solemn Mass of thanksgiving was sung in Santa Maria del Fiore, and "the whole of Florence," says Vespasiano, "went to see so worthy a sight."[56]

But long before this, Fra Bernardino, with his bundle of sermons under his arm and the faithful Fra Vincenzo behind him, had returned to his cell at La Capriola. There, at last, he was again at home.

IX. THE REFORM OF THE OBSERVANTS

AT the time of Bernardino's arrival as a young novice in the
remote little convent of Il Colombaio, the branch of the
Franciscan Order which practised the "Strict Observance" of St.
Francis' Rule was just beginning to gather strength again, after a
long period of conflict and obscurity.

Thirty-three years before, a little community of Franciscans headed by a nobleman of Foligno, Paoluccio de' Trinci, had received
permission to live, in a lonely hermitage in the hills above their
city, San Bartolomeo da Brogliano, a life as strict and as austere
as that of the *Porziuncola*¹ – observing the precepts of utter poverty bequeathed to them by their founder – "without gloss, without gloss, without gloss," but with the approval of the Church and
within the discipline of the Franciscan Order. This experiment followed upon a similar one in the same place some forty years earlier –
under the guidance of the Franciscan Spiritual Angelo Clareno and
the leadership of Padre Giovanni della Valle – but this earlier community, having accepted some members suspected of heresy, had
been dissolved by the Pope's orders, and now Paoluccio, who as a
young man had been a lay brother there, had returned with a few
chosen followers to the same hermitage, to attempt to fulfil the
same dream. It was not a spot to which, by choice, most men
would have returned twice in a lifetime. It stood on a wild and
lonely hillside; a plague of frogs and snakes infested the house from
the marshes below and even crawled into the friars' beds, and the cold
was so intense that they were obliged, after obtaining due dispensa-
tion, to wear goatskins on their shoulders and the peasants' wooden

clogs upon their feet. One by one, indeed, Paoluccio's first companions fled away, "and the poor man was left alone";[2] but others came to take their place, and among them Fra Giovanni da Stroncone, who, at the time of Fra Bernardino's novitiate, had become the Superior of Il Colombaio. Thus an unbroken chain linked the men who had first followed St. Francis in search of "Our Lady Poverty" with the young novice of Il Colombaio. It was he, Fra Bernardino, who was to complete the return to the strict Rule according to St. Francis' own words, and to deserve the title of second founder of the Franciscan Order.

Before, however, we attempt an account of his work, it is necessary to glance back at the chequered story of the observance of St. Francis' Rule, on which the reformed Observants, like their founder, based their lives. "The brothers shall appropriate nothing for themselves," said the essential passage, "neither house nor place nor anything whatever. And as pilgrims and strangers in this world, serving the Lord in poverty and humility, let them beg confidently for alms, nor should they be ashamed, for the Lord himself made himself poor in this world for our sake. . . . Let this be your portion, which leads to the land of the living."[3] The friars were to live only by the trade unto which each one had been called, and those who had not, should learn one. "I have worked," said St. Francis, "and wish to work, with my hands, and I firmly desire that the other brothers should have some work. . . . And when the price of our labour is not given us, we will turn to the Lord's table, begging for alms from door to door."[4] They were to live upon the road and to rest, when they must, not within the stone walls of a convent, but in little *luoghi* ("places"), in huts of clay or reeds – "so that all things may sing to them of pilgrimage and exile."

> *Povertade è nulla avere,*
> *E nulla cosa poi volere,*

Et omne cosa possedere
In spirito di libertade.[5]

And that this was indeed the impression given in early days by the life of the friars, is recorded by more than one impartial witness. "Living in groups often or even in towns or communes, possessing nothing at all, subsisting according to the Gospel, observing extreme poverty in food and dress and going barefoot, they give the greatest example of humility.... They keep no food over for the next day, so that the poverty which flourishes in the mind, may live in the sight of all."[6] So wrote Roger of Winburne, Prior of St. Albans, and Cardinal Jacques de Vitry gave a very similar account. "I believe," he commented, "that the Lord, through these poor and simple men, means to save many before the end of the world."[7]

It was not until after St. Francis' death that the trouble began. His successor, Brother Elias, at once began to build the great basilica at Assisi, and soon protests from all over Christendom reached Pope Gregory IX. The essence of the problem, of course, did not lie in the building of the church, but in the whole interpretation of St. Francis' Rule, which the more zealous of the friars demanded to follow without any modification. The first Bull issued by the Pope upon the subject, only four years after St. Francis' death – *Quo elongato a saeculo* – attempted a reasonable compromise. He declared that though the friars should own no property, either in common or particular, they might have the *use* of books, tools, etc. while those who wished to give alms to the Order might do so through a third person, a trustee, who would administer this money for the community's needs. This solution was welcomed by many of the laxer friars, but the extremists bitterly resented the denial of St. Francis' testament, declaring that the Bull was a betrayal of his intention – and even, they said, of the will of Christ himself.

So St. Francis' family was divided into two. The Conventuals grew in numbers and power – but it was the fanatical Zealots or Spirituals who claimed that they carried out St. Francis' will. Even the clothing of the two branches was different – the Conventuals wearing sandals and the long black habit which made people call them *frati corbi* (brothers crow), the Spirituals going barefoot, in a short ash-coloured habit, which was often both dirty and ragged. Their aspiration, in the words of their leader, Angelo Clareno, was "To live according to the Cross, and to bear the naked Cross after Him, and for ever to desire the possession of nothing under the sky save Christ Jesus Himself – poor, humble, crucified for men."[8]

To say that the two branches of the Order quarrelled with each other, is a considerable understatement, and this is not the place for the full story to be told, but at least a short account of it is necessary, to understand the part which Bernardino played later on in the reform of the Observants. The Spirituals had at first a leader of great ability and saintliness in Fra Pietro Giovanni Olivi of Languedoc and their position was also strengthened by the Bull *Exiit qui seminat* (August 14, 1279) of Pope Nicholas III, interpreting the Rule in a much stricter sense than his predecessor had done. Olivi and his followers, however, insisted not only on the total renunciation of property, but also on the restriction of the *use* of such necessities as food and clothing to the bare minimum required to keep alive – for had not St. Francis himself declared that to accept more than what was necessary was as bad as to steal? When he accepted a cloak, he took it only "as a loan, until we come upon someone poorer than we." "I have never been a thief," he said, "with regard to alms.... Always I have taken less than I needed, lest I should defraud some poor man of his share."[9] Such an attitude admitted of no compromise, and the words *usus pauper* became a summary of the Spirituals' way of life.

Then, in 1290, a very odd event occurred: the election to the papal throne of a man who was neither a statesman nor a theologian, but was simply considered a saint – a very old hermit from the Abruzzi called Pietro da Morrone, who took the name of Celestine V. At once the Spirituals took heart again and turned to Celestine for protection, and he not only granted it but added that – as their life was precisely the one that he himself had always desired to lead – he would give them permission to follow it forever, absolved from obedience to the head of their Order, and directly under his own authority. Henceforth, he said, they would no longer use the name of Friars Minor, but would be called the "Poor Hermits of Pope Celestine."

A new era for the Spirituals might perhaps have begun. But when, only five months later, Pope Celestine made his *gran rifiuto*,[10] renouncing the office for which he considered himself unfit and returning to his bare hermit's cell, his successor, Boniface VIII, declared his decrees to be null and void, and the Poor Hermits were again adrift.

Their leader in Italy was now Angelo Clareno, a true spiritual descendant of St. Francis. More than once condemned for heresy, he suffered, owing to his unswerving devotion to the cause of "holy poverty," long periods of imprisonment and exile and even spent some years (which he himself said he hated "more than any other punishment")[11] at the Papal Court in Avignon, to further the Spirituals' cause. But he saw his work undone by the extremists of his own branch, popularly known as *Fraticelli*,[12] who identified themselves with the Ghibelline party, preaching in and out of season that the temporal power should be in the Emperor's hands alone, and the spiritual power be awarded to a new Pope of their own election – a *papa angelico*, of whom, they claimed, St. Francis had been the forerunner. It is hardly surprising that the Church should have determined at all costs to suppress these doctrines and those who held them. On December 30, 1317, Pope John XXII issued at Avignon

209

the Bull *Sancta Romana*, which included the following clause: "Certain seculars commonly called *Fraticelli*, *Bizocchi*, *Beguins* or the like . . . have the impudence to wear a religious habit, call themselves children of St. Francis, and please themselves by observing his rule literally, although they are not authorized by either the Church or their Founder. They claim that they were formally authorized by Celestine V of saintly memory, but they offer no proof, and even if they did it would be worthless."[13]

So the *Fraticelli* were cast out of the Church. Four of them, who refused to make their submission, were condemned to be burned in Avignon, and all over Southern France their communities were broken up. But in Italy they still persisted – some of them, under the leadership of Angelo Clareno, leading austere and visionary lives in lonely mountain hermitages, some, even as late as the end of the fourteenth century, dying at the stake for their beliefs. But others became pure vagrants, bringing the whole sect into disrepute by their unruly behaviour, their ragged appearance, and the fanatical intolerance of their opinions.

Many of them, moreover, were responsible for spreading the Messianic prophecies of a Second Coming and of the dawn of a new "kingdom of the spirit" first proclaimed by the visionary abbot of Calabria, Gioacchino da Fiore, nearly two hundred years before, and subsequently elaborated by his Franciscan commentators, especially Fra Gerardo da Borgo San Donnino, in a work called *The Everlasting Gospel*.[14] These prophecies divided the history of the world into three epochs: the first, from Adam to Christ, had been the reign of the Father, the era of Justice; the second, the reign of the Son, was the era of Grace; the third, which was about to dawn, would be the reign of the Holy Ghost. The first era had been one of fear, the second of faith, the third would be one of charity, in which mankind, inspired by the Holy Ghost, would walk in freedom.

The duration of each epoch was estimated at forty-two generations, each of thirty years, and the third had been due to dawn, with the coming of the Messiah, in 1260.[15] The great year came and went, but long afterwards, in Fra Bernardino's time, some of the *Fraticelli* – in the austere mountain hermitages to which the persecution of the Conventuals and their own intransigence had driven them – were still comforting themselves for the corruption of the Church and of their Order by the belief that a new kingdom of the spirit was near at hand.

Moreover, under the influence of these prophecies, other religious sects had also sprung up, still less amenable to the Church's authority, and using, as a justification for their fanaticism and lawlessness, Gioacchino's phrase, "Where the Lord's spirit is, there is liberty."[16]

These had left their spiritual seed behind them. When, in 1417, Fra Bernardino first went to preach in Piedmont, he found there a Dominican preacher, Manfredi of Vercelli, who – although orthodox in all other respects – was so firmly convinced of the imminence of a Second Coming as to teach his followers that the ordinary ties of human society were no longer binding. It was lawful, he said, even for husbands and wives to desert each other, if the inspiration of the Holy Ghost told either partner that this course was necessary for his or her salvation. "If you like not your husband," Fra Bernardino dryly commented "– so say those who say that Antichrist is born – begin to pray, and the Holy Ghost will tell you whether to stay with him or leave him." One lady indeed, in Castelnuovo Scrivia, who had heard Manfredi preach, came to Bernardino's companion, Fra Vincenzo, for further advice, asking whether she might indeed leave her husband to save her soul before the coming of Antichrist – whereupon Fra Bernardino promptly brought the matter to the attention of the Dominican Inquisitor in Alessandria.[17]

In another Piedmontese valley he discovered another sect, the

Nicolaiti – so called after the early deacon Nicholas, who, it was said, had left his wife, telling her that she was now free to give herself to anyone she pleased – and their behaviour pleased him still less. They, too, he said, lived in sexual promiscuity – men and women, "*tutto un brodetto*" (all one soup) – and he added, with a credulousness only too similar to that which he criticized in others, that they also practised a rite called "*del barilotto*" (of the little barrel) which consisted in placing in a wine-barrel a powder made of the bones of a murdered baby, and then handing the barrel round for each member to drink. One is irresistibly reminded of the scandalous tales told in pagan Rome about the rites of the Early Christians. We know little about the *Nicolaiti*, but certainly Fra Manfredi – according to both St. Antoninus of Florence and Pope Martin V, who ordered a thorough investigation into this preacher's doctrines and manner of life – was both a learned and a God-fearing man (*peritus et timens Deum*) whose disciples led lives of virtue, poverty and humility, and whose only fault lay in too great a faith in his own visions. But Fra Bernardino maintained that it was precisely credulousness such as this that brought discredit upon the religious orders as a whole, and fostered the rise of new false prophets. And he told his congregation about a wild friar who, in 1412, had suddenly appeared out of the woods near Fermo in the Marches at the head of a large company of men and women, whom he ordered to strip themselves naked, promising to lead them to Jerusalem dryshod, for the earth would open at his bidding. "And when this story reached the ears of Messer Ludovico, the Seigneur of Fermo, he cast them all into prison."[18]

Is is hardly surprising that Fra Bernardino should have looked with a sardonic eye at incidents such as these, and should have felt inclined to dismiss all the Messianic prophecies of his day, whatever their origin, as "Pentecostal smoke." "We have been stuffed with predictions," he cried, "until we are sick, such as those about the coming of Antichrist and of the Day of Judgement, to which some sober and decent men have given more belief than they should.[19] Ever since I was a little boy I have heard of the birth of Antichrist – what am I saying? Already in the time of the Apostles it was said that he was born, and also in that of St. Bernard . . . and a short time ago it was firmly believed. . . ."[20] And he added elsewhere that "Even if such predictions were true and authentic, God's servants might find many matters in which they could be engaged more fruitfully."[21]

There was, indeed, no lack of fruitful work for God's servants to perform. The little community of Brogliano, of which we spoke at the beginning of this chapter, had flourished, avoiding both the Pope's censure and the resentment of the Conventuals – who had, indeed, some cause for irritation, since ten of their convents rapidly went over to the strict Observance, including three of those which had been best loved by their founder: Le Carceri above Assisi, Greccio, where on Christmas Eve St. Francis had made the first Crib with living figures in a stable, and Fonte Colombo, where he had received, in a vision, his Rule. Moreover, during one of the violent conflicts between the lax Conventuals and the fanatical *Fraticelli* in Perugia, Paoluccio de' Trinci had been called upon as a mediator, with such success that he had been rewarded with the gift of another fine convent, that of Monteripido, outside Perugia. In 1373 Pope Gregory XI had signified to the friars of Brogliano his full approval of their manner of life, and soon afterwards, Paoluccio had been appointed Commissioner General over the convents reformed by him and had sent his disciples, Giovanni da Stroncone and Antonio da Monteleone, to spread the work in Tuscany. At the time of his death, in 1393, twenty-three Conventual communities had gone over to the Observants.

The essence of this revival of the Franciscan Rule was moderation. The men who visited Brogliano from other communities, returned home to their own convents "to remove abuses by their example and gradually introduce a spiritual renewal . . . in so gentle a manner, without forcing themselves or rendering themselves singular in the cloth, colour or fashion of their habit, that no disturbance arose within the Order on their account."[22]

One can hardly doubt that this is the kind of reform that St. Francis himself, the peacemaker, would have approved – and it was in this spirit that Fra Bernardino, too, set to work. In 1416 or 1417 he was transferred to the convent of Fiesole, which had also been donated recently to the Observants, and from there he set forth, as has been told, for his first years of preaching in Northern Italy. There – while the number of the Observant convents in Tuscany and Umbria was increasing to thirty-two and Pope Martin V had given permission for new communities to be founded in Morocco, Russia and the Levant – Fra Bernardino was founding others in Northern Italy and, after his return to Tuscany, in Florence and Pisa. In 1421 he was nominated Vicar of the Observants of Tuscany and Umbria and seventeen years later, in 1438 – to his own great dismay – he was appointed by the Minister General of the Franciscan Order as Vicar General of all the convents of the Observance in Italy.

Much of his time was now spent at La Capriola; it was there, in his bare cell, that most of his sermons were set down, and that he administered the convents over which he ruled. His work as a reformer of the Observants can never have aroused in him the same "delight" that he felt in his mission as a preacher, yet in the history of the Franciscan Order it plays quite as important a part. The Minister General's letter of appointment, which was approved by a Bull of the Pope's, referred to Fra Bernardino's "praiseworthy life, zeal for the Order and for justice, pleasant sociability, outstanding discretion, prudent circumspection and great experience," and gave him full authority to reform the communities of the Order and its individual members, with power "to visit, call, summon, admonish, correct, punish, deprive of office and suspend," whenever he might see fit.[23] All this he faithfully carried out. His object was to renew, not the letter of St. Francis' Rule, but the spirit – adapting it to the needs of his own time.

With regard to the much vexed question of poverty, he showed himself far less extreme than the fanatical Spirituals of the past – since he always maintained that it was not poverty itself that was a virtue, but the disregard of riches. He therefore permitted the friars the "moderate use" of such worldly goods as had been bestowed upon them, and even to live in the fine, well-furnished buildings which had come to them, when some of the Conventuals had passed over to their branch.[24] In such matters he was, as always, a realist. "Three things are needful," he said, "for the spiritual life: one within you, one beside you and one without. Within, your own good will is needful; beside you, good company, for he who falls down cannot get up alone. And the third need, externally, is a suitable place – for one cannot meditate in the Mercato Nuovo!"[25] He was lenient, too, in the matter of clothing, especially with the older friars, or those who had been appointed to especially cold places, permitting them to wear sandals or clogs and "such clothing as you need . . . according to discretion"; and he did not forbid meat in the refectory (except of course on fast-days), nor wine "tempered with water." But such bodily necessities were a very different matter from the love of pomp and show for its own sake, and he sternly reproved those friars who – to obtain some fine vessels for the Church – would go about begging "for old rings and broken silver to make chalices and crosses," saying that they were no sons of his. "If any of them comes your way," he told his congregation, "do not believe him. . . . By the ring of their coins you will know if they are my disciples or not!"[26]

He vehemently expressed his disapproval, moreover, of the ac-

ceptance of any public office by his friars, even the post of treasurer of the City Council, which since the early Middle Ages had
generally been held by a Religious. "You believe," he said, "that
your lay treasurers of the Commune stole from it, and therefore
want the friars to do this. But do friars never steal? . . . What do
you think a Religious does, when he is made treasurer? All night
he dreams of counting money, and sometimes in his sleep he says,
four, six, eight, and goes on counting. I believe that I myself, if I
were given that office, would steal more than any other man! . . .
And is it right that, after this, he should say Mass?"[27]

The life in the communities into which Fra Bernardino's direct
influence had penetrated must have had, for all its austerity, a great
appeal. It was penurious, but it had about it that atmosphere of
freedom and cheerfulness which St. Francis, too, had bestowed on
those who lived with him. We even find Pope Eugenius granting
the friars permission to take off their habit, not only in order to
wash or patch it, but also to fish.[28] And there always seems to have
been a lot of talk and story-telling and of "pleasant sociability." At
any table at which Fra Bernardino sat – even during the painful
journeys of his last years, when he was often too ill to eat – the food
was flavoured with laughter.

Even when he described the hardships that he expected his friars
to bear, he did so gaily and half-ironically, calling the life that he
imposed on them (and on himself) "the joyous life of the Friars
Minor," and pointing out all the advantages that their very privations brought to them. "The Rule of the friars is this, to go barefoot. . . . Certainly this is a delight: in the winter you acquire merit,
and in the summer you are cool. . . . You must have no money; and
this is a pleasure, for the man who has no money, has also no cares.
I never have had any since the day I became a friar – and there is
not one of you seculars here, who has spent a single day without
tormenting himself about collecting money and possessions. . . . You

must sleep in your clothes, and this is a luxury. Shall I show you how? . . . In winter, if you undress, you must get out of warm clothing into the cold; and when you get up, you get out of the warm into the cold. I myself feel all broken when I sleep in a bed – as sometimes I must do, out of complaisance to my host. . . . The friars must go begging; and this is a greedy morsel – for you can get every kind of bread. If you like it fresh, you get it, and also if you like it well baked or too little baked. And so with wine of every kind – rough or heavy – or sometimes gone sour . . . and your only labour is to go and fetch it!"

He added – and one feels that he was speaking from his own experience – that there is only one thing that is not easy: the suppression of one's own personality. "One must *appallottolarsi*" – roll oneself up into a ball – "like a beetle's little ball of dung, which rolls now this way and now that. If you are with a proud man, you must become humble; if with a melancholy one, you must be gay. Always, if you see the scales weighed down on one side, put your weight on to the other, to make it even – and this from obedience. You must bear with everyone, as others must bear with you – for we are not alike. Some eat more, some less; some can fast and others cannot; one is apt at contemplation and another not, one at study and another not. . . . And all must be equal. . . . Religion [by which he meant, a religious Rule] is like a river, in which there are many stones: the stream bears them on."[29]

There was one field, however, in which reform was urgent: the gross ignorance of many of the friars. In this matter Fra Bernardino was entirely of the opinion of St. Jerome. "Holy rusticity," he quoted, "benefits itself alone," and he issued a decree depriving all unlettered friars of the right to hear confessions and to give absolution, and instituted a course of scholastic theology and canon law in the convent of Monteripido, beginning the lectures himself with a course on ecclesiastical censures.[30] Many of his hearers were then horrified to discover for the first time in how many ways excommunication might be deserved, and began to be tormented by scruples as to whether they had not sometimes given absolution wrongly – so that the matter had to be taken before the Pope himself (Eugenius IV), who very practically decided that the absolutions given in the past were valid, but ordered the establishment of other schools for the instruction of priests and friars in canon law.[31] But meanwhile the more ignorant friars – deprived of the right of confession and bewildered by all the complicated ideas that were being introduced to them – violently protested, telling Fra Bernardino that he was going against the will of their founder, who had always found room among his disciples for simple, unlettered men, and indeed had preferred to keep them so.[32] Their Vicar, however, firmly replied that the times had changed. "Our Father St. Francis, seeing mature men of coarse intellect coming into the Order, ordained in his Rule that the unlettered should not try to learn, because he saw them more likely to fall into danger, than to acquire knowledge. But our Fra Bonaventura . . . in reply to a friend who had said that the friars were not to study, said that this was meant by St. Francis for men who were not fit to learn, but not for the young who were able to do so. Those who are able to learn and to do honour to the Church of God and to our Order, are following God's Will."[33]

This resolute attack on unlettered monasticism – coming at a moment when, in popular opinion, the word "friar" was all too often coupled with the adjectives "ignorant" or "corrupt," was based on Fra Bernardino's deep conviction that many of the worst ills of his time were caused by sheer ignorance.

How necessary it was for the priests and friars of his day, whom Wadding describes as "*viri simpli, abiecti, illiterati,*" to learn a little more about the doctrines they were supposed to teach, is often illustrated in his sermons. He described the venal priests, "who sell their Masses for a golden florin," and the unlettered, "who on Christmas morning say the Whitsunday Mass or that of the Resurrection or of All Saints' Day.... And those Masses are called the Masses of ignorance."[34] And he told the story of a Tuscan priest who reproved one of his fellows for saying "*Hoc est corpus meum*," saying that the right words were "*Hoc est corpusso meusso*" – whereupon a third priest, whose opinion they asked, replied that he himself got out of the difficulty by merely saying, at the moment of the Elevation, a Hail Mary![35]

Stories such as these explain the violent attacks upon the ignorance and corruption of both the clergy and the monastic orders which had become a commonplace, not only among those humanists who preferred Stoicism or Epicureanism to Christianity, but also among many devout, but shocked and bewildered believers. Such attacks were not rare even in the pulpit – a fact which Fra Bernardino deplored, saying that this was an easy, but dangerous, device to gain a congregation's favour. "If, during the sermon," he remarked, "the people are bored or hot or cold, it is enough for the preacher to say a word against the priests and prelates for the sleepy to wake up and the bored to be cheered.... Even hunger and thirst are forgotten. And the consequence of this abuse is this – that the greatest sinners, comparing themselves to the prelates, feel themselves to be just and holy!"[36]

He told his friars that any reproof to a Religious must be given not from the pulpit, but in private – "not from fear, but to avoid scandal: let it be between him and you." And he added, with his customary realism, that it was better to have poor priests than none at all. "If all the bad ones were turned out, only a few good ones would remain. Take what is good from them – the Sacraments and their dignity – and leave the bad. God will provide."[37]

To sceptical laymen, however, the monastic orders were an even easier target than the clergy, and, in particular, the Observants –

partly no doubt on account of their external resemblance to the fanatical *Fraticelli*, and partly because of the marked favour which Eugenius IV was showing to them. Moreover, they were so unfortunate as to incur the personal dislike of a scholar whose biting tongue was singularly merciless, even towards his friends: the humanist Poggio Bracciolini. His grievance originated in a gift from Carlo de' Ricasoli to Fra Bernardino, for a convent, of a villa in the Valdarno which Poggio had coveted himself and in which he had often entertained his literary friends. This villa he now saw occupied by barefoot, unlettered friars, who even cut down the charming wood beside it. Plato, he sourly remarked, had chosen for his Academy an unhealthy spot, so that the soul should grow stronger as the body became weaker, but the friars preferred to follow Christ "in voluptuous and pleasant places, which make the heart glad." "They call themselves Mendicants," he said elsewhere, "although they seem to be more likely to bring other men down to the beggar's staff.... The greater part of those who call themselves Minorites and attribute to themselves the title of Observants, consist of rough peasants and venal poltroons, whose interest lies not in the sanctity of their life but in the avoidance of work." And he went on to say that in their sermons these friars did not seek to save souls, but only to gain applause from the foolish crowds who came to them for entertainment – most of them resembling monkeys, rather than preachers.[38] "It is not enough," he wrote, in a *Dialogue on Hypocrisy*, "that they [the friars] should be shut away in a cloister, dressed in coarse garments and doing the public no harm; I ask of what use they are to the faith or what advantage they bring to the people. I don't know what they do, except to sing like cicadas, and they seem to me too well paid for this exercise of their lungs. They exalt their labours as if they were those of Hercules, because they get up in the night to sing God's praises. Certainly, it is a great merit to get up and sing psalms – but what would they say if they had to get up and plough, often barefoot and ill-dressed, in the rain and wind?"[39]

And indeed that the peasants would sometimes grumble to this effect, is told us by Fra Bernardino himself. "'We work all day,' they say, 'with the hoe and spade, in cold, heat, wind, snow, hail, storms; we run short all the year and can never put anything away, for when we have finished toiling, we must buy again at great cost the bread and wine we have grown.... You rest all day; sometimes you read and sometimes you write. When you are hot, you sit in a cool place; when it is cold, by the fire.... If you want bread, you can have it fresh every day, and the same with wine and everything you need.'" Fra Bernardino, as usual, replied with a story – ("one that is not written in St. Gregory's *Dialogues*, for one can some-times tell stories which are not written down"). A peasant, he said, who had gone to one of his convents with these complaints, had been invited by the Superior to stay there for eight days as a guest and share the friars' life. "That evening he arrived in the convent and they gave him his supper and took him to sleep, fully dressed, on a straw pallet with only a coarse blanket over it, and perhaps it was full of fleas. At midnight they went to knock at his door. 'Get up for Matins, brother, get up.' He got up and went to church with them and the Superior gave him a rosary, saying, 'You don't know the Office, but you shall stay here and say the Lord's Prayer so long as we are saying Matins. When we sit down, you sit down, and as we stand up, you stand up, too.' ... The man was not accustomed to stay awake and he began to nod. 'Sit up, brother, sit up, don't go to sleep!' ... After a while, he leant back, and the rosary fell out of his hand. And the friar, 'Pick it up.' In short... after he had been woken up several times, he said, 'Do you do this every night?... By the Gospels, I will have no more of it!' And so, in one night he had enough of the fine life we lead and getting up, said, 'Open the door, I want to go away!'"[40]

It was also perhaps partly in answer to attacks like Poggio's that Fra Bernardino defended, in another sermon, the monks and nuns belonging to cloistered orders or living in remote hermitages, who spent their days not in good works, but in prayer. "Many ignorant men . . . say that they are good for no one but themselves, but I say that these prayers are very acceptable to God. . . . Woe unto you, ye laymen, if you had no one to pray to God for you! . . . One of the Lord's Prayers they say is worth more than all the alms you give them."[41] Nevertheless it is plain that his own inclinations lay strongly in the direction of community life, and – perhaps remembering the aberrations of some of the *Fraticelli*, who had come very close to madness in their mountain hermitages – he was careful to warn his friars of the possible consequences of too much loneliness for those who had had no previous spiritual discipline. "To take the path of solitude is a great danger, unless you have experience."

Fra Bernardino's reforms were not limited to the communities of the Observants: they also extended to some women's convents, in particular one near Milan, in which the nuns, though calling themselves Poor Clares, were following the Rule of the Augustinians and whom he brought back to that of their foundress, and some other communities without any Rule, whose members were also persuaded to accept that of St. Clare. And he also actively encouraged the development, both among men and women, of the Third Order – saying that, if he had still been a layman, he would have joined it himself.[42]

Humility – to make oneself small, common, almost invisible – that was the keyword of his teaching and his life – to place oneself wholly, unquestioningly, in the hands of God. "I would be capable of committing every evil sin," he said of himself, "if the Lord God did not hold me beneath His holy hand."[43] To the friar who asked him for a rule of life, he answered with a single word: "*Abbasso, abbasso*" (down, down), and when Fra Alberto was riding on a fine

222

horse to Florence on his way back from a mission in the Levant, dressed in the fine robes of a Nuncio and followed by the Jacobite abbot of St. Anthony in Egypt and his priests, whom he had persuaded to make their submission to the Pope, Fra Bernardino placed his little donkey across his path. "Fra Alberto, Fra Alberto," he cried, "lower your eyes! Remember death!"[44] Hastily Fra Alberto dismounted and tried to persuade his old Superior to change places with him, while he mounted instead on Fra Bernardino's donkey. But this of course his Vicar would not allow, and bade him continue his journey as he was. The outer trappings were entirely fitting for the Apostolic Nuncio: it was the heart that must keep its humility.

Three times Fra Bernardino was offered, and refused, a Bishop's mitre – once in Ferrara, once in Urbino and, most tempting of all, by his own fellow-citizens. In 1427 the Bishopric of Siena had become vacant, since the previous Bishop, Cardinal Casini, had been transferred to Grosseto, and the Signoria of Siena had implored the Pope to send them a prelate who was "our own citizen, and faithful to our government," also prepared to reside in Siena. The Pope told them to suggest their own candidate and out of nine names proposed by the *Signoria* to the People's Council, Fra Bernardino was unanimously elected, as being "among all our citizens, the one most distinguished for his learning, life, doctrine and honesty." This news was at once taken by an envoy to the Pope. Cardinal Casini, too, was asked to exert his influence, and indeed, on June 4, 1427, Fra Bernardino's nomination took place – but since the Sienese feared he would be reluctant, they thought it advisable to dispatch to Rome yet another envoy to tell him that his appointment was plainly due to the inspiration of the Holy Ghost, "for many men tried to become Bishop, and only he, who did not attempt it, was nominated by our whole people, in complete agreement.... And therefore let him accept, in reverence for God's will and for the comfort and welfare of our city."[45] Fra Bernardino, however, was in no doubt at all as to where his real duty lay: he was a preacher, and a preacher he would remain. "For many years now," he said, "I have toiled at preaching and have renounced every other occupation . . . for I well know that if I tried to do many things, I would do none of them well."[46] And to Michele Bennini – another friend who tried to persuade him – he added: "If ever you see me with another habit than that of St. Francis on my back, say that this is not Fra Bernardino."[47]

The story is told that, on this occasion, he thought he would test the humility of a lay-brother, the gardener of Santa Maria in Ara-coeli in Rome, where he was staying, by telling him that the Sienese wished to make him their Bishop. "Shall I accept?" "No," replied Fra Angeluccio, adding that if he did he would deprive the people of his sermons and himself of much glory in God's eyes. – "But what if the Milanese wanted me for Archbishop? Would you not change your mind?" – "I would not," said Fra Angeluccio. – "But suppose that they make me a Patriarch?" Still the friar held out. "I see," he said, "that your head has been turned by these honours." Then at last, "But suppose the Pope made me a Cardinal!" This at last was too much for Fra Angeluccio. "There is no doubt about the answer to that. Take off your friar's cord, Father, and do what you must." Whereupon Fra Bernardino – somewhat unfairly – stopped joking and scolded the poor man severely for his foolish-ness.[48]

Other people, too, though less naïve than Fra Angeluccio, could scarcely believe that Fra Bernardino would be able to resist so great an honour as the Bishopric of his own city. Even Fra Ambrogio Traversari, who should have known him better, wrote imploring him not to give in. But indeed it is plain that he was not even tempted. When he got back to Siena and began to preach again, he told his fellow-citizens that he had merely stayed on in Rome to make sure that he was not "ensnared." "'Save yourself first!' I said."

xxvii. Il Convento dell'Osservanza.

XXVIII. The Refusal of three Mitres: *Sforza Book of Hours.*

And he added that, had he come back to them as their Bishop, as they had wished, he would never have been able to speak freely to them again. "My mouth would have been half shut – look, like this!"[49] And he pursed his thin lips still tighter together, and laughed.

During all this time, in spite of his heavy administrative duties, Fra Bernardino never ceased to pursue his real calling as a preacher. In the summer of 1438, a few months after his appointment as Vicar General, he went to preach in Aquila (where his congregation saw a bright star suddenly appear over his head) and in September, to Perugia. In 1440, he went to Rome at the Pope's request, to preach in Santa Maria Nuova in honour of Santa Francesca Romana, and then proceeded to Arezzo to destroy the Fonte Tecta. In 1441 he was in Florence, Assisi and Perugia, where he preached for six days in the fine new marble pulpit which had been erected for him in the Cathedral square, and early in the following spring he was again in Lombardy.[50]

His duties as Vicar General, however, were weighing upon him more and more heavily, not only owing to his increasing years and failing health, but because of his distress at the incurable factiousness of his brethren. For some time the old dissensions between the Conventuals and Observants had been smouldering again, and now they seemed likely to burst into flame.

It was, perhaps, not surprising. So long as the reformed Observants had been few and obscure, the Conventuals had borne with them, but now they were not only spreading all over Italy, but had absorbed some of the finest Conventual communities, while the Pope made no secret of his preference for their Rule. "As far as he could," says Vespasiano da Bisticci, "he made the Conventuals accept the Observants' Rule," and he handed over to the latter both the convent of La Verna and that of Santa Maria in Aracoeli in Rome, as well as the Franciscan communities in Palestine.[51] It was the Observant Giovanni da Capistrano whom the Pope sent on a mission to Constantinople, and Alberto da Sarteano to the Holy Land. All this the Conventuals found very hard to bear. The obvious measure, of course, would have been the one for which Fra Bernardino, as a man of peace, had always hoped – the unification of both branches of the Order – but his usual clearsightedness also enabled him to realize that this was not yet possible. Such an attempt had already been made in 1430, under Pope Martin V, when a new Constitution had been drawn up at a General Chapter in Assisi, which had restored, with certain modifications, St. Francis' original Rule for both branches and had placed all the Franciscan convents, whether in Italy or abroad, under the rule of a single Minister General. This new Rule (which had been drawn up chiefly by Fra Giovanni da Capistrano) was received with enthusiasm, but it soon faded, and within two years the Conventuals and Observants were again at odds with each other, as they had always been. In 1440, indeed, Father Nicholas of Osimo (who had become the Vicar of the Observants in Southern Italy) tried to persuade the Pope to exempt his brethren from even the nominal control of the Conventual Provincial – a measure of which Fra Bernardino openly disapproved. So much, indeed, did he deplore any step which might still further widen the breach, that he even cast into prison in Campania a lay-brother called Constantine, for agitating once more in favour of the complete separation of the two branches.[52] Fra Bernardino's own friars began to grumble, and the Conventuals continued, as before, to harass their brothers in Christ with a hundred pin-pricks.

Finally, thoroughly disheartened, Fra Bernardino attempted to resign, and it was only a personal appeal from Pope Eugenius, expressed "with the affection of [the Pope's] whole heart," that caused him, in the spirit of obedience, to persevere. He did however, call in, with the Pope's permission, Giovanni da Capistrano as his assistant, and with him confronted a new crisis. The Minister General of the Franciscans, Guglielmo da Casale, who had done all he could to keep the peace, had recently died and in 1442 a General Chapter was convoked in Padua, not only to elect his successor, but to attempt, once again, to achieve the union of the two branches – and now, for the first time, the most likely candidate for the post was not a Conventual, but an Observant, Fra Bernardino's own disciple Fra Alberto da Sarteano.

This plan, which had the Pope's approval, seemed to Fra Bernardino to be predestined to failure – and so indeed it proved. At the Chapter meeting the Conventuals, who considered that their hand was being forced, started a free fight in which – crying "freedom! freedom!" – they tore from Fra Alberto's hand the Bull authorizing him to preside, and succeeded in expelling ("with hands and sticks") both him and his supporters from the meeting-place.[53] In the end Fra Bernardino was able, by his own quiet impartiality, to restore a semblance of order, but he wisely gave his vote to the Conventual candidate, Fra Antonio Rusconi (who was indeed elected) – and was therefore considered something of a traitor by his own friars. A few months later the Pope himself reluctantly confirmed the decree, and appointed – according to a plan drawn up by Giovanni da Capistrano – two separate Vicars for the Observants – one for the region called *Cismontana* (which included Italy, Austria, Hungary, Poland and the Balkans) and the other, the *Ultramontana*, for the rest of Europe.

By this time, however, Fra Bernardino had at last succeeded in persuading the Pope to accept his resignation, and to appoint Fra Alberto da Sarteano in his stead. During his lifetime – of which only two more years remained – he had seen the convents of the Observants increase from twenty-three to over two hundred, and their members from 130 to over 4000.[54] Some of this achievement was undoubtedly due to the zeal and skill of his followers – Giovanni da Capistrano, Alberto da Sarteano and Giacomo della Marca – men who possessed the qualities of which statesmen and nuncios are made. But no one can doubt that the driving force which brought the Observant movement to life again, was Fra Bernardino's own. His moderation, his natural sense of balance, his personal humility and warm humanity, though they could not reconcile the Conventuals and the Observants completely (a task perhaps beyond human reach), did at least persuade them to live side by side, and enabled St. Francis' Rule to be observed again within the framework of the Church, while after Fra Bernardino's death his followers – in particular Giovanni da Capistrano and Alberto da Sarteano – carried on his mission, until there was hardly a Catholic country which the Observants had not reached. Thus Fra Bernardino's work – which had brought so much distress and so poignant a sense of failure to himself – regenerated not only one branch of the Franciscans, but the whole Order. In the words of a modern biographer: "The Conventuals had been too worldly, the Spirituals too ascetic; the first had neglected God for man, the second, man for God. San Bernardino avoided both extremes."[55] Above all, he rekindled the fire that can only be lit by the pure in heart. It was St. Francis' own spirit that he renewed.

X. THE LAST JOURNEY

Povertade muore in pace.
JACOPONE DA TODI*

THE last stage of Fra Bernardino's life had now begun. The appointment of Fra Alberto da Sarteano, in the summer of 1424, as his successor as Vicar General of the Observants allowed him to throw off all administrative cares and to return to his own true vocation. It even seemed as if he might allow himself a little rest at La Capriola – "to study and meditate, and to prepare for Heaven" – but only a few months later a great sorrow came to him: the sudden death of his closest friend, Fra Vincenzo da Siena, who had been his companion in all his travels for more than twenty-two years. "Nought but death could have parted him and me."

During the first years of his preaching, Fra Bernardino had had a very irritating companion, a friar who would come up to him just as he was leaving the pulpit, to point out the things that he might have said more effectively. "And though," according to one biographer, "this distressed him when he was tired by preaching, yet he put up with this companion most patiently for twelve years."[1]

Fra Vincenzo was a very different sort of man. "We always took pleasure," said Fra Bernardino, "in each other's company." He became, according to Wadding, the great preacher's "intimate, faithful partner, the sharer of all his secrets" – a man of whom he himself spoke as Dante did of Virgil: "*Tu magister meus, tu doctor meus, tu ductor et rector meus*"[2] – "you were my teacher, doctor, guide and ruler . . . first my friend, and then my brother in religion." It was Fra Vincenzo who took upon himself all the cares of food and lodging on their travels, so that Fra Bernardino might be free for meditation and for a few hours' rest, "for in his humility he believed that my sleep would bear greater fruits than his." In the panegyric

229

which Fra Bernardino pronounced upon him after his death, he spoke not only of his friend's humility and faithfulness, but of how much he had always depended on his strength and steadiness of purpose. "I was weak and often seriously ill, and he always encouraged and sustained me. I was afraid, and he comforted me; lazy and negligent of the Lord's Will, and he inspired me; forgetful and improvident, and he admonished me." This was Fra Bernardino's version of their friendship; but we have already described how Fra Vincenzo's own tears upon his deathbed were not caused by any fear of dying, but merely by the fact that his death had come too soon, before he had been able to testify to all the proofs of his companion's saintliness which only he had known. "Had I only survived him by a short time, I would have been relieved from the vow by which he had bound me, and could have revealed things which would have filled the world with admiration and amazement."[3]

Now that he was gone, Fra Bernardino became fully aware of how much he had owed to him. "Where shall I look now for advice when I am uncertain?" he cried. "To whom shall I turn in trouble? Who will bear the burdens and face the dangers? . . . I confess I have had no other teacher in the Order but you, in the doctrine of God's word. . . . You came to my help in all things, more than any other man: in small things and great, in public matters and private, within and without." And, turning to his fellow-friars, he added: "You who knew him, know that I speak the truth."[4]

For a little while longer he remained at La Capriola, mourning his friend – "my right hand, light of my eyes, my very tongue" – and still unable to realize fully that he had gone. "When anything new occurs, I look for Fra Vincenzo, and he is not there." Then, in response to a pressing invitation from the Duke of Milan, he gathered up his courage and set forth to give a last course of sermons in Northern Italy.

He himself has left us a portrait of himself at that time, after forty years of preaching, privations, and travel. "When a man . . . approaches his sixtieth year, he begins to become very small and bent; his eyes become rheumy and heavy-lidded; he walks with his head bent down towards the ground; he becomes deaf and sees less well; he has lost his teeth."[5] Fra Bernardino, indeed, had lost every tooth but one, which has been described as dangling in his mouth "like a little bell," and he had been suffering for years from gravel, dysentery, inflamed kidneys and piles, as well as from gout and podagra, the latter probably caused by his meagre diet.[6] "And though each of these infirmities, by its very nature, generally makes a man become strange and disagreeable, he was not changed in any respect, but bore them all most patiently.[7]" Even now, when he began to preach, his strength came back to him. He arrived utterly exhausted in Milan, but as soon as he began to speak, he felt the old fire blaze up within him. "Yesterday I was almost dead and today I am alive. I was in such a condition that I thought I could not preach today, and now I feel like a lion."[8]

On the occasion of this visit to Milan he was also acting as the unofficial envoy of Siena, having presumably been chosen for this mission in view of the personal esteem which the Duke of Milan was supposed to feel for him. He was to dispel any suspicions that might have arisen in the Duke's tortuous mind with regard to the loyalty of the Sienese Republic, by asking his advice as to what course Siena should follow "in the new state of affairs that has arisen in these parts from the peacemakings, truces, agreements or quarrels of the Italian rulers and captains, all of which are of great importance and cannot be readily understood, even by those who are very learned and well acquainted with these matters." In short, Fra Bernardino was to attempt to find out what Filippo Maria himself intended to do, and above all, whether he was about to send his troops again – under his *condottiere* Niccolò Piccinino – to fight against his old enemy, Florence, and meanwhile to assure him that "this community is devoted and faithful to his Lordship and can never feel as much trust in anyone as in him." Furthermore, the envoy was to try to discover "what opinion the aforesaid and illustrious Seigneur has of our community and if he still feels towards it the true benevolence that he used to feel," and on his way home again, by way of Florence, he was also to visit the Pope, who was then in Tuscany, and to commend Siena to *his* protection, "as seems opportune to your prudence."⁹ Siena, in fact, was anxious to keep on good terms with both the great powers in Italy, and had chosen for this purpose this man of peace, and, in order that he might be able to send home confidential news safely, provided him with a cypher, containing, in addition to the letters of the alphabet, symbols for the Duke of Milan and the Count of Urbino, for the Pope and the Antipope (Felix V), for the *condottieri* Niccolò Piccinino and Francesco Sforza, and for the Florentines, the Sienese and the Bolognese.

We do not know how this mission was accomplished, but we do know that Fra Bernardino remained on good terms with the Duke, since he pressed him to stay on until February and to give a course of Lenten sermons – which unfortunately he could not do, as he had already promised to preach in Lent in Padua. Meanwhile, however, he had become involved in a disagreeable controversy with a teacher of mathematics, Amedeo de Landris, who in his opinion was teaching heretical doctrines to his pupils and whom, in consequence, the Milanese inquisitor compelled to recant. De Landris, however, secretly succeeded in reaching the Pope's ear with a complaint, in which he craftily refrained from mentioning Fra Bernardino's name, but merely said that he had been slandered "by certain members of the Mendicant Orders," and the Milanese canon to whom the Pope entrusted the consequent investigation fully acquitted the mathematician, declaring that his accuser ought to be obliged to declare his innocence in public. By then Fra Bernardino had left Milan, but the matter arose again after his death, delaying the process of his canonization.[10]

It was early in February when Fra Bernardino, who was going to give some Sermons in Ferrara, went to Padua, where – although he was so exhausted on the way, that he had to be carried on to the barge on which he travelled down the Po for the first part of his journey – he preached no less than forty Lenten sermons, all on a single theme, that of Love. This was the famous course of sermons entitled *Seraphim*. It appears that on each of these forty days the sun shone, except on the one on which the speaker spoke of lust. "Even the weather," he then said, "wishes to fit itself to our subject: it gives us mud, since we are speaking of mud."[11]

On the last day of the course, without attempting to conceal his own emotion, he said, "Now I want to do what a good father does, who is about to leave his children: I want to make my last testament, and to leave you the most precious jewel I possess, the most devout name of Jesus." He taught his congregation a short prayer to Jesus for each day of the week and then, as they fell to their knees in tears, brought his sermon to an end. "I leave unto you the charity which I have preached towards God, towards yourselves and towards your neighbours. I wish you to remember me in your prayers, so that I may always remain united to you and you to me by the chain of our true love for Jesus Christ, and so that we may one day meet again in Paradise."[12]

When he left, a great crowd followed him along the Brenta, many of them in tears at the thought that they would never see him again. "I saw," said an eye-witness, "the famous jurist, Prosdocimo de' Conti, who, shaken by sobs, had taken the saint's hand and would not let it go." So persistent, indeed, were these admirers that after a while his companion, becoming aware of his friend's exhaustion, went ahead and begged the keepers of the bridge across the river to forbid the passage of anyone except Fra Bernardino and his companions.

It was during the friar's stay in Padua that he foretold to his old Venetian friend, Cristoforo Moro, who was then governor of that city, that one day he would be Doge of Venice – a post then held by Francesco Foscari. When Foscari was deposed, some fifteen years later, Moro at once expected to be elected in his stead, and when he was not, he "somewhat lost his faith in the friar"; but a few years later, when the prediction came true, "his devotion to San Bernardino returned to him," and he ordered that his feast-day should be regularly observed in Venice.[13]

Fra Bernardino then went on to Vicenza, Venice and Verona, preaching in each of these cities, and, after another period of severe illness, spoke again in Padua and perhaps in Bologna and Florence. Each of these sermons, he knew, was his farewell to these towns; he would not go back there again. When at last he got home to La Capriola, worn out, he began to revise his sermons, which he wished to leave to his brothers. But he did not rest for long: he had one more task to perform. There was one region of Italy in which, except for a brief visit to Aquila in 1438, he had never preached: the vast and wild kingdom of Naples and Sicily, often called simply "the Kingdom," which was now ruled by a new king, Alfonso of Aragon. He decided that it was his duty to "evangelize" this region, too – vowing to spend whatever time was still left to him in spreading God's word. And perhaps, he may have thought, if he must soon leave this life, his dead body would do as much to bring men to God, as his living words.

First, however, he decided to bid farewell to his own Tuscany. He preached at Massa Marittima, his birthplace, and healed, as we have already told, a Spanish leper who was wandering, a miserable outcast, round the city walls, and from whom he required a promise never to reveal the story so long as he, Fra Bernardino, was still alive.[14] Then he went back to Siena, and there, too, in the Piazza del Duomo, beneath the walls of the Ospedale della Scala in which, forty years before, he had first tended the sick and first felt the call of compassion, he preached a farewell sermon. The text has been lost, but we know that – as in some of his earlier Sienese sermons – he spoke of justice and *il buon governo*, and rejoiced that his city was at last enjoying a period of prosperity and peace. Perhaps, too, he then said to his fellow-citizens words somewhat similar to those that he had said to his friends in Padua a few weeks before, and to the Sienese at the end of his course of sermons in 1427:

"The doctrine I have preached to you is not mine, but what God told me to say.... When I speak to you, I do not know what I am saying, but it is the Holy Ghost that tells me; so you receive nothing from me, but all from God.... I thank the Magnificent *Signori* for all the charity that they have shown to me, and also every other citizen; and I thank you all most humbly for bearing with my words, and for loving me more than I deserve.... I think I shall leave tomorrow, and I do not know if we shall ever see each other again ... but for the love I have felt and feel for you, I beg you to pray to God for me, that He may give me grace to carry out His will." He blessed the kneeling crowd and his last words were those which brought all his sermons to an end: "I leave with you the peace of Messer Domeneddio."[15]

When the day came to go, he could not bear to face any more parting scenes and, having told no one when he was starting, he stole out of the side door of his convent at dawn, in the company of five Sienese friars and a lay-brother from Milan. It was April 30, 1444. His first stop was at Asciano, where the friars in the convent in which he slept, though they were all Conventuals, went over to the Observants after his visit. Lake Trasimene was only a few miles away, and here he spent two days on the little wooded island on which St. Francis, two centuries before, had spent the forty days of Lent in prayer and fasting, and where he now found an old friend, Fra Giacomo della Marca. Fra Giacomo – who later on was also canonized – was one of the most uncompromising and downright of Fra Bernardino's brethren, and also one of the staunchest and most fervent. By birth a poor shepherd of the Marches, the youngest of eighteen children, his vocation had come to him very young, and he had spent his novitiate among the Observants of La Verna – receiving, as he liked to recall, his vestments from Fra Bernardino's own hands and being encouraged by him, when he found preaching a laborious task, with the good advice never to abstain from eating meat, when he felt exhausted![16] Their friendship thus went back a long way. Fra Giacomo had loyally supported Fra Bernardino when he was charged with heresy and in the difficult years when he was Vicar General; they had been together at Fiesole, in the Marches, in Siena, in Bologna and Assisi – and now, at their last meeting, they went fishing together.

From Lake Trasimene Fra Bernardino went on to Perugia – "the city after my own heart" – and here he was met by a large crowd, imploring him to preach to them once again from the fine marble pulpit which they had built for him beside the door of their Cathedral. But the legend tells that though he climbed up its stairs and raised his thin, trembling old hand in benediction, while the congregation fell on their knees, his voice suddenly failed him, and he came down again from the pulpit without having uttered a single word. "He gave, and He has taken away," he was heard to mutter to himself.[17]

After Perugia, he visited Assisi, to pray before the tomb of St. Francis, and from there he went on to Spoleto and Foligno (where he forgot the cord of his habit) and then to the little lake of Piediluco where St. Francis, too, had preached. Here he was laid low by dysentery, but still managed to address his congregation.

236

During the whole of this journey, his weakness had compelled him to give up walking and to ride on his donkey, and when great crowds came out to meet him, he would smile, saying to his brothers, "See, now that I go on horseback I am honoured ten times as much as I used to be when I went on foot – and the difference is all due to my little donkey!" Everywhere his passage was marked by miracles of healing. At Rieti, where a crowd came out to meet him, bearing torches, and a banquet had been prepared for him in the Franciscan convent above the town, all that he could swallow – since he had again been seized by an acute attack of dysentery – was some bread-crumbs soaked in water, but his spirits were so high that his gaiety infected the whole company.[18]

By now his strength was at very low ebb, but his spirit still spurred him on. *Cor eius flammigeratum*, says Fra Giovanni da Capistrano, *quiescere non valebat* (his fiery spirit would not rest). Before reaching Cittaducale, on May 14, he had a long private conversation with one of his brethren, Fra Bartolomeo Mariani,[19] in which it is said that he prophesied some events that afterwards came true, and he also warned his other companions that his last hour was near, but when he reached the little town, he still found the strength to preach to the crowd in the square, exhorting them to pray for him, that he might be forgiven his sins and granted a good death. It was his last sermon.

Yet he was still determined, as he told his brothers, to lay his old bones in Aquila, and the next day he struggled on. At Antrodoco, fifteen miles away, the people again asked for a sermon, but for the first time he was unable to satisfy them. On the rough mountain tracks through the steep, rocky passes of the Abruzzi, he was obliged to dismount and to lie flat on the ground, and once, burning with fever, he asked for water. As he was sitting in the dusk by a spring to which a peasant had led him, he saw – according to the legend – a strange figure approaching: an old man dressed in a white hermit's gown, but wearing on his head a felt hat which had the shape of a triple crown, and on which a silvery dove had rested. It was Pope Celestine himself, the humble Franciscan who had made *il gran rifiuto* to the Papal throne, who had spent his last years in solitude and prayer in a cave of these mountains, and who now appeared in a vision to this other friar, as pure in heart and as unworldly as he himself had been. In silence he embraced Fra Bernardino and gave him his blessing, and then disappeared again into the shadow of the rocks.[20]

Aquila was now only a few miles away, but Fra Bernardino was so exhausted that he could not reach it, and instead spent the night, sleepless, in the little village of San Silvestro. It was on a litter that, on the following morning, May 20, 1444, his companions carried him into the city to the convent of San Francesco and laid him in the cell in which his brother-friar, Fra Giovanni da Capistrano, usually slept. His brothers said to him, "Fra Bernardino, you are already more in the other world than this; set your affairs in order." And he replied, "I am content to do so, and content to die."[21] Then – for the first time – he asked to be dispensed from receiving the visitors who were thronging at the gates, and to be left alone, to prepare himself in peace "for the great voyage that his soul must make."

The story of his last hours has been recorded in a letter written by a certain Fra Giuliano of Milan to his brothers in Lombardy. After receiving Extreme Unction – *la extrema armadura* – and asking for the prayers of all those who were with him, Fra Bernardino sank into motionless silence. "For an hour and a half," wrote Fra Giuliano, "I saw him make no movement, except to breathe – while I, if I have a slight stomach-ache, cannot stay still, and groan." But his next sentence suggests that Fra Bernardino may have had a slight stroke, for he describes him as "being dead on one side, though always fully conscious."[22] He was sixty-four years old, and had spent forty-two of them in the Franciscan Order.

As he felt the end approaching, he plainly showed by his movements that – like St. Francis himself – he wished to die, not on his bed, but on the bare ground. "Twice his companions tried to put back his legs upon the bed, and twice he himself put them back upon the ground." Then his brothers, folding his cloak upon the paved floor of the cell, laid him upon it. A gentle smile lit up his shrunken features: his last wish had been granted, the wish that had inspired all his life – *abbasso, abbasso.* "If this is how men die," wrote Fra Giuliano, "then death is sweeter than sleep."[23]

It was the Eve of the Ascension, and in the church beside Bernardino's cell, the friars were chanting the Vespers Antiphony, *Pater, manifestavi nomen tuum hominibus.*[24]

XXIX. Fra Bernardino's Vision of Pope Celestine V: *P. A. Mezzastris.*

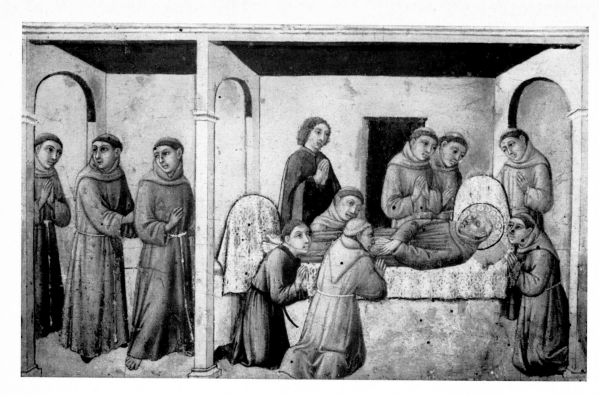

XXX. A. Death of Fra Bernardino: *Sano di Pietro*.

XXX. B. The Cripples beg for a Miracle: *Giacomo da Lodi*.

EPILOGUE

El servo tuo, Signor beato,
Non può stare più celato
Che tu l'hai manifestato
Al grande e al piccolino.

<small>LAMENT FOR SAN BERNARDINO*</small>

HARDLY had Fra Bernardino closed his eyes, than the struggle began as to which city should have the honour of preserving his body. His companions, after weeping for the father they had lost, washed and dressed him, according to the custom of their Order, in another habit, so that they might take home the one he was wearing when he died. Then they placed the body in a rough coffin, nailed it down, wrapped it in a cloth, and were proposing to steal away with it secretly at night, to take it back to Siena.

Someone, however, gave away their plan and at once the people of Aquila hurried to San Francesco, obliged the friars to hand over the coffin to them, and, having drawn out the nails, carried it from his cell to the church. Here the tiny body was exposed to the veneration of the faithful, who kissed Fra Bernardino's hands and feet, and even placed rings upon his fingers. At once, too, the story of the miracles that were taking place spread through the city – the first being granted to two paralysed boys who regained the power to walk, and within the next few days, as the whole population of Aquila hastened to kneel before the corpse, the number of miraculous healings rose to thirty.[1] Thus a prediction in Fra Giuliano's letter was fully confirmed. "I said to the people here," he wrote, "on the night of Fra Bernardino's death, 'Wait and see, he will work miracles.'" And he also added, "If you don't pay him all the honours you can, Messer Domeneddio will soon miraculously remove his body somewhere else!"[2]

So great was the crowd that the Bishop sent for a guard of soldiers, and on Ascension Day, ordered the removal of the coffin to the Cathedral of Aquila. When the procession made its way through the streets, led by the Bishop with the clergy and magistrates, and followed by the silver or wooden crosses of forty religious orders, and all the citizens "bearing torches, as when they followed the Body of Christ" (i.e. at the feast of Corpus Domini), all the city bells began to toll, including that of the Commune, "which they never would do before, even for a Bishop or a King." Then the body was taken back again to San Francesco and, after a funeral oration by an Augustinian friar, was exposed for twenty-six days in a chapel there, while pilgrims came from every remote valley and mountain of the Abruzzi, and the sick continued to be healed.

The first person to become aware of Fra Bernardino's death, at the moment at which it occurred, was his old friend Fra Giacomo della Marca. "In the midst of the Blessed Giacomo's sermon" – writes his biographer – "he suddenly ceased speaking, for the time it takes to say a *Miserere*, and at just that moment, San Bernardino died. And as he [Fra Giacomo] began to speak again, he said, 'A great pillar has just fallen.' ... When he got back to his cell he began to pray with great fervour ... and then sat weeping, saying, 'Oh my father, you said you were going to the kingdom, and I understood, the kingdom of Naples. But you have gone to that of eternal life.'"[3]

Soon the news spread all over Italy, and there was no city to which he had been, that did not grieve. "I do not know whether a father was ever more deeply mourned by his sons, nor a master by his disciples," wrote Fra Sante Boncor, "than now our glorious Bernardino." The list of the cities which held public celebrations in his honour reads like a litany: "Perugia, the strong and magnanimous," "the glorious and magnificent city of Florence," "the marvellous and illustrious power of Milan," "the generous and glorious Bologna," as well as "joyous Ferrara," "famous Padua," "the divine city of Venice" – and, most of all, "the happy city of Siena."[4]

A popular elegy composed by one of his disciples, describes his own city's grief:

> Piangi il tuo dolce e glorioso
> Bernardin, santo e pio,
> Popul sanese mio
> Che se n'è ito al celeste riposo . . .
>
> Non vi ricorda ch'el vedeste andar
> In terra come agniello
> Quel povero vecchiarello,
> Tanto benigno, umile e pietoso? . . .
>
> Pianga ciascun Senese il padre suo,
> Dogliansi grandi, piccoli e mezzani.
> Piangi, Toschana, e 'l gran chonsiglio tuo,
> Anco languischin tutti gl'italiani . . .
>
> Pianghino i frati suoi figlioli diletti,
> Quasi vestiti dalle sagre mani,
> Tutti, o gran parte, povari perfetti;
> Poich'egli è spento el lume de' cristiani.[5]

But the sorrow of the Sienese was tainted by bitterness. They could hardly believe that the holy man who had belonged to them for so many years was now lost to them, and that even his body would not be restored to his own city.

> Aquila ladra innamorata
> Di Bernardin beato!

cried another homely lament, probably written by one of his own friars immediately after his death.[6]

The letter from Aquila bearing not only the official news of his death, but the account of his first miracles, was read aloud on June 10 to the assembled people, and in the following week services were held in his honour, not only in Siena itself, but in the whole territory – the expenses being paid by a special tax on the city's meat.[7] It was also decided to send off two groups of envoys – one to Rome, to beg the Pope to order the return of the friar's body to his own city and to approve his canonization – and the other to Aquila, to fetch his remains.

Both missions failed. The Pope, not wishing to cause trouble in Aquila, refused to order the translation of the friar's body, and the citizens of Aquila indignantly protested that Fra Bernardino had made his own wishes clear enough, by choosing to go there to die. The most that could be obtained from them was that Fra Bernardino's brother-friars might take back with them to Siena as relics the garments he had worn at the time of his death and the objects found in his cell. But when they got home, carrying these effects upon his little donkey, the women of Siena – each of them determined to have a "relic" – nearly skinned the poor beast alive, so as to obtain at least one of its hairs![8]

Few saints have been canonized so soon after their death as San Bernardino, but to the impatient citizens of both Siena and Aquila, as well as to the Observants, the interval of six years seemed too long. At the end of July, two months after his death, the first envoys from Siena were despatched to Rome, taking with them the list of the saint's miracles, but reported that, although "His Holiness was well disposed," he had pointed out that "the Church does nothing with so much solemnity, weight, care and maturity as the canonization of a saint, and that many things are needful." However, soon afterwards the Pontiff, "declaring himself happy that God should have sent such a man during his rule and that he should have died in time for him to canonize him," put the necessary inquiries into the hands of a Commission of three Cardinals. So the envoys handed over the care of Fra Bernardino's interests to a Sienese canon in the Curia, and themselves gladly returned home.[9]

Meanwhile the Observant Order, too, had not been idle. Fra Giovanni da Capistrano at once hurried off to Aquila to investigate Fra Bernardino's miracles himself, and to advise the Aquilani that they, too, would do well to send some envoys to the Pope, but when the next Consistory was held, the canonization examined was not that of Fra Bernardino, but of another holy friar who had died one hundred and forty years before, and who had no less than three hundred miracles to his credit![10] The outlook now seemed so unpromising that Fra Giovanni, on returning to report to the Pope, exclaimed, "Not you, Holy Father, but your successor will complete this work!"[11]

One reason for these delays was probably the fact that Fra Bernardino had sometimes spoken very plainly about the corruption of the high clergy, and among them, about some people who were still alive, and another serious obstacle was now caused by the Milanese followers of the mathematician, Amedeo de Landris, whom, on his last visit there, Fra Bernardino had accused of heresy. These men now proclaimed that, since de Landris had been absolved, Fra Bernardino, who had slandered him, had died guilty, and was therefore certainly not a fit subject for canonization. That these attacks had not been entirely unforeseen, is suggested by Fra Giuliano's letter about the friar's death, since he told his friends to describe all the marvels that had taken place in Aquila, most especially to "that swine of a buffoon with his sect," and "to wash his head without any soap" (i. e. give him a good dressing-down). And although, as soon as Pope Eugenius heard that it was Fra Bernardino who had been de Landris' accuser, he reversed the previous judgment, the episode certainly delayed the canonization.[12]

Meanwhile Pope Eugenius himself was so close to death that

245

Fra Giovanni's prediction was plainly coming true: it would be his successor who would have to take the decision. This was the learned and saintly Nicholas V, who had known Fra Bernardino in Florence and who told the Commission to hasten their study of the documents submitted to them, while the government of Aquila and the City Council of Siena each decided to contribute half of the sum that would be required, some 2.500 florins each.[13] Nevertheless, the matter dragged on for another three years, and just as it seemed to be reaching completion, a most unexpected obstacle arose: the miracles performed by Fra Bernardino's corpse suddenly ceased! On hearing this inconvenient news, Giovanni da Capistrano at once hurried off to Aquila and spent a night in prayer before his master's tomb, imploring him, according to the story told by a contemporary, in the name of Franciscan obedience and of the Holy Ghost, "to perform as many miracles as he could." On the following day, we are told, all the sick who hastened to San Francesco were again miraculously healed, and when the final complete list of miracles was supplied to the Commission, it filled six large folio pages.[14] It was even said that Fra Giovanni, in his devotion to Fra Bernardino's cause, had gone yet one step further – imploring the corpse of Fra Tommaso da Firenze, another holy Franciscan friar who was performing miracles after his death and whose canonization was being considered, to desist from his marvellous deeds until Fra Bernardino's cause was won![15]

Finally Fra Giovanni, in the name of all the impatient Observants, returned again to Rome, to implore the Pope to allow no further delay. Kneeling before him, he even begged that the old mediaeval test of fire should be applied: that Fra Bernardino's corpse should be placed upon a burning pyre, and his own living body beside it. "If the flames consume us, put it down to my sins; but if they do us no harm, you will recognize the will of God!"[16]

We are not told what the Pope replied to this proposal, but we do know that at last, in the spring of 1450, success began to be in sight, for another envoy from Siena reported that Fra Bernardino's canonization would be celebrated on Whit-Sunday, when the General Chapter of the Franciscan Order would also be held in Rome.[17] And at last, on May 14, two other Sienese envoys were able to communicate the long-awaited decision.

When Whit-Sunday came, the celebrations were all that the saint's most ardent disciples could have wished. To celebrate the abdication of the Antipope Felix V and the end of the last chapter of the Great Schism, Nicholas V had ordered a Jubilee Year, and Rome was so full of pilgrims scurrying from church to church that Giannozzo Manetti, who was there, could only compare them to a procession of ants. "One saw innumerable hordes arriving," wrote a Sienese chronicler, "French, German, Spanish, Portuguese, Greek, Armenian, Dalmatian and Italian, all singing hymns in their own tongue," each of them wearing the traditional coarse pilgrim's robe and hat, with a shell round his neck and a staff in his hand. According to Aeneas Silvius Piccolomini, they numbered 40.000, and the whole city was so overcrowded that, when summer came, there was an outbreak of the plague.[18]

Over three thousand Franciscans, too, had come to Rome from every part of Europe – both for the General Chapter of the Order, to elect a new Vicar General, and for the canonization. On that day their procession was so long, according to an eye-witness, "that when the leaders were entering St. Peter's, the last had not yet left the convent on the Capitol," and inside St. Peter's there was so large a crowd "that no one could move independently, but we all had to move together in a single direction, like a wave of the sea." The Pope himself pronounced the panegyric and had composed the official Bull of canonization, *Misericordias Domini*, in which he affirmed "that this holy man served Christ and followed Christ."

In almost every city where San Bernardino had been, great celebrations followed those in Rome, the most magnificent being in Perugia, Aquila and Siena. In his own city, as soon as messengers from Rome had brought back the happy news, the various quarters of the town vied with each other in decorating their streets with garlands and arches of greenery, and altars were set up out of doors for Masses of thanksgiving. Images of San Bernardino and of his emblem were placed in the squares and fluttered on banners in the wind. As for the Campo itself, it was turned into a vast, decorated drawing-room, hung with brocades and banners and lit with torches. A chapel was erected beneath the Palazzo Pubblico and here, on June 14, the Bishop said Mass, and that night, at the *podestà's* high window, a most elaborate "Paradise" was constructed (presumably with figures of angels and saints) "adorned with fine cloths and a wheel of lights and fireworks, in which the image of San Bernardino went to Heaven, accompanied by every musical instrument that we could find." "And so," the chronicler ends, "San Bernardino was led to the feet of God."[19]

In Perugia, after similar celebrations, the wax torches used in the procession were laid aside to start a fund for the erection of a temple in the saint's honour: the Oratory of San Bernardino, with the exquisite bas-reliefs by Agostino di Duccio which still adorn it.

Aquila, too, on the proposal of Fra Giovanni da Capistrano, decided to build a new church worthy of housing the saint's body, but after his departure the plan was opposed by the local Conventuals, who did not want it to leave their own church, and who persuaded the Observants to agree merely to build a new chapel for the same purpose in San Francesco. When, however, this news reached Fra Giovanni – who was then preaching in Cracow – he sent an angry letter of protest, deliberately appealing both to the civic pride of the Aquilani and to their self-interest. "Your city has become very fat, thanks to San Bernardino – and you are provoking God to make it lean again! I, a poor old man in foreign lands, have caused fourteen convents to be built in the course of three years, and eight of them dedicated to San Bernardino, and does the magnificent Council of Aquila only intend to build a little chapel?"

On receiving this letter, the magistrates of Aquila at once hastened to San Bernardino's tomb to beg for his forgiveness, but then began to quarrel among themselves again as to the site of the new church, until a visit from Fra Giacomo della Marca decided the question. Walking through the city at the head of a procession, he stopped by an open space beside the city hospital and, declaring it to be God's will that the church should rise on that spot, himself marked its outline on the ground. As he joyfully wrote to Fra Giovanni: "I, unworthy servant of God and of San Bernardino, took a hoe and with the first blow I invoked the name of God Almighty." This was at the head of the Cross. With the next blows, marking the two arms, he called upon the Son and the Holy Ghost, and at the centre of the Cross, upon the Virgin Mary, "and finally at the foot of the Cross I called upon the name of our blessed father Bernardino, with such delight and so many chants and rejoicings as no tongue can ever describe.... Rejoice then with me, a little old man, you who have also grown old in foreign parts, having been sent from Italy to preach the gospel of peace unto those peoples."[20]

The building of the church was delayed by an earthquake, but in 1471 it was finished and consecrated and in the following year the saint's relics were transferred there.

When, after twenty-eight years, his coffin was opened, his body was found intact. It was clothed (which would certainly have caused him great discomfort) "in a damask robe with a golden cord" and placed in "a crystal urn, with clasps of silver and gold." Nine years later, however, in 1481, this urn was replaced by a still more splendid silver one, a gift from the King of France, and finally an ornate marble monument was erected to contain it.[21] Here at last the friar's tired little body was allowed to find rest.

249

Almost every city in which San Bernardino had preached or lived, laid claim to some precious relic of his – and the authenticity of some of them is very doubtful. Both Aquila and the convent of Monteripido near Perugia say that they possess his staff; Foligno, Perugia and Viterbo claim the cord of his girdle; Aquila, Florence and the Compagnia di San Bernardino in Siena, his vitals, and several other convents in various parts of Italy, one of his habits, a cap or a cloak. In Florence, the convent of Ognissanti still preserves the tablet which he used when preaching there, and Assisi has his standard. And in 1609 some members of the Compagnia di San Bernardino of Siena made a journey to Aquila, to see if they could not find some further relic there, and – "having offered rich gifts" – triumphantly returned with the knife with which their saint had been cut open, which they presented to the Signoria of Siena.

After his death the Duke of Milan asked for one of his caps and a pair of his spectacles, in the hope that they might restore his own fading sight, and these were sent to him by the Sienese government, with a letter asking him to intercede with the Pope on behalf of San Bernardino's canonization. They were kept for some time in the castle of Pavia, but were then broken, and have now completely disappeared.

It is in Siena, however, and in its territory, in which almost every village and hillside knew his footsteps, that most of the indisputably authentic objects may still be found which San Bernardino wore or used. The rough, tiny deal pulpit from which he preached his first sermon may still be seen in the small country church of Santa Maria dell'Osservanza, near Montalcino; his spectacle-case and one of his habits, as well as his chalice and paten – both of tin – in the Oratorio di San Bernardino at Seggiano, beneath the hill on which stands the ruined convent of Il Colombaio. The confraternity of San Sebastiano in Siena still treasures the Crucifix of gnarled, knotted wood, which he held up before his congregation. And the few personal possessions which were with him in Aquila when he died, together with a few books, Pope Eugenius' Bull of Exculpation and his own sermons, may now still be seen in the place which was nearest to being his earthly home, the Convento dell'Osservanza near Siena. The sight of these objects is very moving: the patched habit that the Saint was wearing when he died (inscribed by one of his companions: "This is the habit that San Bernardino wore, when he rode about on his little donkey"), his socks and linen stockings and slippers, a fragment of the cord which formed his girdle, his cap, a pair of thick felt leggings "which he seldom wore," some white linen socks "which he wore when he went to preach upon his donkey, because he was old," and the unbleached cloak in which his friars wrapped him, when they laid him on the ground to die. There was also an hour-glass of sand in a leather case, two pairs of spectacles in their cases, and a small "portable breviary," its parchment binding and pages almost transparent from daily use. All these objects – poor, small, seemly and well-worn – are very like their owner. They lie in the anteroom to the cell which – though destroyed by shellfire during the War – has been rebuilt exactly as it was, and over the door of which one of his brothers had inscribed: "Here I will take refuge from the turmoil of the world, rest, study and meditate; here I will prepare for Heaven."

At the end of the story, we are left with the fundamental question: what was the quality in Bernardino degli Albizzeschi which made his contemporaries so very sure that they were in the presence of a saint, and which, after five hundred years, still conveys itself to us?

He was not a subtle theologian, but merely followed, as he himself said, the path which "the Doctors" had laid down before him; he was not, like St. Francis or St. Catherine, a great mystic; he had not the halo of a man who has suffered persecution or a martyr's death. Yet there was in him some quality which was instantly recognized by widely different kinds of men: by the suspicious tyrant of Milan and the ironic Aeneas Silvius Piccolomini, by the ambitious Emperor Sigismund and the austere Pope Eugenius IV, by the purse-proud merchants of Siena and Florence, the humanists of Padua, the soldiers of fortune upon the roads, and the poor and humble everywhere. What was the common touchstone?

A part of his appeal may have lain in his physical appearance: the thin, worn little body, the drawn look of self-imposed privations which men were accustomed to associate with a saint. He certainly had great personal magnetism. And there was, of course, his gift of words, a talent to which the crowd is always susceptible, and especially in Italy. But the outstanding gift which drew so many thousands to hear him, and often changed their lives, was surely one to which Dante had already given a name – *l'intelletto d'amore* (the understanding of love). He understood the men and women to whom he spoke, and he understood them because he loved them.

He did not, indeed, himself believe that any other kind of comprehension was possible. He said quite openly – even if he happened to be addressing eminent philosophers or shrewd businessmen – that, where knowledge of another human soul is concerned, the capacity of the mind is extremely limited: true knowledge comes only from the heart. "How can one tell a woman who loves her husband from one who does not? . . . By the knowledge that comes from love. The one who loves her husband knows what ails him as soon as she sees him, in the twinkling of an eye, and provides what he needs and believes what he says. . . . And so it is with God. A man will know God, in so far as he loves Him. A man knows as much as he loves."[22] So, too, with our fellow-creatures. "There is a great difference between thinking, understanding and feeling. There are many who can think, fewer who can understand, and fewer still who can feel. . . . Here is an example, which is both simple and subtle. If a man is hanged in the open square, a great multitude of

XXXI. "Rotulo Bernardiniano": *Pietro di Giovanni.*

XXXII. Death Mask of Fra Bernardino.

people will see him, and will think about the things he did. And a few, who have greater understanding, will understand the man himself, and the great pain there is within him. But if his mother or father or son are there, they will suffer in their own selves the pain of the man who is being hanged.... This is what Master St. Paul meant us to understand about Christ Crucified. He did not say that we should understand Him, but that we should feel within ourselves, as He felt on the Cross. *Hoc enim sentite in vobis.* And this is the difference between feeling a thing from outside it, from inside it, or from partaking in it oneself."[23]

It was this inner, costly participation – compassion in its original sense – which was never lacking in San Bernardino. When the name of some saints is mentioned – in particular the great mystics – what immediately comes to mind is their relation to God: but there are others of whom we first remember what they did, through God, for men. San Filippo Neri and St. Vincent de Paul are among these, and so is San Bernardino. Over and over again he reminded other men that God's grace was waiting for them – but only if they sought it of their own free will. "If you open the window of your consent, you will find there the warmth of God's charity. Prepare yourself to receive it, like the baby swallows in their nests, when they open wide their beaks, to be fed." "*Messer Domeneddio* says," he told them, "'Set your own measure. If you will entrust yourselves to me greatly, I will help you greatly; if moderately, I will help you moderately, and if a little, a little.'"[24] Moreover he made his hearers feel that he himself had sometimes found the steps to Heaven very steep, that he was not only their monitor, but their companion. "Faith," he said, "is acquired with toil, hope with toil and charity with toil . . . Let the man who wishes to say that he possesses these virtues, add, 'I have acquired them with great toil.'"[25]

It was perhaps the complete simplicity, the unmistakeable ring of humility and truth in such words as these, that caused their echo to spread so far. Never, even in his sharpest reproofs, did he dissociate himself from the men to whom he preached, or lose his awareness of the infinite value of each one of them. "God," he had said, and it echoes through all his teaching, "God loves one soul more than all the churches in the world. Christ would have come on earth to die . . . to save one single soul."[26]

San Bernardino's love for his flock was, as we have seen, neither soft nor sentimental; he had no illusions about either their follies, their sins or their desires. He loved them not at all with the withdrawn impersonal benevolence of some monastics, a fire at which no man could warm his hands, but with a fault-finding, perceptive, humorous family love which never, in condemnation of the sin, lost sight of the sinner. He scolded and he mocked, but he also felt a quite unmistakeable tenderness for those chattering, mendacious women in their silly hats, those stout, tight-fisted shopkeepers, those unlettered friars, those quarrelsome, vain young men, those starving and sometimes thieving peasants. Certainly they were ungrateful, deaf and blind – but that is the human condition. The sins which he could not bear – which twisted his thin mouth into a grimace of disgust and made his sharp chin tremble – were all sins against lovingkindness: factiousness, blasphemy, avarice, cruelty and the practices of witchcraft, which brought death to little children and played upon the credulity of simple men. The other sins – those of ignorance and poverty, of youth and vanity – he could not blame very severely in his heart, whatever harsh words he might feel bound to use. "You will go to the hot house, to the Devil's house!" he thundered. "You will have a visit from Brother Rod!" But close behind the threat there was a smile, prompted by an affection very like that of his master, St. Francis – "a tender love, like a mother's – not like a father's, which is a little tougher." He was kind – unlike most saints – even to himself. "If you speak to God," he told his fellow-citizens, "speak with charity; if you speak of yourself, speak with charity. See to it that within your heart there be nothing but love, love, love."[27]

Caritas, to his mind, was "the lightest merchandise in the world, needing no ships nor donkeys, no mules nor carriers." And it was also the bridge between this world and the next, the only virtue that, when we have left this life, will still remain with us. "When we are over there in Paradise – may God grant us this grace – the only virtue that will go with us is charity. We shall no longer need faith in the things divine, for we shall see them face to face, and we shall no more hope for the things unseen, for we shall have obtained all that we hoped for. But charity . . . will remain with us even in Paradise."[28]

PRINCIPAL ABBREVIATIONS OF TITLES USED IN BIBLIOGRAPHY AND NOTES

AASS	ACTA SANCTORUM (these include the Lives of San Bernardino by Barnabò da Siena, Maffeo Vegio and Lodovico da Vicenza).
AB	ANALECTA BOLLANDIANA (these include the Life by Leonardo Benevoglienti and the *Leggenda del Frate Anonimo*, and the first list of the miracles of San Bernardino).
AFH	ARCHIVUM FRANCISCANUM HISTORICUM, Quaracchi.
BANCHI	*Le prediche volgari di San Bernardino da Siena dette nella Piazza del Campo l'anno 1427*, ed. Luciano Banchi, Siena, 1880-88.
BARGELLINI	*Le prediche volgari del 1427 in Siena*, ed. Piero Bargellini, Milan, 1936.
BSB	BOLLETTINO DI STUDI BERNARDINIANI, Osservanza, Siena, 1935-1950.
BSStP	BOLLETTINO SENESE DI STORIA PATRIA, Siena, 1893-1900.
CANNAROZZI	*Le prediche volgari di San Bernardino*, ed. Prof. Padre Ciro Cannarozzi, Vols. I & II, Pistoia, 1934, Vols. III, IV & V, Florence, 1940.
CANNAROZZI, SIENA	*Le prediche volgari, predicazione in Siena*, ed. Prof. Ciro Cannarozzi, Vols. I & II, Florence, 1958.
FACCHINETTI	Padre VITTORINO FACCHINETTI, *San Bernardino da Siena*, Milan, 1933.
HOWELL	A. G. FERRERS HOWELL, *San Bernardino of Siena*, London, 1923.
OPERA	SANCTI BERNARDINI SENENSIS OPERA OMNIA, ed. Père De La Haye, Venice, 1745. (This also includes a Life of San Bernardino by Fra Giovanni da Capistrano and one by Lorenzo Surio.)
PACETTI	*Le prediche volgari inedite*, ed. Padre Domenico Pacetti, Siena, 1935 (a selection from the sermons in 1424 and 1425 in Florence and Siena, subsequently published in full by Padre Cannarozzi).
WADDING	LUCAS WADDING, *Annales Minorum seu Trium Ordinum a S. Francisco institutorum. Rome, 1731-45.*

SOURCES AND BIBLIOGRAPHY

SOURCES

The main sources for the Life of San Bernardino are:

A. His own works, both in Latin and Italian.

B. The lives of him written shortly after his death, and the descriptions of him or of events in which he took part, by contemporary historians or chroniclers.

C. The documents concerning him in the Archivio di Stato of Siena.

D. The official documents concerning him.

A. WORKS OF SAN BERNARDINO

I. PRINCIPAL WORKS IN LATIN

For a full account of these works, see Padre Pacetti, *Gli scritti di San Bernardino*, in "Saggi e ricerche nel V centenario della morte" (Milan, 1944), Howell, Chapters III and IV, Facchinetti, Part II, Chapter V, *La dottrina del Santo*, and *Bollettino bibliografico di San Bernardino* in "Aevum," A. IV, fasc. 3., and Domenico Ronzoni, *L'eloquenza di San Bernardino e della sua scuola* (Siena, 1899).

References to the Latin sermons in this book are to the edition used by Howell and Facchinetti: Père De La Haye, *Sancti Bernardini Senensis Ordinis Seraphicum Minorum Opera Omnia* (2nd edition, Venice, 1745).

It is necessary to distinguish between the sermons written out by San Bernardino himself in Latin (the Lenten courses *De christiana religione* and *De Evangelio aeterno*, the treatises *De vita christiana*, *De beata Vergine*, *De beatitudinibus* and *De Spiritu Sancto*, the *Sermones de tempore* and *Extraordinarii*) and those which we only have as reported by persons who heard them (in particular, the Lenten course *Seraphim*, given in Padua in 1443 and probably written down by one of the scholars or doctors of the University, the course given in Siena in 1425 – of which there is also an Italian version – and the courses delivered in Perugia and Assisi in 1425). The Lenten course *De pugna spirituali* (also published by De La Haye) is now considered spurious, as is the *Commentary on the Apocalypse*. Cf. Pacetti, op. cit., pp. 64-8.

2. PRINCIPAL WORKS IN ITALIAN

Le prediche volgari di San Bernardino da Siena, dette nella Piazza del Campo, l'anno 1427, ed. Luciano Banchi, Siena, 1880-8. These are the 45 sermons set down by Benedetto di Maestro Bartolomeo, quoted from a manuscript in the Biblioteca Comunale, Siena (Cod. U. I. 4), collated with two other manuscripts in the same library (Codices U.I.5 and 6) and one in the Biblioteca Comunale of Palermo (20. q: C. 38).

Le prediche volgari di San Bernardino da Siena, ed. Padre Ciro Cannarozzi (1934-58). Of these, Vols. I-II (Pistoia, 1934) contain the course of 58 Lenten sermons in Florence, 1424; Vols. III-V (Florence 1940) the course of 64 Lenten sermons in Florence in 1425;

and Vols. VI-VII (but renumbered I-II and therefore referred to in this book as Cannarozzi, *Siena*), the course of 47 sermons in Siena in April-June 1425. For the manuscripts used, see the Prefaces to Vols. I and III.

In addition, P. Enrico Bulletti has published (in BSB, VIII, 1942) a sermon *Sul Santissimo Nome di Gesú* (probably given between 1419 and 1421).

A more recent edition of the sermons in Siena is: *Le prediche volgari del 1427 in Siena*, ed. Piero Bargellini, Milan, 1936.

Selections from the sermons are contained in: *Le prediche volgari, Campo di Siena, 1427*, and *Le prediche volgari inedite*, ed. Padre Pacetti, Siena, 1935, and

Le più belle pagine di Bernardino da Siena, ed. Piero Misciattelli, with an excellent preface. Padre Pacetti also published a collection of San Bernardino's minor works in the vulgar (stories, treatises, parables): *Operette volgari integralmente edite*, Florence, 1938. For other courses of sermons (some of them incomplete or doubtfully authentic), see Padre Pacetti, op. cit., in "Saggi e ricerche nel V centenario della morte."

3. LETTERS

Only sixteen of San Bernardino's letters remain, of which four in the vulgar. One of these, in his own hand, is preserved in the Augustinian Convent of Siena and one in the Collezione Piancastelli of the Museo Civico, Forlì. The others are dictated.

B. LIVES OF SAN BERNARDINO BY HIS CONTEMPORARIES

1. Barnabò da Siena, *Vita S. B.*, finished only ten months after the saint's death, and principally valuable for the years 1418-19. AASS, Vol. IV, pp. 739-46.
2. Leonardo Benevoglienti, *Vita S. B.*, finished in May 1446 and published by Van Octroy in AB Vol. XXI, fasc. I, pp. 51-8. It deals especially with the saint's early years.
3. Maffeo Vegio, *Vita S. B.*, written in 1453. AASS, Vol. C, pp. 749-766.
4. The Life by "a contemporary," generally known as *Il Frate Anonimo*, who was San Bernardino's companion on some of his journeys. Published in AB, XXX (1906), from a 15th century copy in the Bibliothèque Nationale, Paris.

MINOR WORKS

1. San Giovanni da Capistrano, *Vita S. B.* Published as a preface to De La Haye's 1745 edition of the *Opera*, it is rather a panegyric than a biography.
2. The anonymous Life included in Lorenzo Surio's *Vitae Sanctorum*, written some time after the saint's death.
3. Fra Sante Boncor, *Vita di San Bernardino da Siena*, a panegyric rather than a Life, in ungrammatical Italian, dealing particularly with the saint's death and canonization. Published by Padre Serafino Gaddoni, Arezzo, 1912.

4. Fra Lodovico da Vicenza, *Vita S. B.*, which adds very little to the other biographies. AASS, Vol. c.

5. Vespasiano da Bisticci, *San Bernardino da Massa*, in his *Vite degli uomini illustri del secolo XV* (ed. by P. d'Ancona and E. Aeschlimann, Milan, 1951). Further information about the Saint and his times may also be found in other Lives in this volume, notably in those of Pope Eugenius IV, Maffeo Vegio and Giannozzo Manetti.

In addition, portraits of the saint or references to him may be found in Archbishop Antoninus' *Chronica*, XXII-XXIV (Nuremberg 1490), in Aeneas Silvius Piccolomini's *De viris illustribus* (quoted in *Opera*, I) and in the Sienese chronicler Agostino Dati's *Opera* (also quoted in *Opera*, I, pp. 48-51). The various panegyrics of the saint (by San Giovanni da Capistrano, the Blessed Michele da Carcano, Fra Roberto da Lecce and San Giacomo della Marca) add little or nothing to our previous knowledge, but much interesting information is to be found in Wadding's *Annales Minorum* (Rome, 1731-45), in *La Franceschina* by Giacomo Oddi of Perugia (ed. Padre Cavanna, Florence, 1931) and in the *Cronache degli Ordini istituiti dal P. S. Francesco* by Marco da Lisbona (Italian translation by O. Diola, Venice, 1582).

C. DOCUMENTS IN THE ARCHIVIO DI STATO OF SIENA

These consist chiefly of the correspondence between Siena and Rome concerning Fra Bernardino's appointment as Bishop of Siena (*Concistoro*, copia-lettere 1628 and 1912 and *Notuli di commissioni ad ambasciatori*, *Concistoro* 2411), of the instructions given to him by Siena on his mission to the Duke of Milan in 1444 (*Lettere ad ambasciatori*), of a letter about Fra Bernardino to the envoy of Siena in Milan, Giovanni da Massa (*Concistoro* 2411), of Fra Bernardino's cypher, of the list of his miracles and of the inventory of his books and possessions.

D. OFFICIAL DOCUMENTS

These documents, previously scattered in Wadding, *Analecta Bollandiana*, De La Haye, etc. have now been collected in: *Bullarium franciscanum*, Vol. I, *continens Constitutiones, Epistolas, Diplomata Romanorum Pontificum Eugenii IV et Nicolai V ad Tres Ordines S. P. N. Francisci spectantia*, ed. by Fr. U. Hüntemann, O.F.M. (Quaracchi, 1929). These contain: a) information about the saint's life, b) the process of his canonization and the Bull announcing it, and c) the history of his cult.

BIBLIOGRAPHY

A. MODERN BIOGRAPHIES AND STUDIES (A selection of the most important.)

ALESSIO, F., *Storia di San Bernardino e del suo tempo*, Mondovì, 1899 (the best of the 19th century biographies, though somewhat hagiographical).

BARGELLINI, Piero, *San Bernardino da Siena*, Brescia, 1933.

BONTEMPELLI, M., *San Bernardino da Siena*, Genoa, 1911. (A lively portrait, rather than a Life.)

FACCHINETTI, Padre VITTORINO, O.F.M., *San Bernardino da Siena, mistico sole del secolo XV*, Milan, 1933. (The most complete Life, with a full bibliography up to 1933 and numerous illustrations).

FERRERS HOWELL, A. G., *San Bernardino of Siena*, London, 1912.

HEFELE, K., *Der heilige Bernhardin von Siena und die franziskanische Wanderpredigt in Italien während des XV Jahrhunderts*, Freiburg in Breisgau, 1912.

STICCO, MARIA, *Pensiero e poesia in San Bernardino da Siena*, Milan, 1945.

THUREAU-DANGIN, P., *Un prédicateur populaire dans l'Italie de la Renaissance*, Paris, 1896.

B. MONOGRAPHS AND ARTICLES

Interesting articles regarding especial aspects of the saint's life and thought (referred to specifically before the Notes at the end of each chapter) are to be found in the following periodicals:

1. *Analecta Bollandiana* (AB), founded in Brussels in 1882.
2. *Miscellanea Franciscana* (MF), Assisi, from 1886.
3. *Bollettino Senese di Storia Patria* (BSStP), Siena, since 1893.
4. *Archivum Franciscanum Historicum* (AFH), Florence, Quaracchi, started 1908.
5. *Études franciscaines*, Paris, 1908.
6. *La Diana*, Siena, 1926-1930.

More recently, much valuable new material, both biographic and iconographic, has been published in the *Bollettino di studi bernardiniani* (BSB) founded by Padre E. Bulletti, Siena, 1935-50, and in *San Bernardino da Siena, Saggi e ricerche nel V centenario della morte*, Milan, 1944.

C. GENERAL WORKS

BURCKHARDT, J., *The Renaissance in Italy*, translated by S. G. C. Middlemore, London, 1904.

GARIN, E., *Il Rinascimento italiano*, Milan, 1941.

GREGOROVIUS, F., *History of the city of Rome in the Middle Ages*, Vol. VII, translated by A. Hamilton, London, 1894.

Paschini, P., *Roma nel Rinascimento*, Vol. xii of the *Storia di Roma*, Istituto di Studi Romani, Rome, 1940.

Pastor, L., *History of the Popes*, Italian edition, *Storia dei Papi dalla fine del Medio Evo*, translated by Prof. Angelo Mercati, Rome, 1910.

Voigt, F. L., *Il Risorgimento dell'Antichità classica*, translated by Valbusa, Florence, 1897.

The Cambridge Mediaeval History, Vol. vii, Cambridge University Press, 1949.

D. ICONOGRAPHY

There is no complete work on the iconography of San Bernardino, which is extremely rich and varied. Various aspects of it are treated in the following works:

Barbetti, Mons. Telemaco, *Le arti senesi e San Bernardino*, appendix by the Italian translator to Thureau-Dangin's *Un prédicateur populaire dans l'Italie de la Renaissance*, Paris, 1896.

Cartwright Ady, Julia, *San Bernardino in Art*. This is the last chapter of A. G. Ferrers Howell's *San Bernardino of Siena*, London, 1912.

Facchinetti, Padre Vittorino, *L'omaggio della liturgia e dell'arte* (the last chapter of his Life).

Gallero, Padre T., *Per l'iconografia bernardiniana nella pittura ferrarese*, BSB, a. ii, 1936, nos. 3-4.

Gallero, Padre T., *Il santo senese nell'arte del Monferrato*, BSB, a. iv 1938 no. 1.

Isnard, E., *Deux primitifs français représentant Saint Bernardin de Sienne*, in "Revue d'histoire franciscaine", Vol. v, pp. 168-170, Paris, 1920.

Lusini, A., *Un rotulo bernardiniano*, "La Diana," a. iv, no. 2.

Marri Martini, L., *Affreschi bernardiniani sull'Amiata*, BSB, a. iii (1937), no. 1.

Marri Martini, L., *Una vita illustrata di San Bernardino del '600*, BSB, a. v. (1939) nos. 3-4.

Masseron, A., *Contribution à l'iconographie de Saint Bernardin*, BSStP, a. xxvi, no. 2.

Misciattelli, Piero, *Iconografia bernardiniana*, in "La Diana," a. vii, no. 4.

Misciattelli, Piero, *Arte antica senese*, in "La Diana," a. vi. no. 1.

Misciattelli, Piero, *La maschera di San Bernardino da Siena*, in "Rassegna d'arte senese," a. xviii, nos. 1-2.

Rimbotti, G., *San Bernardino nell'iconografia milanese*, BSB, iv (1938), nos. 3-4.

Rogati, F., *L'arte e San Bernardino da Siena*, BSStP, a. xxx (1923) no. 1.

Catalogo della Mostra Bernardiniana, Siena, 1950.

NOTES
AND ADDITIONAL BIBLIOGRAPHY

PREFACE

Notes

1. Of gilded brass, it was made by the famous Sienese goldsmith Tuccio di Sano and his son Giovanni. The same emblem was also painted inside the Palazzo Pubblico, on the wall of the Sala del Mappamondo, by Maestro Battista of Padova.
2. Three copies of this bust exist. One (Plate II) is in the church of Fontegiusta in Siena, one in San Giobbe in Venice, and one in the Convento dell'Osservanza, near Siena. The one at Fontegiusta appears to be the original and is certainly in the best condition.
3. See Bibliography.
4. *Saggi e ricerche nel quinto centenario della morte di San Bernardino*, Milan, 1944.
5. Cf. *Catalogo della Mostra Bernardiniana*, Siena, 1950.

CHAPTER I: THE FALSE AND THE TRUE VOCATION

1. Additional Works consulted

CANNAROZZI, C., Introduction to Vols. I and III of *Le prediche volgari*, Pistoia, 1933 and Florence, 1940.

MISCIATTELLI, PIERO, Preface to *Le più belle pagine di Bernardino da Siena*, Milan, 1924.

PACETTI, P. D., *La predicazione di San Bernardino in Assisi del 1425* Assisi, Collegium S. Laurentis.

PACETTI, P. D., *La predicazione di San Bernardino in Toscana* in AFH, XXX, nos. II-IX Quaracchi, Florence, 1941.

RIMBOTTI, G., *San Bernardino da Siena a Milano*, in BSB, a. VI (1941), no. 1.

RONZONI, D., *L'eloquenza di San Bernardino da Siena e della sua scuola*, Siena, 1899.

SCARONGELLA, MICHELE, *Contributo allo studio della lingua di San Bernardino da Siena* in BSB, a X, (1944-50).

2. Notes

1. This bell was called after the little city of Sovana in the Maremma from which it had come, when that city was deserted on account of malaria. The bells of Siena played a great part in the city's life: they not only called citizens to prayer, but signalled the beginning and end of the day's work, summoned the fighting men to arms, and called the members of the city council to their meetings. "The bell," said San Bernardino, "is the trumpet of the soul." Falletti-Fossati, *Costumi senesi nella seconda metà del secolo XIV*, p. 116.

2. Banchi, *Prediche volgari*, I, p. 7.

3. Sano di Pietro's picture is in the Capitolo del Duomo of Siena, Neroccio's panel in the Palazzo Pubblico.

4. Benedetto was a *cimatore*, i. e. a man who clipped the rough cloth before it was dyed, and again before it was pressed. Cf. F. Edler, *Steps in the Manufacture of Woollen Cloth in Italy*, in *Glossary of Mediaeval Terms of Business*, pp. 324-9.

5. See Banchi, op. cit. Preface.

6. Banchi, II, p. 35 and III, pp. 257 and 427.

7. The *Mangia* – the great bell-tower which still stands in the Piazza del Campo, beside the Palazzo Pubblico – owed its name to its first bellringer, whose nickname was *mangiaguadagni* (literally "eat-up-savings," i. e. spendthrift).

8. Banchi, II, p. 270. The Fonte Gaia, with its exquisite bas-reliefs by Jacopo della Quercia (now in the Loggia of the Palazzo Pubblico), had been placed there only shortly before, and owed its name to the people's rejoicing on this occasion.

9. Quoted by Bontempelli, *San Bernardino*, p. 53.

10. Banchi, III, p. 168.

11. Banchi, II, pp. 351-3.

12. Ibid., p. 197.

13. Cannarozzi, IV, p. 426 and Howell, *San Bernardino of Siena*, p. 87, quoting Leonardo Benevoglienti, *Life of San Bernardino*.

14. Cannarozzi, III, pp. 305 and 319.

15.
    "Sinners, here in this hour – weep with His Mother Mary
      Who is in great adversity –
    For that she sees her Son – hanging upon the Cross –
      And has no consolation.
    'O, my angelic Son – who knew no mortal sin –
      And art in such distress!'
    In her great grief she falls – unconscious on the ground –
      And can feel no more pain . . ."
                    Penitential *Laude* of the 14th century.

These *Laudi* or hymns (literally praises) of which the most famous is Jacopone da Todi's *Pianto della Madonna*, were sung in the 13th and 14th centuries throughout Central Italy by religious confraternities such as these, and many of them developed into veritable mystery plays, which were given, on the appropriate feast-days, in the churches and open squares, often arousing scenes of great religious fervour. Fra Bernardino, however, unlike many other preachers of his time, refused to make use, in his maturity, of emotional and dramatic appeals of this nature.

16. Banchi, III, p. 295, and II, p. 385.

17. Howell and Padre Pacetti place the meeting of San Bernardino and St. Vincent Ferrer some years later, in 1406 or 1407, but Facchinetti points out that it must have been before 1402, since in that year St. Vincent left Italy and never returned there again. Facchinetti, op. cit., pp. 52-4.

18. Facchinetti, op. cit., p. 52, quoting the version given in Surio's *Vitae Sanctorum*. The one given by Maffeo Vegio is slightly different.

19. He divided his property in Siena into three parts, one for the Ospedale della Scala, one for dowries for poor girls, and one for alms, and gave his land at Massa Marittima to the Convent of Santa Chiara in that city, the deed being made out in the name of one of the nuns.

20. Banchi, III, p. 39 and II, p. 240.

21. This story is entirely in accordance with the mediaeval tradition by which people who might be required later on to bear witness about an important matter (often young children), were given a cuff on the ear or even dipped into a pond beforehand, so as to impress the incident upon their memories!

22. Howell, op. cit., p. 18, quoting Opera III, p. 194, *Seraphim*. Facchinetti, op. cit., p. 262, quoting a sermon by Beato Michele da Carcano, who knew Bernardino in his youth.

23. Banchi, III, p. 312.

24. The story is told both by Maffeo Vegio and Giovanni da Capistrano.

25. Banchi, III, p. 5. "Poverty travels light, In joy and without pride". Jacopone da Todi.

26. Banchi, I, pp. 223-4, and Bargellini, *Le prediche volgari del 1427 in Siena*, p. 184, "And so," the preacher added, "though so small, he begins to taste the bitterness of life."

27. Banchi, I, pp. 323 and 188, and Cannarozzi, *Siena*, I, pp. 280-282.

28. Facchinetti, op. cit., p. 80, quoting both Maffeo Vegio and Fra Giovanni da Capistrano.

29. Lodovico da Vicenza in AASS, pp. 728-9. In 1411 Fra Bernardino had a severe abscess in his throat at La Capriola, and it may well have been the bursting of such an abscess that performed this "miracle."

30. Cannarozzi, preface to *Prediche volgari*, Vol. III, p. CIII, quoting Barnabò da Siena. The adjectives used by Maffeo Vegio for Fra Bernardino's voice were *lenis, clara, sonora, distincta, explicita, solida, penetrans*.

31. The precise date at which he was transferred to La Capriola is not known. The convent, destroyed by bombs in 1943, has been rebuilt precisely as it was.

32. Fra Vincenzo da Fabriano, in AFH, no. 3, pp. 319-20.

33. Facchinetti, op. cit., p. 89, gives the slightly differing versions of both Wadding and *l'Anonimo*.

34. Padre Facchinetti believes that Fra Bernardino went straight to Milan, arriving there in the autumn of 1417 and only visiting Liguria and Piedmont in the following year. I have however followed the itinerary of P. Pacetti, *Cronologia bernardiniana*, in "Studi Francescani", a. XV (1943), nos. 3-4.

35. "This prince," writes Pietro Verri, "believed in astrology; it was indeed perhaps the only rule that guided his morals and all his actions. When the moon was in conjunction with the sun, he would shut himself up in the most remote corner of the palace, and would not answer anyone, nor let anyone speak to him . . .

265

and he had his astrologers, who were his dearest counsellors." P. Verri, *Storia di Milano*, p. 445.

36. Maffeo Vegio of Lodi also wrote a celebrated treatise on humanist education, in which he developed ideas very similar to those of Vittorino da Feltre.

37. Leonardo Benevoglienti, AB, XXI, p. 64.

38. This series of 48 sermons in Latin was the one to which San Bernardino gave the title of *Seraphim*, because their starting-point was the appearance to St. Francis at La Verna of the winged Seraphim who brought him the stigmata.

39. Donati, *Notizie su San Bernardino*, BSStP., I, p. 53, quoting Lodovico Domenichi, *Facezie* (1588).

40. From the panegyric of San Bernardino by Bernardino da Feltre, on May 19, 1493, published by P. Carlo da Milano, in BSB, a. III (1937), no. 2, p. III.

41. Facchinetti, op. cit., p. 298.

42. Quoted by Facchinetti, op. cit., pp. 313-4, from *l'Anonimo*.

43. Ibid., pp. 330-1

44. Ibid., p. 337, quoting from *Seraphim*, *Opera*, III, p. 340.

45. Banchi, II, p. 326.

46. Banchi, I, pp. 60-1 and 223.

47. Padre Cannarozzi remarks that San Bernardino's ideas of brevity, although not ours, were consistent with the taste of his own time. His sermons lasted three or four hours – but some of his fellow-preachers, after preaching for a whole day, would tell their congregation to return on the next, for the end of the sermon! Cannarozzi, III, p. XCVIII.

48. Cannarozzi, III, pp. 263-5. Prof.ssa Sticco points out that these requisites are practically the same as the ones described by Cicero in his *Orationis partitiones*, which San Bernardino had probably read at school. Sticco, *Pensiero e poesia in San Bernardino da Siena*, p. 257.

49. Banchi, I, p. 63, *Opera*, II, 61, *De Evangelio aeterno*, and Banchi, I, p. 66.

50. Ibid, quoting *Opera*, I, pp. 263 ff. Cf. also Howell, op. cit., p. 301. Bernardino pointed out that the Scriptures, too, sometimes described incidents in which a single generous impulse had not led to a change of behaviour. Rahab the harlot, he said, did a good deed in hiding the spies whom Joshua sent into Jericho, "but we do not read that she thereupon forsook the trade of harlot."

51. Cannarozzi, III, pp. 263-4, and Misciattelli, *Le più belle pagine di Bernardino da Siena*, p. III.

52. Cannarozzi, II, p. 3.

53. Banchi, II, p. 38.

54. "Where are you from, comrade? – I come from Milan. – And what is your trade? – I know how to make cloth."

55. Cannarozzi, I, p. 278.

56. Banchi, III, p. 456.

57. Banchi, II, pp. 368-70.

58. Howell, op. cit., pp. 219-20, quoting *Opera*, II, 396, and IV, 214. San Bernardino's quotation is from Matthew, v.

59. Cannarozzi, I, p. 246.

60. Bargellini, *Prediche volgari*, p. 684.

61. *Legenda S. Bernardini*, di Frate Cristoforo Gabrielli (1517), quoted by Padre E. Bulletti in BSB A. VIII (1942), No. 2, p. 81.

62. Banchi, III, p. 449.

63. Bontempelli, op. cit., p. 11.

CHAPTER II: THE WORLD OF WOMEN

1. *Additional Works consulted*

A. CONTEMPORARY MEMOIRS AND TREATISES.

ALBERTI, L. B., *Della famiglia* (the first three books), ed. F. C. Pellegrini, Florence, 1946.

CERTALDO, PAOLO DA, *Libro di buoni costumi*, ed. A. Schiaffini, Florence, 1945.

BARBERINO, FRANCESCO DA, *Reggimento e costumi di donna*, Bologna, 1875.

DOMINICI, Beato GIOVANNI, *Regola del governo di cura familiare*, ed. Prof. D. Salvi, Florence, 1860.

MACINGHI STROZZI, A., *Lettere ai figlioli*, ed. Guasti, Florence, 1877.

MORELLI, GIOVANNI, *Ricordi*, ed. Vittore Branca, Florence, 1956.

PICCOLOMINI, AENEAS SILVIUS, *Historia de duobus amantibus*, Capolago, 1832.

SACCHETTI, FRANCO, *Novelle*, Florence, 1938.

SACCHETTI, FRANCO, *Sermoni evangelici, lettere varie e scritti inediti*, Florence, 1857.

B. MODERN WORKS.

BIAGI, G. B., *La vita privata dei fiorentini* in "La Vita Italiana nel Rinascimento," Milan, 1896.

BONELLI GANDOLFO, C., *Leggi suntuarie senesi dei secoli XV e XVI*, in "La Diana," a. II, no. 4.

BULLETTI, P. ENRICO, *La Madonna di Porta Camollia*, in BSB, a. I, nos. 3-4.

CASANOVA, E., *La donna senese nel Quattrocento*, in BSStP, a. VIII, no. I.

DEL LUNGO, I., *Le donne fiorentine del buon tempo antico*, Florence, 1906.

MARRI MARTINI, L., *San Bernardino e la Donna*, in "La Diana," a. V., nos. 1-2.

MISCIATTELLI, P., *La donna senese del Rinascimento*, in "La Diana," a. II, no. 4.

NICCOLINI DI CAMUGLIANO, G., *Chronicles of a Florentine Family*, London, 1933.

POLIDORI CALAMANDREI, E., *Le vesti della donna fiorentina nel Quattrocento*, Florence, 1925.

TAMASSIA, N., *La famiglia italiana nei secoli XV e XVI*, Milan, 1910.

2. *Notes*

* What will you say of the women of Siena?
What shall I say? That they were made in Heaven.
Adorned or disadorned, in headdress, cap or veil,
Most beautiful, and filling all the town.

ANTONIO CAMMELLI (1446-1502)

1. *Opera*, III, pp. 140 and 257.

2. Banchi, II, pp. 130-2, I, p. 123 and II, p. 109.

3. Banchi, I, p. 64, II, p. 56, I, p. 77, and II, p. 85.

4. How common this practice was, is shown by the especial praise that Fra Bernardino gave to the city of Perugia, for having abolished it. Banchi, I, p. 350.

5. It was in consequence of such sacrilegious performances as these that Fra Bernardino expressed his disapproval of *any* mystery play. He also, in one of his Latin sermons, quoted some of the students' profane parodies of the prayers of the Mass. Cf. Alessio, *Storia di San Bernardino e del suo tempo*, Chap. xx.

6. Cannarozzi, Preface to Vol. III and Banchi, II, p. 411.

7. Banchi, III, p. 212.

8. Banchi, II, pp. 208 and 43-4.

9. Quoted by P. Misciattelli, *La donna senese del Rinascimento*, in "La Diana," a. II, no. 4.

10. Aeneas Silvius Piccolomini, *Historia rerum Friderici III imperatoris*.

11. Cannarozzi, II, p. 145.

12. Quoted by L. Marri Martini, in "La Diana", a. v, No. 2, p. 104.

13. Banchi, III, p. 209.

14. Banchi, III, p. 66, and II, p. 330. Some fifty years earlier, these sleeves were already considered ridiculous. "Was there ever a more useless and inconvenient fashion?" Franco Sacchetti asked. "None of you can put a glass or a mouthful on the table without soiling her sleeve and the cloth, too, with the glasses she has upset." *Novelle*, CLXXVIII.

15. Banchi, III, p. 211.

16. Banchi, II, p. 210. Working-women and good housewives wore instead plain sandals, with wooden soles, like clogs, or long stockings with a flat leather sole.

17. Quoted by C. Brunelli Gandolfo, *Leggi suntuarie senesi dei secoli XV e XVI* in "La Diana," A. II, No. xv.

18. Banchi, III, pp. 361-2, and p. 176. The explanation of this story is probably that, while the sumptuary laws forbade certain fashions and materials to respectable women, they allowed them to prostitutes and to little girls under twelve, so that, to get the model copied, the woman had to put it on her daughter.

19. Ibid., pp. 187-9. Fra Bernardino also objected to the short soldier's tunic called *giornea*, which was sometimes worn by both young men and women. "It is made," he said, "like a horse's blanket, with fringes at each side and at the hem, so that you are dressed in the same way as a beast." Banchi, II, p. 444.

20. Sermon "On women's vanities." Codex A. 156, Convento dell'Osservanza. Published by L. Marri Martini in "La Diana," a. v, no. 2. We even find, in a confessor's manual of the 15th century, that one of the questions he should put to his fair penitents was "whether she spent too much time in washing her hair and whether she washed it with 'artificial water.'"

21. Banchi, III, p. 206. Agnolo Pandolfini, too, in *Il governo della famiglia*, tried to persuade his young wife to refrain from using cosmetics, telling her about "a neighbour of ours who had few teeth left in her mouth, and those seemed to be

made of worm-eaten boxwood. Her eyes were sunken and always surrounded by dark rims; the rest of her face was white or ashen, and the flesh withered or greasy. The only thing attractive in her was her light fair hair . . . and she was not yet thirty-two years of age, but by reason of her painting had grown old before her time." Cf. also Heywood, op. cit., pp. 100-105, and Falletti-Fossati, *I costumi senesi nella seconda metà del secolo XIV*, pp. 133-6, and Fra Filippo degli Agazzari, *Assempri*, Nos. II, III and IV.

22. Cannarozzi, v, pp. 201-5.

23. Casanova, *La donna senese nel Quattrocento*, in BSStP, A. VIII, no. 1, and Gandolfo, op. cit., p. 278.

24. Banchi, I, p. 356.

25. L. Marri Martini, op. cit., p. 100, and Gandolfo, op. cit., p. 278, quoting the deliberations of the Sienese Council in 1427.

26. The Florentines, who saw in this new industry a dangerous rival to their own *Arte della Seta*, did everything they could to destroy it, even dumping their own silks and velvets on the Siena market at ridiculously low prices and attempting to bribe Nello's workmen to set fire to his workshops; but he was nevertheless successful and in 1481, in his old age, offered to present the Sienese territory with no less than ten thousand mulberry trees. P. Misciattelli, *La donna senese del Rinascimento*, in "La Diana," a. II, no. IV, p. 235.

27. *De christiana religione*, Sermon XLIV, and Banchi, III, pp. 193-4.

28. Ginevra Niccolini, *Chronicles of a Florentine Family*, pp. 77-9, and Alessandra Macinghi Strozzi, *Lettere ai figlioli*, passim.

29. *I primi tre libri della famiglia*, ed. F. C. Pellegrini, Florence, 1946, p. 160.

30. Cannarozzi, IV, p. 117.

31. Cannarozzi, I, Sermons 24 and 25, and Banchi, II, Sermons 19-21. There are also two Latin sermons on marriage in *Seraphim* and two long passages on the subject in *De christ. relig.* (*Opera*, III, pp. 202-6 and 257-61.)

32. Cannarozzi, pp. 381-3.

33. Banchi, II, pp. 95 and 148.

34. Ibid., pp. 95 and 82-9. It may be doubted, however, whether many girls were quite as ignorant as Fra Bernardino thought. Apart from the extreme plainspeaking practised in every Tuscan household, we find some manuals of the 14th century called *Avvertimenti al maritaggio* (advice for marriage) which gave very clear advice about a bride's duties and behaviour. Moreover, it would appear from the ecclesiastical records of the time that all the efforts to keep a girl secluded before marriage did not always fulfil their main purpose, that of keeping her chaste, and at least one popular book, Francesco da Barberino's *Reggimento e costumi di donna*, contained instructions to a bride as to how to *appear* a virgin, even if she was not.

35. Banchi, II, p. 105.

36. Ibid., p. 115. Cf. also Cannarozzi, I, Sermon 24. The preacher also speaks of a man showing greater patience "to the pig, who always grunts and squeals and

dirties his house, than to his wife" – from which one may conclude that the pig, too, was often living with the family.

37. Cannarozzi, IV, p. 178 and I, p. 416.

38. Banchi, II, p. 105 and Cannarozzi, I, p. 416.

39. Banchi, II, p. 52. Yet, only a few years before this sermon of Fra Bernardino's, Fra Giovanni Dominici was still preaching that a woman owed her husband a *total* submission. "Follow his ways and not your own in your ornaments, your food, your talk, your earnings and your prayers. . . . Go out of the house or stay in it, as he commands, and if he forbids it, do not visit even your father or mother or any of your kin. . . . And know that all you earn, is not yours, but his." *Regola del governo di cura familiare*, pp. 89-91.

40. Banchi, II, p. 119.

41. Ibid., pp. 107 and 89 and Cannarozzi, I, Sermon 25.

42. Banchi, III, pp. 359-60. The ritual return of the bride, a week after her marriage, to her father's house – called *la ritornata* – was a custom dating from the days of child-marriage, when often, after the wedding-day, a child-bride returned home until she was old enough to take on a wife's duties. It was still practised in Tuscany, (though it generally only lasted for two or three days) and was celebrated almost as formally as the wedding-day itself.

43. Banchi, II, p. 106.

44. Ibid., p. 117.

45. Ibid., pp. 159-60 and 299-300, and I, pp. 354-5. "Oh you men," he added, "who have fallen into the mire and cannot get out, cry for help to the Mother of all sinners."

46. Banchi, III, pp. 202 and 224.

47. Cannarozzi, II, p. 41, and V, pp. 39-42.

48. Facchinetti, op. cit., p. 222, quoting *De honore parentum, Opera*, I, p. 142.

49. Fra Giovanni Dominici, op. cit., pp. 164-5.

50. Ibid., p. 157.

51. Cannarozzi, I, Sermon XII, pp. 185-6 and 179.

52. Cannarozzi, I, pp. 204-5. "The man who has a misshapen or mutilated daughter," wrote Franco Sacchetti sourly, "gives her to Christ. A little candle for God, a torch for the lords of this world."

53. Cannarozzi, II, p. 467, I, p. 188, and V, p. 50.

54. Cannarozzi, I, p. 186, and Banchi, II, pp. 455-6. Here Fra Bernardino is inventing, as he often did, his own expressions.

55. Cannarozzi, I, p. 205, and Banchi, II, p. 177. These were not merely monastic precepts; Vespasiano da Bisticci, the celebrated bookseller and biographer, and a close friend of the Florentine humanists, gave remarkably similar advice. "Do not let her [your daughter] converse with other silly girls. . . . Keep her from talking to boys, even her own brothers, after the age of seven. . . . Accustom her, above all, to learn everything that is fit for a woman, to sew and run the house . . . and let her never be idle. The mother who has daughters should never let them be

parted from her, until they have found a husband . . . nor stay with friends or relations. They must always be under her eye." Vespasiano da Bisticci, *Quello che si conviene a una donna che abbia marito.*

56. Banchi, II, p. 439.

57. Banchi, III, p. 371. In Sermini's 24th *Novella*, for instance, we find a husband saying to his wife, about their daughter, "Don't you see that she doesn't know how to do anything? If she could learn to sing and dance a little, she would be worth a hundred more florins, when we give her in marriage."

58. Giovanni Morelli, *Ricordi*, ed. V. Branca, Florence, 1956, pp. 209-10.

59. I. Del Lungo, *La donna fiorentina nel Rinascimento*, in "La Vita Italiana nel Rinascimento," pp. 123-4.

60. Banchi, II, p. 196, and Cannarozzi, IV, p. 129.

61. Cannarozzi, IV, pp. 139-40.

62. Banchi, II, p. 193. Sometimes, indeed, a woman was allowed some say in her children's education and in the administration of their fortune, but this depended entirely upon her husband's estimate of her character. Giovanni Morelli, in 1393, advised his son, if he was certain of his wife's fidelity and also of her future chastity, "to leave her free in your will in all her actions, and the disposer of all your property," and Lapo Niccolini, in 1426, bequeathed to his wife, with four sons approaching manhood, "the same power and authority that I have." But such bequests were still exceptional.

63. Cannarozzi, IV, p. 136. Fra Giovanni Dominici considered that a widow must be her children's father "in teaching them and chastising them, until they are twenty-five years old!"

64. Banchi, II, p. 199, Cannarozzi, IV, pp. 131-3, and Banchi, I, pp. 174-5.

65. Banchi, II, pp. 187-8.

66. Ibid., p. 410.

67. This story is told by all Fra Bernardino's early biographers – Barnabò da Siena, Maffeo Vegio and Giovanni da Capistrano – the latter describing the picture as representing "the glorious Virgin and her triumphant Assumption, with the figures of many angels, singing and rejoicing with musical instruments." Bernardino often went to look at this picture, even after he had become a friar, and obtained a copy of it to place on the high altar of the church in the Convento dell'Osservanza. The original remained in the Porta Camollia until the 17th century, when it was replaced by a copy, which may still be seen there. Cf. P. Enrico Bulletti, *La Madonna di Porta Camollia*, in BSB, A. 4 (1935), nos. 3-4.

68. Banchi, I, p. 35. This vision is illustrated in one of the tablets in the *Tavolette di Biccherna* (so-called because these were the account-books – "Bücher" – of the Commune). Attributed to Neroccio di Bartolomeo, it represents the Madonna kneeling before her Son, and holding in her hand a model of the city of Siena, with the inscription, *"Haec est civitas mea."*

69. Banchi, I, pp. 22-3.

70. Cannarozzi, v, p. 123. "I believe," Fra Bernardino added, "that she loved a flea, God's creature, better than you love God Himself".

71.   "In thee is mercy, in thee is piety,
         In thee munificence, in thee is gathered
         All that there is of good in human creatures."
                                             Paradiso, XXXIII, 19-20.

72. Cannarozzi, I, p. 101, and Bargellini, pp. 635 and 535.

73. Banchi, II, pp. 395-6, and Cannarozzi, v, pp. 134-6.

74. Banchi, II, pp. 437-8.

CHAPTER III: THE WORLD OF TRADE

1. Additional Works consulted

CASTELLINI, A., *La legislazione dell'usura e San Bernardino da Siena*, in BSB, a. II (1936), no. 3.

CASTELLINI, A., *Una predica arguta* (containing a story about usury), in BSB, a. IV (1938), nos. 3-4.

DE ROOVER, R., *Appunti sulla storia della cambiale e del contratto di cambio*, in "Studi in onore di G. Luzzatto," Milan, 1950.

DE ROOVER, R., *Il trattato di Fra Santi Rucellai sul cambio, il monte comune e il monte delle doti*, in "Arch. Stor. italiano," 1953.

DE ROOVER, R., *Joseph A. Schlumpeter and Scholastic Economics*, in "Kyklos," 1957, No. 2.

DE ROOVER, R., *The Concept of the Just Price, Theory and Economic Practice*, in "Journal of Economic History," December 1957.

DOREN, A., *Storia economica dell'Italia nel Medio Evo*, Italian translation by G. Luzzatto, Padua, 1937.

FANFANI, A., *Saggi di storia economica italiana*, Milan, 1930.

Lettere di un notaio (Ser Lapo Mazzei) a un mercante (Francesco Datini), ed. C. Guasti, Florence, 1880.

LUZZATTO, G., *Piccoli e grandi mercanti nelle città d'Italia del Rinascimento*, in "Studi in onore di G. Prato", Turin, 1930.

MENGOZZI, N., *Il prestito ad usura in Siena nei secoli XIII, XIV e XV*, in "Il Monte dei Paschi di Siena," Vol. I, Siena, 1891.

SAPORI, A., *Mercatores*, Milan, 1941.

SAPORI, A., *Studi di storia economica medievale* (2ª ed.), Florence, 1946.

2. Notes

★ To reach some rest, I've never ceased to toil
  I hoe in water, sow upon the sand,
  And hope still tempts and ever leads me on,
  Today, tomorrow, and the year goes by.

And under this illusion I've grown grey,
And never have found rest, no single day.

BENUCCIO SALIMBENI, knight and merchant
of Siena (d. 1332), in "La Diana," 1932, no. 1.

★★ The sleep of misers is a restless sleep.

SAN BERNARDINO

1. These sermons were published separately in 1474 under the title *De contractibus et usuris*. An Italian translation entitled *Istruzioni morali intorno all'usura* appeared in Venice in 1774.

2. Cannarozzi, I, pp. 98 ff. and IV, Sermons XLI and XLIV, and Cannarozzi, *Siena*, I, Sermons XV-XVIII.

3. Banchi, III, p. 264.

4. "The *Signori Nove*" (the nine members of the Communal Council), said the new Statutes, "should and must belong to the Merchants of the city of Siena, that is, to the middle class. . . . It is decreed that no nobleman . . . nor any knight nor judge nor notary nor physician . . . may be one of the *Signori Nove*." F. Schevill, *Siena, The Story of a Mediaeval Commune*, pp. 195-6.

5. Cannarozzi, V, pp. 248-253.

6. Banchi, III, pp. 232-240.

7. Ibid., p. 227.

8. R. de Roover, *Joseph A. Schlumpeter and Scholastic Economics*, in 'Kyklos', fasc. 2, 1957, pp. 125-7. I am much indebted to Prof. de Roover for first calling my attention to San Bernardino's outstanding abilities as an economist.

9. See A. Sapori, *Il giusto prezzo nella dottrina di San Tommaso e la pratica del suo tempo*, in "Studi di storia economica," pp. 189-227. He quotes, as an example, St. Thomas' reference to a merchant who had imported wheat during a famine: was or was it not permissible for him to sell this wheat at the current market price (which was, of course, very high) or must he state that he knew some other merchant-ships to be on their way, with more wheat? St. Thomas decided that the merchant was *not* obliged to state this (though of course it would have been more virtuous to do so, and thus to lower the price). In Sapori's opinion, this conclusion clearly shows that St. Thomas considered the "just price" to be not the cost of production, but merely the market price.

10. *ferlino*, according to Banchi (Vol. I, p. 292), was a word coming from the ancient Saxon *feord-ling*, a quarter, and was used to designate either the quarter of a *denaro* (the smallest coin - the French *denier*) or the small metal counters which boys used in some games.

11. Banchi, III, pp. 242-3 and pp. 249-50.

12. De Roover, op. cit. pp. 421 and 426, quoting from San Bernardino's *De Evangelio aeterno*, Serm. 33, art. 2, cap. 5, and referring to a cartulary issued by Charlemagne, but incorporated in the twelfth century into canon law, which stated that parish priests should tell their congregations not to charge more than the market price to

273

wayfarers; if they did, the traveller could complain to the priest, who would set a price "with humanity."

13. Banchi, III, pp. 246 and 249.

14. *Summa theologica*, II, 2, qu. 118, art. I, 3 b.

15. *Lettere di un notaio a un mercante*, vol. II, p. 142.

16. In this, too, he was following St. Thomas Aquinas, who, however, added that the maintenance of a man's family did not include provision for its future, for that belongs to God. *Summa theologica*, 2, II, qu. XXXII, art. V, 4, 7.

17. Banchi, III, pp. 220 and 223, and Cannarozzi, I, p. 160.

18. E. Garin, *L'umanesimo italiano*, pp. 51-2, quoting Poggio's *Historia disceptativa de avaritia* in *Opera*, vol. 7. Other humanist writers went still further, discerning in riches – as in Jacob's flocks – a positive token of the Lord's approval.

19. Banchi, III, pp. 247-9. Cf. also Cannarozzi, I, pp. 103-4, and 223.

20. Cannarozzi, I, pp. 100-102.

21. Domenico di Cambio to Francesco Datini, March 12, 1390. Archivio Datini, Prato. Francesco di Marco Datini, a wool-merchant of Prato, was warned by his friends, as soon as he joined the *Arte del Cambio*, that it would be said that he had become a "usurer." "Francesco di Marco will lose his repute . . . by becoming a money-changer; for there is not one of them who practises no usury in his contracts." Cf. Origo, *The Merchant of Prato*, p. 149.

22. Cf. A. Sapori, *L'interesse del denaro a Firenze nel Trecento*, in "Studi di storia economica," pp. 97-101. Even St. Thomas Aquinas had said that if a creditor could prove that some damage had been caused him (for instance by slowness in repayment), it was licit for the debtor to pay some compensation.

23. Cannarozzi, IV, p. 363.

24. St. Thomas, however, and San Bernardino following him, did admit that sometimes money, by means of investment of capital, could become productive, as seed produces a crop. Cf. R. De Roover, op. cit., p. 110.

25. Cannarozzi, IV, p. 365.

26. An inventory of 1422 – two years before San Bernardino's first sermon in Florence – mentions no less than 72 money-changers' offices around the Mercato Nuovo. Burckhardt, *The Renaissance in Italy*, p. 77.

27. Cannarozzi, IV, pp. 363 and 436. Such transactions were, however, precarious, and it was generally held that it was only *certain* profits that were usurious.

28. Vespasiano da Bisticci, *San Bernardino da Massa*, in *Vite di uomini illustri del secolo XV*, p. 139.

29. De Roover, op. cit., pp. 134-5.

30. *Opera*, III, p. 157, *Seraphim*, 2. Quoted by Howell, pp. 286-7.

31. Banchi, III, pp. 355 and 244.

32. "Usury offends the divine goodness," *Inferno*, XI, 95.

33. Any interest of over 20% was considered "usurious," but this was often exceeded. Cf. Sapori, *L'interesse del denaro a Firenze nel Trecento* in "Studi di storia economica," pp. 112-115 and *Il concetto di "usura"* in op. cit., pp. 119-25.

34. Aldo Lusini, *Il ghetto degli Ebrei*, in "La Diana," 1927, No. 3, p. 195.

35. Christian burial was denied to *usurari manifesti* by the Lateran Council of 1179 and this had been confirmed by the Council of Lyons in 1271. "Their bodies," wrote Fra Filippo degli Agazzari, "should be buried in ditches, together with dogs and cattle."

36. He even goes so far as to lay down that it is a mortal sin to do so, but here he is perhaps thinking of them not only as usurers, but as the men who killed Our Lord. See *Opera*, III, 133 and 334.

37. Cannarozzi, II, pp. 79, 81 and 84.

38. Cannarozzi, I, p. 115. Another similar story, with a very Etruscan flavour, is that of a miser who, on his deathbed, sent not only for his wife and children, but for "his money, his ornaments and his fine horse" – and then, when they were all around him, he "began to lament, saying 'Alas, alas, my wife! alas, my money! alas, my children! alas, my horse! Alas, that I must leave you!'" And there was yet another usurer who, when visited by a friar who wished to lead him to confess, made him bring to him "a basin in which he made him [the friar] put all the money which he kept under his mattress," and so died, clutching the basin and saying only "O, my money! O my money!" Cannarozzi, *Siena*, II, p. 125.

39. Another similar tale (for they are too many and too like each other to repeat them all) was that of the usurer "who dreamed one night that the Devil was carrying him away. And the next morning, waking up with this sight in his mind, he dressed himself in rags and crouched down in a dark corner of the church" [thinking that there, at least, the Devil could not find him]. "But his relations came to take him home, for he seemed out of his mind. On his way home he had to cross a bridge across a stream, and when the usurer was on this bridge, he saw a boatload of devils sailing down it, and when they got under the bridge, they cried to him, 'Come down!' And he flung himself into the water, and the Devil bore him away." Cannarozzi, *Siena*, II, p. 124.

40. Howell, op. cit., pp. 128-9, quoting *l'Anonimo* (AB. XX. 5. 337). This incident took place in Vicenza.

CHAPTER IV: THE WORLD OF THE POOR

1. *Additional Works consulted*

FALLETTI FOSSATI, C., *Costumi senesi nella seconda metà del secolo XIV*, Siena, 1881.

IMBERCIADORI, I., *Il problema del pane nella storia della bonifica maremmana*, in "Atti della Reale Accademia dei Georgofili," 1938.

LEVASTI, A., *Santa Caterina da Siena*, Torino, 1947.

MANACORDA, G., *Mistica minore*, Foligno, 1926.

MISCIATTELLI, P., *Mistici senesi*, Siena, 1913.

RODOLICO, N., *Il popolo minuto, note di storia fiorentina (1343-78)*, Bologna, 1899.

SAPORI, A., *La beneficenza delle compagnie mercantili del Trecento*, in "Studi di storia economica medievale," Florence, 1946.

2. Notes

*Enamoured Poverty / great is thy seigniory!

JACOPONE DA TODI

1. After the first terrible epidemic in 1348, by which four fifths of the population of Siena was carried off, there were other severe outbreaks in 1363, 1378, 1400, 1411 and 1427.

2. This was the dream to which Dante referred when he wrote of *"quella gente vana che spera in Talamone."* "The foolish folk who hope in Talamone" (*Purg.*, XIII, 152).

3. Quoted by Imberciadori, *Il problema del pane nella storia della bonifica maremmana*, from the report of a Commission formed in Siena in 1361 to look into the problem of feeding the population.

4. A *moggio* was about 24 bushels, in Tuscany. The report of another Commission in 1373 commented: "Thus the whole of the Maremma is going into ruin, for if there are no men, there can be no labour, and without labour we shall have neither bread nor wheat." Imberciadori, op. cit., p. 8.

5. Ibid., pp. 4-6. As late as 1554, during the siege of Siena by the Spanish troops of Charles V, the "useless mouths" of Siena – the old, the sick, and even the foundlings of the Ospedale della Scala – were cast out of the gate at Fonte Branda, into the no-man's-land between the enemy and the city walls. Many of them were killed during the night, all were robbed of the little they had, and the next day at dawn the survivors, wounded and half-naked, were again hammering at the gate. Schevill, op. cit., p. 416.

6. Cannarozzi, IV, pp. 407-8.

7. Cannarozzi, V, pp. 15-6.

8. Quoted by Rodolico, *Storia degli Italiani*, p. 130.

9. Banchi, I, p. 234.

10. Giovanni Morelli, *Ricordi*, p. 256. In 1343, during such a riot, 22 palaces and warehouses of the Bardi were sacked, causing damage to the value of 60.000 florins, and in 1360 there was a similar uprising, ending in the execution of the ringleaders.

11. A. Sapori, *La beneficenza delle compagnie mercantili del Trecento*, in "Studi di storia economica medievale," pp. 5-6, and *Il giusto prezzo*, ibid., p. 198.

12. Banchi, III, p. 323.

13. A. Fortini, *Nova vita di S. Francesco d'Assisi*, pp. 131-2, quoting the statutes of Assisi in the time of St. Francis. "Let no leper dare to re-enter the city, and if one of them does, it is permitted to everyone to beat him."

14. P. Misciattelli, *Le più belle pagine di Bernardino da Siena*, p. 258.

15. Banchi, III, p. 34, and II, p. 60.

16. *Lettere di un notaio ad un mercante*, December 6, 1409.

17. "Poverty, poverty, none understand your language
    Long live the holy poverty within our hearts."

18. P. Misciattelli, *Sena Vetus*, in "La Diana," a. VII (1932), no. 1. and in *Mistici Senesi*, p. 108.

19. Levasti, *Santa Caterina da Siena*, p. 85.

20. Banchi, III, p. 321 and II, pp. 316 and 343-5.

21. Cannarozzi, I, p. 243.

22. Sticco, op. cit., p. 214, quoting Codex D. 2. 1330, p. 15; Bibl. Nazionale, Florence.

23. Banchi, III, pp. 295, 299-300, and 311-12.

24. Cannarozzi, I, p. 243, and Banchi, III, pp. 310-13.

25. Cannarozzi, III, p. 343.

26. "Let him be considered a wild beast," said the old Lombard law which had left so strong a trace on Tuscan usage, "and be killed without fear" – *vardus sit et sine pavidi occidatur*.

27. Banchi, II, p. 59.

28. Banchi, III, pp. 153-4, 307 and 336-7.

29. Banchi, III, p. 341, and II, pp. 61-2.

30. *Summa theologica*: Charity, Vol. I, q. XX 5, 3.

31. Cf. G. Manacorda, *San Francesco, le creature e la gioia*, in *Mistica Minore*, pp. 129-38. San Bernardino pointed out that St. Francis' power over beasts, birds, plants and even the elements was the same as that which Adam had, before the Fall – and concluded that St. Francis had the same innocence that Adam had, before he sinned. Banchi, III, p. 37.

32. Banchi, III, p. 453.

33. Cannarozzi, III, p. 343, Banchi, III, pp. 305-6 and p. 196.

34. Ibid., p. 314.

CHAPTER V: THE CHARGE OF HERESY

1. Additional Works consulted

BERTAGNA, Padre M., *Christologia S. Bernardini Senensis*, Rome, 1949.

BULLETTI, Padre E., *Il Nome di Gesú*, predica volgare inedita di S. Bernardino, in BSB, a. III (1937), no. III.

LIVI, R., *San Bernardino e le sue prediche secondo un ascoltatore pratese*, in BSStP, 1900, no. 3.

MELANI, Fra GAUDENZIO, *San Bernardino e il Nome di Gesú*, in "Saggi e ricerche," Milan, 1945.

PELLEGRINETTI, Card. E., *San Bernardino apostolo del Nome di Gesú*, in BSB, a. VI (1942), no. 2.

2. Notes

★ Some wanted me roasted, and some fried.

SAN BERNARDINO

1. According to Alessio, Facchinetti and Père Longpré, Fra Bernardino's summons to Rome occurred in 1427. But the correspondence in 1427 between Siena and the Roman Curia (recently published by Padre E. Bulletti in BSB, 1939, pp. 27-48) makes it almost certain that the summons took place in the previous year (1426), since it seems impossible, or at least very unlikely, that the Sienese should

appoint as their Bishop a man still accused of heresy. See also, P. Gaudenzio Melani, O.F.M., *San Bernardino e il Nome di Gesú*, in "Saggi e ricerche," etc., p. 283.

2. According to the *Anonimo*, some of Fra Bernardino's friends, having been forbidden by him to accompany him, went ahead to plead his cause. The Pope, however, was not well disposed. "Where is that seducer, Fra Bernardino?" he asked, adding, "I will surely have him punished, as soon as he arrives." See Howell, op. cit., p. 149.

3. Card. E. Pellegrinetti, *San Bernardino apostolo del Nome di Gesú*, in BSB, 1942, no. 2.

4. Banchi, III, pp. 31-2.

5. Cannarozzi, II, p. 149.

6. "That at the name of Jesus every knee should bow, of things in heaven, and things on earth, and things under the earth." Philippians, II, 10. The complicated symbolism attached to each feature of the design and described in detail in Bernardino's sermons, adds little to its essential meaning. The three letters represented, in his eyes, simply the first three letters of the Name of Jesus in Greek (not, as was later claimed, the words, *Jesus Hominum Salvator*). Later on the H came to bear a cross over it. The twelve longer rays represented the twelve articles of faith, spread throughout the world by the twelve Apostles. Cf. Howell, op. cit., pp. 158-9, and Facchinetti, op. cit., pp. 358-61.

7. Cannarozzi, II, p. 224.

8. Playing-cards seem to have been first imported by the Arabs into Spain, and from there into Italy, in the second half of the 14th century. (A Florentine decree refers to them as "new" in 1376.) Those called *naibi* were at first a series of simple, instructive picture cards for children, while the *tarocchi* often also had Arabic numerals and represented allegorical or mythological figures, or those of planets or of the zodiac.

9. Barnabò da Siena, AASS, p. 743.

10. Cannarozzi, II, p. 213.

11. *Opera*, II, 282, *Seraphim*, Sermon 40, quoted by Howell, op. cit., p. 138.

12. Cannarozzi, II, p. 208, and Banchi, II, pp. 250-1.

13. The sermons specifically devoted to the subject are two in Latin: Serm. XLIX, *De triumphali Jesu* in the course *De christiana religione*, which was largely based on a 13th century pamphlet, *De laudi melliflui nominis D. N. J. C.* (first attributed to San Bonaventura, but now by P. Efrem Longpré, to Fra Gilbert of Tournai) and Serm. XLIX, *De glorioso nomine D. N. J. C.*, in the course *De Evangelio aeterno*, which was inspired by Ubertino da Casale's *Arbor vitae crucifixae Jesus*.

14. Quoted by Facchinetti, op. cit., p. 356, from the translation into Italian of the sermon *De glorioso nomine Jesu Christi* by Mons. Telemaco Barbetti.

15. Banchi, III, pp. 32-3.

16. *De christiana religione*, Sermon XLIX.

17. Letters from Sandro di Marco di Sandro Marcovaldi to his brother Giuliano, pub-

lished by R. Livi, in *San Bernardino e le sue prediche secondo un suo ascoltatore pratese*, BSStP, 1900, no. III.

18. Cannarozzi, III, pp. 146 and 198.

19. St. Antoninus, *Historia Ecclesiae*, Part III.

20. Donati, *Notizie su San Bernardino*, in BSStP, I, p. 57, quoting Poggio, *Epistolae* (ed. Tonelli), Book III, ep. 26.

21. The pamphlet, entitled *Liber de institutis, discipulis et doctrina Fratris Bernardini Ord. Minorum*, appeared in Bologna in 1427, and was followed by another pamphlet by the same author, *Tractatus ad Barchinonenses de littera 'h' in nomine Jesu*, and by two violent pamphlets by another Augustinian, Fra Andrea da Cascia, in which Fra Bernardino is referred to as Antichrist.

22. Howell, op. cit., pp. 154-5, quoting from the pamphlet of Fra Andrea de' Bigli.

23. The *Anonimo* gives a slightly different account of his interview, stating that it was enough for the Pope to see Bernardino, to realize that he was not merely the ignorant and superstitious friar who had been described to him.

24. By "*Gesù*" the people meant the tablets. The friars who preached this devotion were called "*Gesuati*" or in Sicily "*Gesuari*."

25. Banchi, I, p. 205.

26. Howell, p. 160, quoting Maffeo Vegio.

27. Facchinetti, op. cit., pp. 85-6, quoting Padre Aniceto Chiappini, *San Giovanni da Capistrano e San Bernardino*.

28. Howell, op. cit., p. 162, and Facchinetti, op. cit., pp. 168-9.

29. Cardinal E. Pellegrinetti, op. cit., p. 65. Bernardino's speech was published by Padre Enrico Bulletti from the *Legenda Sancti Bernardini* by Fra Cristoforo Gabrielli, (1517).

30. Banchi, I, p. 98, and II, p. 59.

31. Pellegrinetti, op. cit., p. 75.

32. Banchi, II, p. 418.

33. The Pope reprimanded the Inquisitor and gave orders that the monogram should again be painted above the Cross, or else that a fresh picture should be painted of the Crucifix, with the monogram above it. Both pictures may still be seen in the Convento dell'Osservanza (San Paolo al Monte) outside Bologna.

34. The first of these pamphlets (both recently edited by P. Longpré) was by Maestro Bartolomeo Lappacci of Florence in 1431, the second by an anonymous Dominican. They contain the most complete summary of the charges against Fra Bernardino. Cf. Padre Melani, op. cit., pp. 293-4.

35. Facchinetti, op. cit., pp. 372-3, quoting the Bull *Sedis apostolicae*, dated January 8, 1432.

36. Cannarozzi, III, p. 17, and I, pp. 218-9.

37. This point has remained uncertain. Certainly it appears that in Siena, directly after his trial, Fra Bernardino – although often referring to the devotion to the Holy Name – refrained from exhibiting the tablets, but this may perhaps have been due to prudence rather than to a positive prohibition, and certainly in other cities,

later on, the tablets were again displayed. Cf. Padre Melani, op. cit., p. 285.

38. Another version merely says that Fra Bernardino's accusers asked the Council to examine a *libello* of his (possibly one of his sermons?). Cf. P. Melani, op. cit., pp. 286-7, and Howell, op. cit., pp. 181-5.

39. Pellegrinetti, op. cit., p. 61.

40. One of the charges against Joan of Arc was that she bore upon her banner, together with an image of the Virgin, the name of Jesus. Sainte Colette caused the monogram JHS to be engraved upon her tomb.

CHAPTER VI: STRIFE, CRIME AND PEACEMAKING

1. Additional Works consulted

AGAZZARI, Fra FILIPPO DEGLI, *Assempri*, Siena, 1922.

FALLETTI FOSSATI, C., *Costumi senesi nella seconda metà del secolo XIV*, Siena, 1882.

HEYWOOD, W., *A study of mediaeval Siena*, Siena, 1901.

NESTI, Fra BENEDETTO, *S. Bernardino e l'imperatore Sigismondo*, in BSB, VII (1941), no. 4.

SCHEVILL, F., *Siena, the Story of a Mediaeval Commune*, London, 1912.

ZDEKAUER, L., *Il giuoco in Italia nei secoli XIV e XV*, in Arch. Stor. It., Vol. XVIII (1886).

ZDEKAUER, L., Preface to the *Constituto del Comune di Siena*, Siena, 1896-97.

2. Notes

* I implore for peace, peace, peace.

PETRARCA

1. Misciattelli, *Le più belle pagine di Bernardino da Siena*, p. X 1.

2. Banchi, I, p. 292.

3. Ibid., I, p. 132, III, pp. 84-5 and II, p. 219. The sermons which Fra Bernardino devoted in this course to attacking party strife were four (nos. X-XIII), and to these he added four against calumniators and spies (nos. VI-IX), two on good government (nos. XVII and XXV) and one about the Free Companies (no. XXXVI). In addition, four of his Latin sermons dealt with party strife. Cf. Facchinetti, op. cit., pp. 410-17.

4. Schevill, *Siena, the Story of a Mediaeval Commune*, p. 218, quoting Muratori, XV, 192.

5. Muratori, XV, 238 B.

6. This incident is related by the chronicler Malavolti, of the year 1439. The Statutes, too, supply a similar picture: 50 *lire* was the fine required of a man who hit a fellow-citizen with a stone, stick or iron bar, or who slapped or kicked him; 100 *lire* for throwing a spear, knife or skewer; five hundred, for cutting off another man's hand or foot or tongue or nose, or for pulling out all his teeth or one of his eyes. C. Falletti-Fossati, *Costumi senesi nella seconda metà del sec. XIV*, pp. 160-2.

7. Banchi, I, p. 245.

8. Ibid., pp. 242, 283, and II, pp. 323 and 15.

9. Banchi, I, pp. 262 and 257.

10. "You cannot absolve a man who does not repent." Dante, *Inferno*, XXVII 118.

11. Banchi, II, pp. 233 and 213.

12. "In Siena," writes Prof. Zdekauer in his informative preface to the *Constituto del Comune di Siena* (Part I, p. xxxv), "the duty of revenge was fully recognized by the Commune itself, and from 1223 to 1235 a special register was kept in which all the injuries and offences suffered by the Commune were entered . . . 'so that, when the time is come, you may not delay to return good for good and evil for evil to each, according to his deeds.'"

13. Paolo di Messer Pace da Certaldo, *Il libro di buoni costumi*, para. 270.

14. Banchi, I, pp. 252-3.

15. Fra Filippo degli Agazzari, *Assempri*, no. XLI.

16. Neri di Donato, *Cronaca*, Muratori, XXXX, XII, 18.

17. Banchi, III, p. 68, and I, p. 262.

18. Ibid., pp. 286-7.

19. Cannarozzi, II, p. 239.

20. Facchinetti, op. cit., p. 423 and pp. 443-7.

21. Giovanni Sercambi, *Le Croniche*, Vol. II, p. 34. Cf. also Origo, *The Merchant of Prato*, pp. 313-20.

22. Howell, op. cit., p. 264, quoting *Opera* III, 137, *De inspirationibus*.

23. San Giovanni da Capistrano, in *Opera*, I, p. 35. That some rumour against Fra Bernardino had also reached the ears of the Duke of Milan is suggested by a letter of instructions from the *Signoria* of Siena to their envoy in Milan, Giovanni da Massa, asking him to tell the Duke "about the good and sincere doctrine of Fra Bernardino of the Observance of St. Francis, the most famous preacher," and to ask the Duke "to excuse him if anything has been said against him and tell him not to believe it, but to consider him a most virtuous man and very well disposed towards his Grace. . . ." Archivio di Stato, Siena, Conc. 2411, Nov. 1.

24. Facchinetti, op. cit., pp. 438-440, Howell, op. cit., pp. 176-7 and F. Benedetto Nesti, *San Bernardino e l'Imperatore Sigismondo*, in BSB, 1941, no. 4.

25. Codex F. 6. 1329, f. 24 Biblioteca Nazionale, Florence, and Banchi, III, pp. 260, 269-70 and Cannarozzi, IV, p. 273.

26. Banchi, I, pp. 137-154.

27. Cannarozzi, I, p. 429.

28. Heywood, op. cit., pp. 164-9. They also sometimes had their own companies in the army of the Commune and, according to Villani, their own banner, representing *ribaldi dipinti in gualdana e giuocando* (scoundrels portrayed in a troop and gambling), *Cronica*, VI, 40. In peace-time, they set up this banner beside their booths in the squares.

29. Cannarozzi, *Siena*, I, pp. 174-5.

30. Zdekauer, *Il giuoco in Italia nei secoli XIII e XIV*, in "Archiv. Storico Italiano," Vol. XVIII (1886).

31. "And then one may see the loser cursing with great sighs, with his hand to his jaw, giving and receiving many blows. And then they come to the knife and kill each other, and the whole fair square is in turmoil." Antonio Pucci.

32. Cannarozzi, I, p. 431-7.

33. Heywood, op. cit., pp. 170-9. Similar stories, too, are told in Fra Filippo's *Assempri*.

34. Cannarozzi, I, pp. 428, and 438-40.

35. Banchi, II, p. 270.

36. M. Sticco, *Pensiero e poesia in San Bernardino da Siena*, p. 208, quoting Codex F, 6 1239, Biblioteca Nazionale, Florence.

37. Banchi, II, Cannarozzi, I, p. 5 and III p. 230, and Cannarozzi, *Siena*, II, p. 208.

38. Banchi, II, pp. 297-8.

39. Facchinetti, op. cit., pp. 429-30, quoting Padre A. Fantozzi, *Documenti perusiani di San Bernardino senese*, in AFH, a.xv, vol. xv. Similar organized street-fighting took place in Siena, ending in a dance in the Piazza del Campo at which all the survivors danced round in a ring, "to the sound of instruments." Falletti-Fossati, op. cit., pp. 200-202.

40. Cannarozzi, II, p. 213. It was not, Fra Bernardino insisted, that he objected to harmless pleasures. "One cannot always be studying or practising one's trade or business. To take delight in hawking, hunting, fishing now and then, that is a fine occupation! But afterwards come back to your trade or your studies, if you wish to be a gentleman."

41. Banchi, I, Sermon XIV.

42. M. Sticco, op. cit., p. 220, quoting from Codex D. 2 1330, Biblioteca Nazionale, Florence, and Banchi, II, p. 273.

43. Cannarozzi, V, pp. 15-6. It must be remembered that the *podestà* of a small country town, in Fra Bernardino's time, was generally, to the men over whom he ruled, a "foreigner," sent to them from the chief city of the district, living in an unnatural isolation and resenting the villagers almost as much as they resented him. "Can there be," wrote the novelist Franco Sacchetti in 1385, when he was *podestà* of Bibbiena, to a friend, the *podestà* of Bologna, "a more troubled life than ours?" The man who deliberately sought such a post, he decided, must be impelled to do so either by folly or by immoderate greed. "Otherwise he must indeed be insane, to cease to be the head of his own family, living a gentle and civilized life, and to go off to be, not the master, but the servant of a band of robbers." Sacchetti, *I sermoni evangelici*, etc.

44. Cannarozzi, V, p. 104, and Banchi, II, p. 272.

45. Banchi, p. 384.

46. Banchi, III, p. 373, and Cannarozzi, *Siena*, Preface, pp. XXXII-III. The picture referred to was Lorenzetti's famous fresco entitled *Il Buon Governo*, painted in the "Sala dei Nove" of the Palazzo Pubblico between 1337 and 1339. The frescoes on one wall show the effects of a strong and peace-loving government, a city filled with flourishing tradesmen and merrymakers and a prosperous countryside, while the other wall shows a ruined city and ravaged fields.

47. Banchi, III, p. 385.

48. Howell, who repeats the story as told by Wadding (*Annales*, XI, 194) comments

that it is strange that Fra Giuliano, who was present at San Bernardino's death and wrote a long letter describing it, should not have mentioned this "miracle." But it certainly became incorporated very quickly in his legend, and is, of all the stories told about him, one of the most characteristic.

CHAPTER VII:
THE PRETERNATURAL AND SUPERNATURAL WORLDS

1. Additional Works consulted

GARIN, E., "La crisi del pensiero medievale" and "Considerazioni sulla magia," in *Medioevo e Rinascimento*, Bari, 1961.

GIANNINI, G., *Una curiosa raccolta di segreti e di pratiche superstiziose del secolo XIV*. Città di Castello, 1898.

GILMORE, Prof. MYRON G., *Freedom and Determinism in Renaissance Historians*, Central Renaissance Conference, Columbia, Mo., 1955.

GRAF, *Il diavolo*, Milan, 1889.

KRAMER & SPENGLER, *Malleus maleficarum*, trans. Montague Summers, London, 1948.

PANNIZZI, G., *Un'apparizione di San Bernardino*, in BSB, 1943, No. 1.

PIANA, Padre CELESTINO, O.F.M., *San Bernardino teologo*, in "Saggi e ricerche nel V centenario della morte di San Bernardino," Milan, 1950.

RONDONI, G., *Tradizioni popolari e leggende di un comune medioevale*, Siena, 1890.

SANESI, G., *Un'accusa di eresia nel 1383*, in BSStP, III (1896).

2. Notes

> ★ Understanding is given of both good and evil
> And a free will.
> *Purgatorio*, XVI, 72.

1. Banchi, I, p. 39.
2. G. Villani, *Cronica XI*, 2.
3. *I Dialoghi di Giovanni Pontano*, ed. C. Provatera. Cf. Prof. Myron C. Gilmore, *Freedom and Determinism in Renaissance Historians*.
4. Francesco Guicciardini, *Opere*, p. 431 (ed. V. de Caprariis, Milan, 1953). Even the celebrated humanist, Poggio Bracciolini, while scoffing at the ignorance and folly of monks and priests, made no secret of his own belief in ghosts, devils and strange prodigies.
5. Cf. Facchinetti, p. 281. Unlike St. Bernard and Duns Scotus, Fra Bernardino did not admit that there was a distinction in person between angels, but only a numerical one.
6. Banchi, III, p. 406, I, p. 46, and Cannarozzi, I, p. 212.
7. Banchi, I, p. 294.
8. The belief in this story had spread so wide that Cardinal Dominici, the great Dominican preacher, sent two of his friars to the village in the Apennines where the incident was supposed to have taken place, to find out precisely what did occur. The story was told by Fra Bernardino in *Seraphim, Opera*, III, p. 250.

9. Cannarozzi, *Siena*, I, pp. 94-6.

10. This anecdote was told by Fra Andrea de' Bigli in his pamphlet attacking Fra Bernardino's manner of preaching. See Howell, op. cit., p. 153.

11. Rondoni, *Tradizioni popolari e leggende di un comune medioevale*, p. 179.

12. Banchi, III, p. 262.

13. Howell, op. cit., p. 122, quoting *Opera*, III, *Seraphim*, Sermon 40. In the *Assempri* of Fra Filippo Agazzari, too, the devil was constantly changing his shape.

14. Cannarozzi, II, pp. 157-8, and Banchi, III, p. 120.

15. Rondoni, op. cit., pp. 155-6, quoting the 14th century *Libro di Astrologia*, Biblioteca Comunale, Siena, IX, 40.

16. Cannarozzi, II, p. 77, Cannarozzi, *Siena*, II, pp. 55 and 187-8, and V, p. 126, and Banchi, II, p. 92.

17. The unlucky dates apparently varied according to different astrologers. Rondoni (op. cit., pp. 152-3) gives a list of those observed in Siena in the 14th century, while a different set of dates is given by Sacchetti in his *Zibaldone*, and yet another in one of Antonio Pucci's sonnets. *"E però cose nuove – Non far in questi venti-quattro giorni, – Se tu non vuoi che contro te ritorni."* Quoted by G. Giannini, *Una curiosa raccolta di segreti e di pratiche superstiziose*, pp. 104-5.

18. Cannarozzi, II, p. 187.

19. Cf. *Enciclopedia Treccani*, vol. IX, 759: *Ceppo*. To this day, in remote country places, people believe that the *ceppo* blazes "to give light to *Gesú Bambino.*"

20. Cannarozzi, II, p. 164. It is interesting to compare this list of superstitions with those which, according to a 14th century Florentine manuscript, a confessor should tell his penitents to eschew. He was to ask them "whether he [the man seeking absolution] has believed in sorcerers who foretell the future by the use of belts, candle-ends, or the nails of a virgin child, or in the magical properties of eggs laid on Ascension Day. . . . Whether he has believed in dreams . . . or in the song of birds or the barking of dogs or the sneezing of men or the buzzing of ears. Whether he has believed that animals take the name of God in vain on the day of the Epiphany . . . whether he has bowed to the moon . . . whether he has put a piece of iron in his mouth, when the first bell tolls on Holy Saturday. . . . Whether he has tried to foretell the future from the lines of the palm."

21. Cannarozzi, II, pp. 168-9, 180l-1 and 186.

22. The most famous book by Avicenna (in Arabic, Ibn Sina), 980-1037, "The Canon of Medicine," had already been translated into Latin at the end of the 12th century. It was studied in all the chief European Universities and still exercised a great influence during the early Renaissance, where his neo-Platonic mysticism was particularly in harmony with the *Zeitgeist.*

23. Quoted by Garin, "Considerazioni sulla magia," in *Medioevo e Rinascimento*, p. 174.

24. Cannarozzi, II, pp. 180-2.

25. "Before the fire is out – May you come to my door – May my love come to pierce you – As I now pierce this heart."

26. Aeneas Silvius Piccolomini, *Opera*, I, Ep. 46, p. 552.

27. Banchi, II, pp. 125-6. A possible explanation of this story is that this girl, like many others, had been captured by slave-traders in the Balkans as a child and then sold by them in the slave-markets of Venice or Genoa.

28. Cannarozzi, III, pp. 208-11.

29. Banchi, III, pp. 121-5.

30. *Malleus Maleficarum*, pp. 126-7. The form of a cat was chosen as "an animal which is, in the Scriptures, an appropriate symbol of perfidiousness, just as a dog is the symbol of fidelity."

31. G. Sanesi, *Un'accusa di eresia nel 1383*, in BSStP, III (1896).

32. Howell, op. cit., pp. 139-40. This action of Fra Bernardino's would doubtless have obtained the approval of those of his fellow-citizens who, only a few years before, in a sudden attack of Puritanism and superstitious terror, after a series of calamities, had torn down from the Fonte Gaia in the Piazza del Campo the exquisite Greek statue of Venus Anadyomene which they themselves had placed there. The Madonna, they cried, must be punishing them for placing a heathen goddess in their midst – and they shattered the statue into small fragments, and caused them to be buried in Florentine soil. Heywood, op. cit., pp. 94-5.

33. Banchi, II, p. 375, Cannarozzi, I, p. 216, and Banchi, II, pp. 267.

34. Banchi, II, pp. 377-8.

35. *Opera*, 176-7. Quoted by Howell, pp. 239-40. The *Malleus Maleficarum* got around the difficulty that some of the Devil's "miracles" – such as healing the sick by a charm – *seem* supernatural, by saying that "when the Devil seems to do things that are beyond his power, such as causing the dead to rise or the blind to see," what he has really done is to produce an "illusion." "For when he appears to do the former [i. e. raise the dead] he either enters into the dead body or else removes it, taking its place himself . . . and in the latter case he removes a man's sight by an illusion and then similarly restores it, by taking away the disability he had caused." Op. cit., pp. 162-3.

36. Misciattelli, *Le più belle pagine di Bernardino da Siena* p. 242.

37. Howell, op. cit., p. 180, and Facchinetti, op. cit., p. 302.

38. G. Panizza, *Un'apparizione di San Bernardino* in BSB, 1943, no. 1. The writer is a descendant of the family at whose door the saint knocked, and adds that the householder, realizing too late that he must have refused to give shelter to two saints, followed them to beg for their forgiveness, whereupon they granted to him and to all his family the faculty of curing people afflicted by jaundice – a faculty which they retained for many years.

39. Facchinetti, op. cit., pp. 401-2.

40. Banchi, II, p. 353. The whole subject was discussed by the preacher again in his Latin sermons. Men who are so presumptuous, he said, as to try to perform miracles are in danger of the gravest form of spiritual pride: they are assuming divine power. On the other hand, like St. Augustine, he considered *true* miracles to constitute one of the decisive proofs of the truth of the Christian faith, and he made known to his congregation St. Augustine's celebrated argument that if we believe that

Christ's miracles did not take place, we must then admit that the divulgation of the Christian faith throughout the world took place without the aid of a miracle – which is the greatest miracle of all. "Take it that the apostles performed no miracles and were twelve coarse men, rough fishermen, subject to bodily passions and danger of thirst and other extremities – and they converted the whole world." Cannarozzi, II, p. 99.

41. Banchi, II, p. 350.
42. Facchinetti, op. cit., p. 488, quoting Wadding.
43. Banchi, II, p. 286, Cannarozzi, II, p. 248 and Banchi, I, p. 24.

CHAPTER VIII: THE WORLD OF LETTERS

1. Additional Works consulted

BARGELLINI, PIERO, *Il Concilio di Firenze*, printed for the Cassa di Risparmio di Firenze, Vallecchi, 1961.

BRACCIOLINI, POGGIO, *Epistolae*, Florence, 1852-59.

BURCKHARDT, J., *The Renaissance in Italy*, English transl. by S.G.C. Middlemore, 1904.

CHASTEL, ANDRÉ, *Art et Humanisme à Florence au temps de Laurent le Magnifique*, Paris, 1959.

GARIN, EUGENIO, *Il Rinascimento italiano*, Milan, 1941 (texts of the Renaissance humanists, with transl.).

GARIN, EUGENIO, *L'umanesimo italiano nel Rinascimento: Filosofia e vita civile*, Bari, 1950.

GARIN, EUGENIO, *Il pensiero pedagogico dell'umanesimo*, Florence, 1959.

GILL, Father JOSEPH, S. J., *The Council of Florence. A Success that failed*, in "The Month," April 1960.

PICO DELLA MIRANDOLA, GIOVANNI, *De hominis dignitate*, ed. B. Cicognani, Florence, 1941.

SALUTATI, COLUCCIO, *Epistolae*, ed. F. Novati, Rome 1891-1905.

VESPASIANO DA BISTICCI, *Vite di Uomini Illustri del secolo XV*, ed. Paolo d'Ancona and E. Aeschlimann, Milan, 1951.

VOIGT, GEORG, *Il risorgimento dell'antichità classica*, Italian translation by D. Valbusa, 2 vols, Florence, 1888.

WOODWARD, W. H., *Vittorino da Feltre*, Cambridge, 1905.

2. Notes

* No enterprise, however small it be, can have a beginning or an end without these three things: ability, knowledge and a joyful will.

1. M. Sticco, *Pensiero e poesia in San Bernardino da Siena*, p. 234, quoting F. 6 1329, f. 37, Biblioteca Nazionale, Florence and Cannarozzi, IV, p. 25.
2. "The man who does not praise beauty," wrote Lorenzo Valla, "is blind either in his body or his soul."
3. "It is Greek, Donatello saw it and gave it the highest praise."
4. Vasari, *Vite*, ed. Torchiani, p. 87.

5. Cannarozzi, I, p. 168. "All the things that God has made in the world," he said elsewhere, "are His books." *Prediche volgari*, ed. Bargellini, p. 365.

6. Cf. Sticco, op. cit., pp. 134-7. Fra Giovanni's attack upon humanist education was contained in a book published in 1405 in reply to a defence of humanist studies by Coluccio Salutati, entitled *Lucula noctis*.

7. Vespasiano da Bisticci, *Nicola V, Papa*, in op. cit., p. 27. Tommaso Parentucelli became the first great humanist Pope, Nicholas V.

8. Niccolò Niccoli, well known for his fine taste and his caustic tongue, was perhaps the leading Florentine humanist after the death of Coluccio Salutati. A collector of manuscripts, pictures, sculpture, gems, mosaics, coins, he extended his taste in art to his way of life, sweeping through the streets of Florence in a long scarlet gown, eating out of antique bowls and drinking from a crystal cup. His collection of 800 manuscripts was bequeathed to the friars of San Marco, for the benefit of all his fellow citizens, and is now in the Biblioteca Laurenziana, Florence.

9. Leonardo Bruni of Arezzo, also called Leonardo Aretino, a pupil, like Guarino, of Chrysoloras, was a Greek scholar and historian who, like Salutati, believed that men of letters should put their culture at the service of the Republic. He was a close friend of Fra Bernardino's and greatly admired him.

10. Carlo Marsuppini, who succeeded Bruni as chancellor of the Florentine Republic, differed from most of the other humanists of his time in being an open disbeliever in the Christian faith.

11. Giannozzo Manetti, also a close friend of Fra Bernardino's, was one of the most profoundly orthodox of the scholars who frequented Vespasiano's bookshop and would declare that "the truths written and approved by the Church are as true as that a triangle is a triangle." Humanist, politician, historian, translator from the Greek and the Hebrew, his works have now fallen into oblivion, except for his treatise, *De dignitate et excellentia hominis*.

12. Vespasiano, *Poggio fiorentino*, in op. cit., p. 293. Poggio Bracciolini, a member of the Papal Chancery, was chiefly famous for his unequalled flair for unearthing ancient manuscripts and for his archaeological discoveries in Rome.

13. The accusations and insults which these learned men aimed at each other were of an unparalleled virulence and malice, whether the controversy was on a matter of such moment as the truth or falsity of the Faith, or a trivial point of grammar. They would accuse each other in turn of theft, treachery and immoral practices, and would extend these accusations even to their opponents' wives and children. Cf. Voigt, *Il risorgimento dell'antichità classica*, I, p. 300.

14. Bontempelli, op. cit., p. 15.

15. "Petrarca, Salutati and Bruni placed themselves, with the whole of Italian humanism, under the protection of the Fathers of the fourth century." André de Chastel, *Art et humanisme à Florence au temps de Laurent le Magnifique*, pp. 84 and 106. Giannozzo Manetti, a Hebrew scholar as well as a humanist, used to say that he knew three books by heart: St. Paul's *Epistles*, Aristotle's *Ethics* and St. Augustine's *De civitate Dei*.

16. Letter from Guarino Veronese to Fra Giovanni da Prato, April 7, 1450, printed by Garin in *Il pensiero pedagogico dell'umanesimo*, p. 415. St. Basil's treatise on the profit to be drawn from learning Greek was translated, in Florence, by Leonardo Bruni, in 1420. "For several hundred years," he wrote, "no one in Italy has known any Greek; yet it is the source of all doctrine."

17. Cannarozzi, III, p. 300.

18. Coluccio Salutati, *Epistolario*, ed. F. Novati, I, pp. 178-9.

19. Quoted by Garin, *L'umanesimo italiano*, pp. 44-5.

20. Pico della Mirandola, *De hominis dignitate*, ed. B. Cicognani, p. 8.

21. Cannarozzi, V, pp. 47-8.

22. Letter from Guarino to Girolamo Gesualdo, whose son Esopo was Guarino's pupil, June 1423. Published by Garin, *Il pensiero pedagogico* etc. pp. 332-4.

23. Guarino's Preface to his translation of Plutarch's Life of Themistocles, published by Garin, op. cit., pp. 318-22.

24. He remained, however, upon excellent terms with his old master, who referred to him as "my one-time pupil, and now my master in preaching," and dedicated to him a work on St. Ambrose.

25. The school of Vittorino da Feltre was founded in 1423 at the request of Gianfrancesco Gonzaga, Marquis of Mantua, for the education of his sons. The boys educated there – amongst others, Ludovico Gonzaga and Federigo da Montefeltro, Duke of Urbino – as well as their children and grandchildren, became the rulers of the courts of Mantua and Urbino, of Ferrara and Milan, in which the civilization of the Renaissance reached its finest flowering. If the moral climate of some of these courts was a very different one from that inculcated on the playing-fields of La Giocosa, Vittorino did succeed in transmitting to all his pupils a certain fineness of taste – in life as well as in art – such as has perhaps never been acquired to so high a degree anywhere else in Europe.

26. Cannarozzi, IV, pp. 205-12.

27. Banchi, III, p. 247.

28. Cannarozzi, *Siena*, II, pp. 296-7 and 300-1.

29. Cannarozzi, III, p. 297.

30.   Four winds blow from the sea – which will disturb the mind:
         Their names are joy and grief – and fearfulness and hope.

                                                            JACOPONE DA TODI
    Banchi I, pp. 43-5.

31. Cannarozzi, III, Sermon XVII. Much of Fra Bernardino's advice on education is based on the rules laid down by San Bonaventura.

32. The classical authors referred to in Fra Bernardino's sermons include Aristotle, Plato, Homer, Cicero, Virgil, Seneca, Quintilian, Vitruvius, Juvenal and Apuleius, but of these the Greek authors are probably quoted at second hand. Cf. Howell, op. cit., p. 234.

33. Cannarozzi, *Siena*, I, p. 54.

34. Cannarozzi, III, pp. 305-6.

31. In the same year as the foundation of Fra Bernardino's course in Perugia, the University of Siena founded a faculty for the study of theology.

32. "*Armaverunt se contra illum et articulaverunt eum mirabiliter.*" Francesco da Rimini, quoted by Facchinetti, op. cit., p. 474.

33. Sticco, op. cit., pp. 42-3, quoting Codex D. 2.1330, f. 30, Biblioteca Nazionale, Florence.

34. Idem, p. 244, quoting Cod. Magliabechiano, Cl. xxv-244, f. 190, Biblioteca Nazionale, Florence.

35. Banchi, II, pp. 127-8.

36. Bargellini, *San Bernardino da Siena*, p. 102.

37. Cannarozzi, I, p. 219.

38. Quoted by Pastor, *Storia dei Papi*, I, 31-2.

39. Poggio Bracciolini, *Epistolae*. Quoted by Voigt, op. cit., vol. II, p. 210. An almost equally violent attack upon the Observants was made by the philosopher Leonardo Bruni in his treatise *Contra hypocritas*, in which he describes their pale faces, their furtive glances, and the tales of dreams and visions with which they entertained unlettered men and foolish women – while Filelfo, too, described a friar of this type in most venomous tones in one of his Satires. Cf. Voigt, op. cit., III, pp. 206-7.

40. Misciattelli, *Le più belle pagine*, etc., pp. 50-2.

41. Sticco, quoting from Codex D. 2.1330, Biblioteca Nazionale, Florence.

42. Facchinetti, op. cit., pp. 463-4, and Banchi, II, p. 44.

43. Pacetti, op. cit., p. 462.

44. Howell, op. cit., pp. 190-1, quoting the chronicle attributed to Graziani in "Arch. Storico Italiano," XVI, I, p. 470.

45. Padre E. Bulletti, *Per la nomina di San Bernardino a Vescovo di Siena*, in BSB, 1939, no. I.

46. Banchi, II, p. 368.

47. Vespasiano da Bisticci, op. cit., *XV*, p. 139.

48. Wadding, X, 117.

49. Banchi, II, pp. 69-70. What the Sienese thought of it all, they said in some popular verses after San Bernardino's death: "*Tu cercasti povertadi – Non curasti l'amistadi – E schifasti vescovadi – Pel tuo libero stato.*" (You looked for poverty, heeded not your friends, and made scorn of Bishoprics, to keep your free condition.) A. Lusini, *Un rotulo bernardiniano*, in "La Diana," 1929, no. 2.

50. On disputed points I have followed Padre Pacetti's *Cronologia*.

51. Vespasiano da Bisticci, op. cit., p. 12.

52. Howell, p. 75, quoting Fra Francesco da Rimini.

53. Fra Ilarino da Milano, O.F.M., op. cit., p. 396 (quoting *Speculum Minorum* and Wadding) and Howell, pp. 78-9.

54. The figures are Giovanni da Capistrano's, but are accepted by Facchinetti and other modern biographers.

55. Facchinetti, p. 475.

CHAPTER X: THE LAST JOURNEY

1. *Additional Works consulted*

ALESSIO, F., *Storia di San Bernardino da Siena*, Mondovì, 1899.

DONATI, F., *Notizie su San Bernardino da Siena*, in BSStP, a. I, nos. 1-2.

PACETTI, Padre DIONISIO, O.F.M. *Cronologia bernardiniana*, in "Studi Francescani," a. XV (1943), nos. 3-4.

2. *Notes*

★ Poverty dies in peace.

JACOPONE DA TODI

1. AB, XXXV, 315, quoted by Howell, pp. 194-5.
2. "*Tu duce, tu Signore, e tu maestro.*" *Inferno*, II, 140.
3. Wadding, XI, p. 189, Cf. Howell, p. 194 and Facchinetti, pp. 487-8.
4. This panegyric of Fra Vincenzo was introduced into the third of San Bernardino's Latin sermons on the Beatitudes, on the text "Blessed are they that mourn." A part of it was directly borrowed from St. Bernard's lament, in his *Expositio in Cantica Canticorum*, for his own beloved friend, the Venerable Gérard of Clairvaux – almost as if Bernardino, in the intensity of his grief, felt that no words of his own could be fine enough. Cf. Facchinetti, op. cit., p. 486, n. 1.
5. Banchi, III, p. 365.
6. Sante Boncor, *Vita inedita*, VI, p. 8, quoted by Facchinetti, op. cit., p. 486, p. 1.
7. Vespasiano da Bisticci, op. cit., p. 140.
8. Banchi, II, p. 389.
9. From a memorandum, dated September 27, 1442, sent by the *Signoria* of Siena to San Bernardino. Archivio di Stato, Siena, *Concistoro* 2413, c. 541-2. In 1433 peace had been concluded between the Florentines and the Venetians on the one hand, and Milan and Siena on the other – but on terms which were unsatisfactory to Siena, who had to hand back to Florence several towns which she had taken from her.
10. Howell, p. 196. The whole story was told in the Bull of Exculpation of Fra Bernardino issued by Pope Nicholas V in 1447 and printed in Wadding, XI, 275.
11. Bargellini, *San Bernardino da Siena*, p. 326.
12. Alessio, op. cit., pp. 381-2.
13. Donati, *Notizie su San Bernardino*, in BSStP, a. I, nos. I-II, quoting the Venetian chronicler Cicogna.
14. Wadding, XI, 189.
15. Banchi, III, p. 504.
16. Panegyric of San Bernardino by Fra Giacomo della Marca, quoted by Facchinetti, op. cit., p. 463.
17. The story is told by Bargellini, op. cit., p. 342, but he does not give the source.
18. AASS, p. 761.

19. Fra Bartolomeo wrote an account of the journey, which has unfortunately been lost, but which has in part come down to us, in Wadding, XI, 190 ff.

20. This legend is told only by Wadding and by Marco da Lisbona.

21. Letter from Fra Giuliano of Milan to a convent of the Observants in that city, published by F. Donati in BSStP, a. I, nos. I-II.

22. Fra Sante Boncor reports at length the sayings of the dying man, but the account of Fra Giuliano, who was present, suggests that these are apocryphal. Cf. Facchinetti, op. cit., p. 449.

23. All his biographers agree as to the joy in his face, just before his death. *"Feliciterque e corpore excessit,"* wrote Surio, and Fra Lodovico da Vicenza, *"laeto vultu quasi ridens, gloriosum emisit spiritum."*

24. "Father, I have made your Name known unto men."

EPILOGUE

1. Additional Works consulted

BULLETTI, Padre E., *Per la canonizzazione di San Bernardino da Siena*, Carteggi inediti in BSB, a. x. (1940),

CHINI, M., *La chiesa e la tomba di San Bernardino in Aquila degli Abruzzi*, in BSB, a. III (1937), No. 2.

DONATI, F., *Notizie su San Bernardino*, in BSStP, a. I, nos. 1-2.

LIBERATI, A., *Le vicende della canonizzazione di San Bernardino*, in BSB, a. II (1936), no. 1.

2. Notes

★ O blessed Lord, your servant – Can no longer be concealed
You have made him manifest – To the great man and the small.
Lusini, *Un rotulo bernardiniano*, in "La Diana," a. IV, fasc. 2.

1. The people then healed, according to the testimonies reported to the Curia, were twelve paralytics, eight cripples, four deformed men, two blind persons, two deaf and dumb, and two men suffering from stone. In addition a woman "possessed of a devil," having kissed the saint's feet, was freed from her obsession.

2. F. Donati, *Notizie su San Bernardino*, in BSStP, a. I, nos. 1-2, in which the full text of Fra Giuliano's letter is given.

3. Life of San Giacomo della Marca by Fra Vincenzo da Fabriano, in AFH, a. XVIII.

4. Facchinetti, op. cit., pp. 508-9, quoting Fra Sante Boncor's *Vita Inedita*, XII, pp. 13-14.

5. "Weep, my people of Siena, for your sweet and glorious, holy and pious Bernardino, who has gone to his eternal rest. Do you not remember how you saw him pass on earth like a lamb, that poor little old man, so kindly, humble and compassionate? Let each *Sienese* weep for his father – the great, the burghers and the poor – let Tuscany weep the loss of his wise counsel, let every Italian join in the lament.

Weep, you friars who were his beloved sons, whom he dressed with his own holy hands – all of you, or nearly, perfect in poverty – for the light of Christianity has been blown out." Quoted in *Miscellanea Storica Senese*, a. 1., fasc. 2.

6. This was one of fourteen laments contained in a parchment scroll belonging to the Palmieri family of Siena, published by Aldo Lusini in "La Diana," A. IV, fasc. 2. The miniature at the head of the scroll is attributed to Pietro di Giovanni.

7. Facchinetti, op. cit., p. 510.

8. Aeneas Silvius Piccolomini (Pius II), *De viris illustribus*.

9. F. Donati, *Notizie su San Bernardino*, quoting *Commissioni ed Ambasciatori del Comune di Siena*, Biblioteca Comunale, Cod. A. v. 34, p. 282, and Liberati, *Le vicende della canonizzazione di San Bernardino*, quoting letters in the Arch. Sergardi, A. II, nos. 21, 24, 25 & 28.

10. Liberati, op. cit., quoting Arch. Sergardi, a. II, No. 46.

11. Wadding, *Annales*, XI, para. v, p. 274. The question of Bernardino's canonization was eventually examined in four "processes": one in 1445 in Aquila, a second in 1447 in Aquila, a third in 1448 in Rome and in several other towns where he had been, and finally a fourth in Aquila and Rieti in 1449. P. D. Pacetti, O. F.M., *Cronologia bernardiniana*, in "Studi Francescani", a. XV (1943), Nos. 3-4.

12. Howell, op. cit., pp. 214-5.

13. Liberati, op. cit., p. 117. This "expense" appears to have included the "gift" to one of the cardinals of the Commission, of a house worth 800 florins.

14. An old Life of San Bernardino, that of Padre Amadio of Venice, divides these miracles into the following categories: 13 corpses brought back to life, 12 dying persons cured, 14 wounded men healed, 15 persons cured of blindness and 10 of deafness, 17 cripples given back the use of their limbs, 7 persons possessed by devils healed of their obsession, and 20 sick persons cured of various diseases, including leprosy. Sometimes even the saint's habit alone, or his girdle, or one of his images, could work the miracle; and in one case he even showed his power over inanimate matter, putting back into the barrel some wine that a poor shepherd in Rieti had spilt, "so that the barrel overflowed." Facchinetti, pp. 529-30.

15. Facchinetti, p. 528, quoting both P. Cristofano da Varese, in *Acta Sanctorum*, p. 510, and Wadding, *Annales*, Vol. XI, para. XXXVII, p. 279.

16. Ibid., p. 526, quoting P. Cristofano da Varese, op. cit., p. 510.

17. Liberati, op. cit., pp. 121-3. The envoy added that it would be desirable for the Sienese to purchase all the wax that would be required, since it was cheaper in Siena than in Florence. It must be sufficient to make 100 candelabras (*doppieri*) of 11 lbs each, besides candles for all the cardinals, patriarchs, prelates, officials and envoys, and twelve torches to be lit at the moment of the consecration. The full expense of the canonization seems to have amounted to about 7.000 florins. Cf. Pastor, *Storia dei Papi*, I, p. 387.

18. Facchinetti, p. 532, quoting Fra Bernardino da Fossa, *Chronica fratrum*, p. 38. Cf. also Pastor, *Storia dei Papi*, I, pp. 386-8.

19. Liberati, op. cit., p. 123, n. 2, quoting from the unpublished chronicle of Facini

31. In the same year as the foundation of Fra Bernardino's course in Perugia, the University of Siena founded a faculty for the study of theology.

32. *"Armaverunt se contra illum et articulaverunt eum mirabiliter."* Francesco da Rimini, quoted by Facchinetti, op. cit., p. 474.

33. Sticco, op. cit., pp. 42-3, quoting Codex D. 2.1330, f. 30, Biblioteca Nazionale, Florence.

34. Idem, p. 244, quoting Cod. Magliabechiano, Cl. xxv-244, f. 190, Biblioteca Nazionale, Florence.

35. Banchi, II, pp. 127-8.

36. Bargellini, *San Bernardino da Siena*, p. 102.

37. Cannarozzi, I, p. 219.

38. Quoted by Pastor, *Storia dei Papi*, I, 31-2.

39. Poggio Bracciolini, *Epistolae*. Quoted by Voigt, op. cit., vol. II, p. 210. An almost equally violent attack upon the Observants was made by the philosopher Leonardo Bruni in his treatise *Contra hypocritas*, in which he describes their pale faces, their furtive glances, and the tales of dreams and visions with which they entertained unlettered men and foolish women – while Filelfo, too, described a friar of this type in most venomous tones in one of his Satires. Cf. Voigt, op. cit., III, pp. 206-7.

40. Misciattelli, *Le più belle pagine*, etc., pp. 50-2.

41. Sticco, quoting from Codex D. 2.1330, Biblioteca Nazionale, Florence.

42. Facchinetti, op. cit., pp. 463-4, and Banchi, II, p. 44.

43. Pacetti, op. cit., p. 462.

44. Howell, op. cit., pp. 190-1, quoting the chronicle attributed to Graziani in "Arch. Storico Italiano," XVI, I, p. 470.

45. Padre E. Bulletti, *Per la nomina di San Bernardino a Vescovo di Siena*, in BSB, 1939, no. I.

46. Banchi, II, p. 368.

47. Vespasiano da Bisticci, op. cit., *XV*, p. 139.

48. Wadding, x, 117.

49. Banchi, II, pp. 69-70. What the Sienese thought of it all, they said in some popular verses after San Bernardino's death: *"Tu cercasti povertadi – Non curasti l'amistadi – E schifasti vescovadi – Pel tuo libero stato."* (You looked for poverty, heeded not your friends, and made scorn of Bishoprics, to keep your free condition.) A. Lusini, *Un rotulo bernardiniano*, in "La Diana," 1929, no. 2.

50. On disputed points I have followed Padre Pacetti's *Cronologia*.

51. Vespasiano da Bisticci, op. cit., p. 12.

52. Howell, p. 75, quoting Fra Francesco da Rimini.

53. Fra Ilarino da Milano, O.F.M., op. cit., p. 396 (quoting *Speculum Minorum* and Wadding) and Howell, pp. 78-9.

54. The figures are Giovanni da Capistrano's, but are accepted by Facchinetti and other modern biographers.

55. Facchinetti, p. 475.

CHAPTER X: THE LAST JOURNEY

1. Additional Works consulted

ALESSIO, F., *Storia di San Bernardino da Siena*, Mondovì, 1899.

DONATI, F., *Notizie su San Bernardino da Siena*, in BSStP, a. I, nos. 1-2.

PACETTI, Padre DIONISIO, O.F.M. *Cronologia bernardiniana*, in "Studi Francescani," a. XV (1943), nos. 3-4.

2. Notes

★ Poverty dies in peace.

JACOPONE DA TODI

1. AB, XXXV, 315, quoted by Howell, pp. 194-5.
2. "*Tu duce, tu Signore, e tu maestro.*" *Inferno*, II, 140.
3. Wadding, XI, p. 189, Cf. Howell, p. 194 and Facchinetti, pp. 487-8.
4. This panegyric of Fra Vincenzo was introduced into the third of San Bernardino's Latin sermons on the Beatitudes, on the text "Blessed are they that mourn." A part of it was directly borrowed from St. Bernard's lament, in his *Expositio in Cantica Canticorum*, for his own beloved friend, the Venerable Gérard of Clairvaux – almost as if Bernardino, in the intensity of his grief, felt that no words of his own could be fine enough. Cf. Facchinetti, op. cit., p. 486, n. 1.
5. Banchi, III, p. 365.
6. Sante Boncor, *Vita inedita*, VI, p. 8, quoted by Facchinetti, op. cit., p. 486, p. 1.
7. Vespasiano da Bisticci, op. cit., p. 140.
8. Banchi, II, p. 389.
9. From a memorandum, dated September 27, 1442, sent by the *Signoria* of Siena to San Bernardino. Archivio di Stato, Siena, *Concistoro* 2413, c. 541-2. In 1433 peace had been concluded between the Florentines and the Venetians on the one hand, and Milan and Siena on the other – but on terms which were unsatisfactory to Siena, who had to hand back to Florence several towns which she had taken from her.
10. Howell, p. 196. The whole story was told in the Bull of Exculpation of Fra Bernardino issued by Pope Nicholas V in 1447 and printed in Wadding, XI, 275.
11. Bargellini, *San Bernardino da Siena*, p. 326.
12. Alessio, op. cit., pp. 381-2.
13. Donati, *Notizie su San Bernardino*, in BSStP, a. I, nos. I-II, quoting the Venetian chronicler Cicogna.
14. Wadding, XI, 189.
15. Banchi, III, p. 504.
16. Panegyric of San Bernardino by Fra Giacomo della Marca, quoted by Facchinetti, op. cit., p. 463.
17. The story is told by Bargellini, op. cit., p. 342, but he does not give the source.
18. AASS, p. 761.

19. Fra Bartolomeo wrote an account of the journey, which has unfortunately been lost, but which has in part come down to us, in Wadding, XI, 190 ff.
20. This legend is told only by Wadding and by Marco da Lisbona.
21. Letter from Fra Giuliano of Milan to a convent of the Observants in that city, published by F. Donati in BSStP, a. I, nos. I-II.
22. Fra Sante Boncor reports at length the sayings of the dying man, but the account of Fra Giuliano, who was present, suggests that these are apocryphal. Cf. Facchinetti, op. cit., p. 449.
23. All his biographers agree as to the joy in his face, just before his death. "*Feliciterque e corpore excessit,*" wrote Surio, and Fra Lodovico da Vicenza, "*laeto vultu quasi ridens, gloriosum emisit spiritum.*"
24. "Father, I have made your Name known unto men."

EPILOGUE

1. Additional Works consulted

BULLETTI, Padre E., *Per la canonizzazione di San Bernardino da Siena*, Carteggi inediti in BSB, a. X. (1940),
CHINI, M., *La chiesa e la tomba di San Bernardino in Aquila degli Abruzzi*, in BSB, a. III (1937), No. 2.
DONATI, F., *Notizie su San Bernardino*, in BSStP, a. I, nos. I-2.
LIBERATI, A., *Le vicende della canonizzazione di San Bernardino*, in BSB, a. II (1936), no. I.

2. Notes

★ O blessed Lord, your servant – Can no longer be concealed
You have made him manifest – To the great man and the small.
Lusini, *Un rotulo bernardiniano*, in "La Diana," a. IV, fasc. 2.

1. The people then healed, according to the testimonies reported to the Curia, were twelve paralytics, eight cripples, four deformed men, two blind persons, two deaf and dumb, and two men suffering from stone. In addition a woman "possessed of a devil," having kissed the saint's feet, was freed from her obsession.
2. F. Donati, *Notizie su San Bernardino*, in BSStP, a. I, nos. I-2, in which the full text of Fra Giuliano's letter is given.
3. Life of San Giacomo della Marca by Fra Vincenzo da Fabriano, in AFH, a. XVIII.
4. Facchinetti, op. cit., pp. 508-9, quoting Fra Sante Boncor's *Vita Inedita*, XII, pp. 13-14.
5. "Weep, my people of Siena, for your sweet and glorious, holy and pious Bernardino, who has gone to his eternal rest. Do you not remember how you saw him pass on earth like a lamb, that poor little old man, so kindly, humble and compassionate? Let each *Sienese* weep for his father – the great, the burghers and the poor – let Tuscany weep the loss of his wise counsel, let every Italian join in the lament.

Weep, you friars who were his beloved sons, whom he dressed with his own holy hands – all of you, or nearly, perfect in poverty – for the light of Christianity has been blown out." Quoted in *Miscellanea Storica Senese*, a. I., fasc. 2.

6. This was one of fourteen laments contained in a parchment scroll belonging to the Palmieri family of Siena, published by Aldo Lusini in "La Diana," A. IV, fasc. 2. The miniature at the head of the scroll is attributed to Pietro di Giovanni.

7. Facchinetti, op. cit., p. 510.

8. Aeneas Silvius Piccolomini (Pius II), *De viris illustribus*.

9. F. Donati, *Notizie su San Bernardino*, quoting *Commissioni ed Ambasciatori del Comune di Siena*, Biblioteca Comunale, Cod. A. V. 34, p. 282, and Liberati, *Le vicende della canonizzazione di San Bernardino*, quoting letters in the Arch. Sergardi, A. II, nos. 21, 24, 25 & 28.

10. Liberati, op. cit., quoting Arch. Sergardi, a. II, No. 46.

11. Wadding, *Annales*, XI, para. V, p. 274. The question of Bernardino's canonization was eventually examined in four "processes": one in 1445 in Aquila, a second in 1447 in Aquila, a third in 1448 in Rome and in several other towns where he had been, and finally a fourth in Aquila and Rieti in 1449. P. D. Pacetti, O. F.M., *Cronologia bernardiniana*, in "Studi Francescani", a. XV (1943), Nos. 3-4.

12. Howell, op. cit., pp. 214-5.

13. Liberati, op. cit., p. 117. This "expense" appears to have included the "gift" to one of the cardinals of the Commission, of a house worth 800 florins.

14. An old Life of San Bernardino, that of Padre Amadio of Venice, divides these miracles into the following categories: 13 corpses brought back to life, 12 dying persons cured, 14 wounded men healed, 15 persons cured of blindness and 10 of deafness, 17 cripples given back the use of their limbs, 7 persons possessed by devils healed of their obsession, and 20 sick persons cured of various diseases, including leprosy. Sometimes even the saint's habit alone, or his girdle, or one of his images, could work the miracle; and in one case he even showed his power over inanimate matter, putting back into the barrel some wine that a poor shepherd in Rieti had spilt, "so that the barrel overflowed." Facchinetti, pp. 529-30.

15. Facchinetti, p. 528, quoting both P. Cristofano da Varese, in *Acta Sanctorum*, p. 510, and Wadding, *Annales*, Vol. XI, para. XXXVII, p. 279.

16. Ibid., p. 526, quoting P. Cristofano da Varese, op. cit., p. 510.

17. Liberati, op. cit., pp. 121-3. The envoy added that it would be desirable for the Sienese to purchase all the wax that would be required, since it was cheaper in Siena than in Florence. It must be sufficient to make 100 candelabras (*doppieri*) of 11 lbs each, besides candles for all the cardinals, patriarchs, prelates, officials and envoys, and twelve torches to be lit at the moment of the consecration. The full expense of the canonization seems to have amounted to about 7.000 florins. Cf. Pastor, *Storia dei Papi*, I, p. 387.

18. Facchinetti, p. 532, quoting Fra Bernardino da Fossa, *Chronica fratrum*, p. 38. Cf. also Pastor, *Storia dei Papi*, I, pp. 386-8.

19. Liberati, op. cit., p. 123, n. 2, quoting from the unpublished chronicle of Facini

(Arch. di Stato, Siena, Mss. D. 35) and Facchinetti, op. cit., quoting the *Storia senese* of Agostino Dati and the *Diario senese* of Allegretti.

20. Facchinetti, pp. 541-4, quoting from Fra Giovanni's and Fra Giacomo's letters as published by Faraglia, in *La chiesa primitiva ed il monastero di San Bernardino in Aquila.*

21. Mario Chini, *La chiesa e la tomba di San Bernardino in Aquila degli Abruzzi.*

22. M. Sticco, op. cit., p. 84, quoting Cod. Magliabechiano, Bibl. Nazionale, Florence, xxxv, 8, 240, f. 151.

23. Cannarozzi, II, pp. 479-480.

24. Cannarozzi, V, p. 81, and III, p. 154.

25. Misciattelli, op. cit., p. 263.

26. L. Marri Martini in "La Diana," a. v. (1930), no. 2, quoting San Bernardino's sermon on "the vanity of Sienese women."

27. Banchi, III, p. 452, and I, p. 226.

28. Cannarozzi, *Siena*, I, p. 10, and III, p. 77.

INDEX

Since San Bernardino and Siena appear on almost every page,
they are not included in the index.

299